The Power of the Professional Person

Edited by

Robert W. Clarke
and
Robert P. Lawry

UNIVERSITY
PRESS OF
AMERICA

Lanham • New York • London

The Center for Professional Ethics
Case Western Reserve University

BJ
1725
.P67
1989

Copyright © 1988 by

University Press of America,® Inc.

4720 Boston Way
Lanham, MD 20706

3 Henrietta Street
London WC2E 8LU England

All rights reserved

Printed in the United States of America

British Cataloging in Publication Information Available

Co-published by arrangement with The Center
for Professional Ethics at Case Western Reserve University

Library of Congress Cataloging-in-Publication Data

The Power of the professional person / edited by Robert W. Clarke and
Robert P. Lawry.
p. cm.
Papers from a series of conferences held at Case Western Reserve
University during the 1985-1986 academic year, sponsored by the
University's Center for Professional Ethics.
1. Professional ethics—Congresses. I. Clarke, Robert W., 1922–
II. Lawry, Robert P., 1941– . III. Case Western Reserve
University. Center for Professional Ethics.
BJ1725.P67   1988
174—dc 19   88–840 CIP
ISBN 0–8191–6955–2 (alk. paper)
ISBN 0–8191–6956–0 (pbk. : alk. paper)

All University Press of America books are produced on acid-free
paper which exceeds the minimum standards set by the National
Historical Publications and Records Commission.

CANISIUS COLLEGE LIBRARY
BUFFALO, N.Y.

DEDICATION

This book is dedicated to the many people who have created, nurtured and supported the Center for Professional Ethics since its inception in 1977:

To that little band of students and faculty members who studied together and sponsored the Center's first conference in 1978 and their successors who have given leadership to the Center ever since;

To those who have shared their experiences as speakers;

To those professional practitioners who have contributed from their experience the need for ethical searching and decision-making;

To those University administrators who have shared the financial resources of their office;

To the several foundations who have enabled us to provide the leadership and the underwriting of our program activities;

To the Office of Student Affairs and the Development Office of the University who have labored on our behalf on the campus and in the larger community;

To all of these committed people we dedicate this book.

Acknowledgments

While many people are responsible for the advent of this book, we extend our special thanks to Kimberli Diemert, the Center's Administrative Assistant, for the extensive preparation of the pages of this book, and Elizabeth Clarke and Bridget Metz for their careful proofreading of the text.

Table of Contents

Preface	ix
Chapter 1	1
The Social Worker	
Presenter: Thomas P. Holland	1
Practitioner: Deborah M. Miller	17
Chapter 2	23
The Engineer	
Presenter: Lynn J. Ebert	23
Practitioner: Edward A. Steigerwald	41
Practitioner: Barry A. Rogers	49
Chapter 3	59
The Nurse	
Presenter: Violet M. Malinski	59
Practitioner: Gail E. Bromley	73
Consumer: Carol J. Rottman	83
Chapter 4	93
The Manager	
Presenter: John D. Aram	93
Practitioner: Robert J. Lally	109
Consumer: Susan Coverdale	115
Chapter 5	119
The Physician	
Presenter: Mary B. Mahowald	119
Practitioner: Hugh J. Leslie, Jr.	133
Chapter 6	139
The Professor	
Presenter: Sandra W. Russ	139
Practitioner: Eldon Jay Epp	145
Consumer: Daniel J. Linke	155
Chapter 7	159
The Lawyer	
Presenter: Robert P. Lawry	159
Practitioner: James R. Skirbunt	183
Chapter 8	193
The Dentist	
Presenter: Glenn L. Keiper	193
Practitioner: Daniel Verne	207
Consumer: Marla Comet-Stark	213
Appendix I: Biographical Data	221
Appendix II: Programs of the Center for Professional Ethics	233

PREFACE

The Center for Professional Ethics (CPE) at Case Western Reserve University in Cleveland, Ohio, was founded in 1978 to fill a perceived need across the campus and the wider community for a forum where professionals (scholars, practitioners and students) could meet to exchange concerns and ideas about ethics which cut across disciplinary lines. Through the end of the 1986-1987 academic year some 56 educational conferences and seminar sessions have been held under CPE auspices. Usually the meetings are deliberately cross-disiplinary and cross-professional in scope. Often the keynote speaker is a philosopher with a special interest in applied ethics. The responders and other participants are invariably nurses and engineers, lawyers and managers, dentists and doctors, social workers and teachers. Our strategy is to take a subject -- "confidentiality" or "lying" or "conflict of interest" -- and to offer some provocative comments as the beginning of a dialouge between and among a variety of professionals who are deeply concerned about ethics and professional responsibility.

During the 1985-86 academic year, the Center tried something different. Rather than an isolated conference on a subject in which we bring together different professional groups, we went into each of the eight schools of the University with a theme, "The Power of the Professional Person", and conducted sessions vertically rather than horizontally. In each school we engaged a distinguished scholar to prepare and deliver a paper on the ethical problems embedded in the use of the specialized "power" professionals identified with that school wielded in his or her field. A distinguished practitioner was asked to comment on the scholar's paper. That format was followed at the School of Applied Social Sciences, the Medical School and the Law School. In the School of Engineering, a second practitioner was added. A consumer ("client") was asked to comment at the Schools of Nursing, Dentistry, and Management, and at our undergraduate liberal arts college.

The twenty-one papers generated as a result of this effort are collected here and printed, with minor editorial revisions, as they were delivered. The result is different from what we usually obtain when we hold one conference and ask a variety of professionals to dialogue together. There is more variety here; more vistas opened on to more horizons. We still were able to play off voice against voice, although in a manner less provocative than often is the case, say, when doctor and lawyer square off. Nevertheless, we believe we have achieved a fair sampling of what can happen when professionals from different fields are asked to come together (if only through the magic of a book) and dialogue about a given issue. The question of the use of power by professionals is a vast and complex one. We believe anyone interested in that subject or in the general field of professional and applied ethics will profit by reading the papers included in this volume. We at the Center for Professional Ethics invite you to participate in our efforts at cross-fertilization and to try similar projects at your own institutions. We believe much can be gained by examining a topic from a variety of professional points of view. After reading what we have gathered here, we hope you will agree with us.

       Robert W. Clarke
       Robert P. Lawry

       Co-Directors
       Center for Professional Ethics
       Case Western Reserve University

       January, 1988

Chapter 1

THE SOCIAL WORKER

THE PRESENTER:
THOMAS P. HOLLAND, Ph.D., A.C.S.W.

Power, Paternalism and Professional-Client
Relationships in Social Work Practice

The interactions between social workers and their clients involve a variety of ethical dimensions. The profession itself came into existence as an expression of the society's moral concerns of beneficence and has been characterized as "humanitarianism in search of a method." (Cohen, 1958) In recent years, however, the profession has been attacked for supporting narcissistic egoism, encouraging deviance, and using its skills and power to undermine the very society that produced it. As Siporin (1982) notes, "social workers have been criticized as being amoral or immoral and as encouraging immoral behavior in their clients and people in general." These are disturbing charges indeed for a profession that has long defined itself in terms of values.

The clients of this profession are among the most troubled and vulnerable people in our society. In order to help them address their personal needs and problems constructively, the profession has developed a variety of practice skills and methods for use with individuals, families, groups, and communities. However, despite the claims of many, the uses of the profession's expertise and influence have not always been guided by clear and consistent moral values. The imbalances of power, risk, and responsibilities in relationships with clients have contributed to abuses and led to dilemmas in practice for which little guidance has been available. The sometimes careless use of influence has fueled political conflicts with the community and served to diminish the confidence of both social workers and lay persons alike in this profession.

Efforts to deal with concerns over values and power have taken a variety of directions, from the formulation of numerous theories and models for practice to the refinement of the profession's Code of Ethics. (1980) However, there is little consensus in the field regarding such issues. For example, a conflicted exchange on the meaning and usefulness of our Code of Ethics appears in a recent issue (September-October, 1985, pp. 451-453) of Social Work, the major professional journal of the National Association of Social Workers.

It is widely acknowledged that we have a great need for clarification of the nature of the work that this profession does and guidance regarding the appropriate uses of its power in human lives. Such issues are not ours alone, however. They proceed from some deeper, unresolved questions regarding how we work together as a society to provide for our mutual well-being (Hampshire, 1985) and how the profession of social work is expected to contribute to those goals. (Reamer, 1982)

Toward the end of understanding our situation better, let us briefly examine some of the current approaches to conceptualizing the relationship between social workers and their clients as well as the assumptions and implications of each approach regarding roles, responsibilities, power, and the values guiding professional practice. Following these assessments, we will consider an alternative formulation that has promising potential for advancing our efforts to find a morally and socially responsible model for practice.

The Issues in Context

While efforts at mutual aid are as old as human communities, the notion of professionalizing our fraternal responsibilities is a twentieth century invention. Formal training programs for social workers are scarcely three generations of age. At the time of their establishment, social workers were involved with immigrants and the under-class of our large urban centers. Through Charity Organization Societies and settlement houses they offered guidanace, socialization, and some limited material resources. They sought to help the poor learn the habits necessary to allow them to take their place in a growing industrial society.

In the decades that followed World War I, the

field of social work sought earnestly to develop the requisites of professionalism. For a knowledge base, it chose to model itself after psychiatry and to seek intra-psychic determinants of social problems. In subsequent years, some members of the field turned outward to a more political stance, viewing human suffering as a result of structural inequities in the society. More recently, there have been efforts to develop a blending of intra- and inter- personal perspectives into a variety of ecological or interactive theories to guide practice.

Throughout these struggles to solidify the foundations of this profession, a few basic questions have recurred in various guises. First, what is the nature of the <u>work</u> the profession does? Does it seek to help people adapt to their social circumstances or does it seek to help redesign the social environment to allow for better individual lives? Some have held that the services it provides are intended only to fill in the gaps, or take care of the few failures, in the basic, free economy -- as in the case of income maintenance for the disabled. From such a perspective, the profession's work is a modest, residual function in the society. Alternatively, others maintain that our mutual needs and interests for well-being involve dimensions other than individual freedom to compete in the economy. A caring community addresses a variety of shared concerns, such as day care for its children, volunteer activities for the retired, or other enrichment programs. From this perspective, the work of this profession is a basic institutional component of the society, an expression of its values.

Another core set of unresolved questions addresses the nature of the power and responsibility of the social work practitioner. Is he or she basically an agent of the society, exercising social control over individuals for the purpose of fitting them into conformity with the existing social order? Or is the practitioner a free entrepreneur, advancing his or her own interests through the exchange of skilled services and advancing the market value of those services by means of a professional trade organization? Or, as some maintain, does the profession derive its legitimacy from its effectiveness in assisting individuals and groups that are seeking their own objectives? From this latter perspective, social workers provide technical expertise to clients in attaining power, resources, or control over their circumstances, to be used in whatever direction the clients may want. Indeed, avoidance of any evaluative judgments regarding clients' choices is stressed widely in the profession. This stance often results in conflicts among the interests of the community, the worker, and the client.

Unresolved questions regarding power and its appropriate application in their work shape the day-to-day interactions of social workers with their clients. Should this worker comply with the law and report a suspected child abuse situations, thus jeopardizing any further relationship with this family, or should he rather attempt to expand the discussions with the parents to include their interactions with the child in the hope that the situation may thus be ameliorated? To what extent should this infirm elderly person's resistance to accept more adequate shelter be honored over a contrary professional opinion? Are there limits to a worker's duty to assist clients in arranging for alternate lifestyles, however deviant from that of the community?

The moral value of client autonomy or self-determination has been given priority in the principles of the profession. The Code of Ethics (1980) states explicity that "the social worker should make every effort to foster self-determination on the part of clients." This principle refers to the assumed right of clients to choose their own life goals and the activities that lead to them. The professional is enjoined not only to respect such choices but to assist clients in making maximum use of resources toward their own ends. The priority placed on self-direction means not only that the worker help the client obtain resourses or information needed, but also that the worker withdraw whenever the client so decides.

The Code further enjoins the worker to promote the general welfare of society and advocate for social justice and improved social conditions. The interests of individuals and the welfare of the community are implicitly assumed to be harmonious, as no attention is given to conflicts between individual and community goals or how to address such tensions. The profession has taken the route of liberal political action to expand the availability of rights and resources for persons in need. The values embodied in the Code are assumed to be self-evidently worthy and beyond need of systematic justification and reconciliation with other values.

While plentiful resources may help solve some problems, they may only serve to mask other dilemmas. The practitioner is left in a quandry when he/she is dealing with a client whose choices violate other norms or values. If the choice is clearly injurious to the client or another, the worker may fall back onto the law. But in less extreme situations, little guidance is provided. How much detail should the social worker disclose to this abused and abandoned child regarding his parents? To what extent does the worker discuss diagnostic information with the person who is recovering from mental illness? Should the community organizer help a neighborhood group mobilize to block the creation of a new half-way house for recovering addicts?

Such dilemmas confront workers with a collision of values between allegiances to client autonomy and beneficence or the well-being of the client, between their own values and the community's norms. By its endorsement of all of these sets of values, our Code of Ethics can be used to support quite contradictory decisions and thus is severely limited in its usefulness as a guide in the many very real dilemmas that arise in practice. The practitioner is abandoned at the very point where help is most needed. As Rhodes (1985) sums up our situation, "...The N.A.S.W. Code of Ethics hides these troubling conflicts from view by its assumption of a unified set of values and by the vagueness of the principles it sets forth. As it stands, it cannot serve as a reliable guide for a consistent social work ethic and is, in fact, misleading in its claim to do so." Little wonder that Felkenes' research (1980) reported that few practitioners found the Code to be of any importance in their professional activites.

Models for Professional-Client Relationships

Efforts to deal with such problems have resulted in a variety of models for the appropriate relationship between social workers and their clients. Numerous alternative perspectives on professional practice have been put forward, each with its own value assumptions about the use of power and the handling of conflicts.

Let us examine some of the major ones, with special attention to the issues of the nature of the work to be performed, the allocation of power and responsibility, and the implications for practice. Among the prevalent models or formulations of the appropriate professional role for the social worker are the following: advocate, contractor, friend, agency representative and therapist.

In the advocacy model of social work practice, the professional seeks purposively to increase the client's power, resources, and success in pursuing the client's own goals. The client seeks out the professional due to the latter's assumed technical expertise, which is enlisted to enable the client better to realize his or her own ends. The worth or value of these ends is not questioned by either party. Both agree that the client is responsible for selecting the goals and that the practitioner is present not to judge them but to lend skill or expert means toward their realization. The professional's power is limited to the domain of technical methods or processes which are to be utilized to enlarge the client's power to attain the ends the client seeks. Increasing the power of the client and attainment of the client's objectives are the emphases of this model.

A somewhat more egalitarian perspective takes as its model a bargaining or contracting relationship. The practitioner and the client are assumed to be peers and to have approximately equivalent power. Each has freedom to enter into explicit agreements both on how they will interact with one another, as well as on the objectives they will seek. The client has needs, interests, and resources, as does the professional. Exchange between them is guided by an explicitly negotiated agreement or contract in which each sets forth his or her expectations, bargains for a desired result, limits the obligations, and then works toward mutually beneficial outcomes.

The objectivity and self-interest emphasized by such a perspective has stimulated others to reformulate this model in the personal terms of friendship. As with a friend, the interaction between professional and client is seen to be appropriately characterized by warmth, mutual esteem, cooperation, and trust. Explicit objectives are purposively de-emphasized. Increasing the power of the client to manage his or her life is a major theme of their interaction. The relationship involves mutual responsibilities and the enjoyment of free, non-directive interaction, which are assumed to lead to self-actualization for both participants. The professional is a benign facilitator, and the process is the product.

A somewhat less personalistic alternative involves emphasis upon the organizational context for the roles of caregiver and recipient. The formal policies and rules of the agency control their interation and the resources available. In this bureaucratic model, the worker is responsible for determining whether the client qualifies for services or resources and then dispenses them, all within the procedural guidelines of the organization. The client may reject these limitations and thus disqualify himself, but within the system the policies are not at question. Supportive maintenance of the client within the limits of compliance with agency policies is emphasized in this approach.

The wisdom and expertise of the professional to guide the client are emphasized by the therapist model. From this perspective, the client is assumed to have some sort of deficit or illness, the nature of which he does not comprehend. In fact, what he thinks to be the problem may actually be only a symptom of a deeper problem, understandable only to the professionally trained expert. Likewise, the client's definition of the desired outcome is open to evaluation and redirection by the therapist, whose insights include possibilities only vaguely known to the layman. The power and responsibility of the professional are clearly emphasized in this perspective. Likewise, the professional alone has the skills necessary to identify the appropriate ends as well as the proper means to reach them. (Reamer, 1983)

The various models of the professional-client relationship understand social work practice from very different sets of assumptions regarding the nature of the work, the appropriate distribution of power and the desirable focus of their interaction. One model separates the power to establish goals from the responsibility for means, while a second model insists on their inseparability. Some presume equality with regard both to effective power and to determining the content of interaction, while others emphasize subjective processes over explicit objectives. Placing a priority on any dimension can lead to a preferred approach to practice. (Holland and Cook, 1983)

In order to compare and contrast such perspectives on professional-client relationships, some key dimensions within them may be drawn out for critical examination. Let us consider but two of them: the locus of power in the dyad and the emphasis of their interaction. Each of these dimensions may be conceptualized as continuua. Power may be seen as concentrated in the role of the professional on the one hand, or in the client on the other. Their interaction may emphasize implementation of appropriate rules, procedures, or it may concentrate upon the attainment of explicit goals and objectives, with less concern for the means. Obviously, there are mixed positions at intermediate points along either dimension. Comparisons across these dimensions allow for the simultaneous examination of alternative combinations. The regions of such a bi-dimensional grid may be identified in terms of the major practice approaches noted earlier, as shown in Figure 1.

Figure 1:

Power and Interaction in Four Roles of the Professional

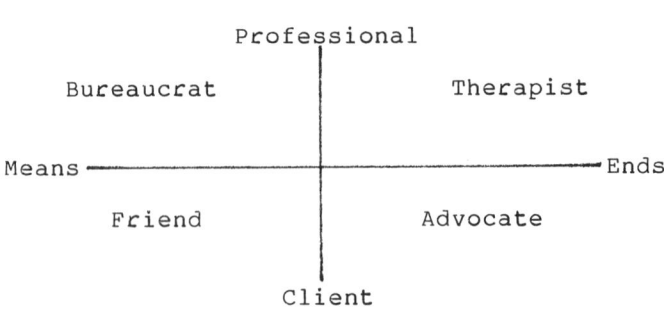

Emphasis of Interaction

Among the numerous professional roles discussed in the practice literature, these four serve to illustrate some of the issues of differential power and emphases of professional-client interaction. The combination of greater power in the role of the professional and an emphasis upon means or processes tends to characterize the role of the bureaucrat. Taken to extremes, this combination can lead to inflexible conservatism, inertia, and atrophy. The combination of client power and emphasis on ends tends to characterize the role of advocate. In extreme forms, this combination can lead to the unprincipled hired gun or anarchy. The combination of power in the professional role and an emphasis on ends is associated with the role of therapist, which, taken to the extreme, may lead to an oppressive big-brotherism. Finally, the quadrant combining client power and interaction, emphasizing processes or means, tends to characterize the friendship model, the extreme forms of which may become anapathetic permissiveness or careless and irresponsible individualism.

The problems encountered at the extremes of these dimensions suggest that balance and equality are crucial to effective practice relationships. Despite the superficial appeal of such an inference, it must be acknowledged that while the professional and the client may be equal in some ways, they are notably unequal in other, quite relevant, aspects. As Veatch (1973) pointed out, they differ significantly with regard to their training, the power they have over the relationship, their risk and vulnerability in the interaction, their freedom to accept or avoid the other, and the interests that are at stake. Treating one another as equals in these respects would seem to require systematic avoidance of characteristics that are, in fact, highly relevant to the relationship and thus tend to undermine trust and responsibility.

Professionals do have more extensive training and experience in dealing with certain types of problems than do their clients. With such a background, professionals may indeed perceive aspects of the clients' situations and possible directions of which the latter are unaware. Being caught up in their situations, clients may be less able to reflect on them thoughtfully, identify and assess their alternatives carefully, and reach objective conclusions. Fatigue, fear, depression, or ignorance are undeniable limitations to optimal problem-solving for anyone. Professionals are presumed to be less clouded by such influences.

Having acknowledged the inequalities and imbalances of power that are inherent in worker-client relationships, we then face the problem of defining the appropriate direction and limits to the exercise of professional power. Relegating to the client all questions of responsibility for goals, as the advocacy model tends to do, narrows the role of the social worker to that of a technician or a hired gun. Practitioners cannot so easily escape moral responsibility for their own evaluation of ends as well as means. Indeed, our discomfort with this model arose precisely because we could not avoid the painful reality that not all goals are equally morally worthy.

Alternately, if it is the case that the professional appropriately carries a larger share of power than does the client, on what grounds do we prevent such a relationship from sliding into an overweening paternalism? How can the social worker foster client self-determination in the midst of a relationship where the professional clearly has more power? Having rejected social workers' efforts to avoid their moral responsibilities, are there any justifiable limits to their assumption of such duties on behalf of their clients, however well-intentioned? In short, we need to find ways to maintain an appropriate balance of power in an inherently unequal relationship.

An Alternative Formulation

One approach to our dilemma would be to consider the conditions under which a person normally may be willing to let another person make an important decision for him or her. Most people recognize that there are various technical problems that clearly warrant outside expert judgments. Likewise, we are aware of times when our physical or emotional state is such that we genuinely need another's care. However, such extremes are atypical situations, and when we are in them we are somewhat more inclined to tolerate paternalistic treatment than we normally would otherwise be.

Under more usual decision-making circumstances, an

individual generally sees his own judgment as important and quite relevant, even if not exclusively so. We may desire to expand the depth of information and the range of choices available to us, but all of that must be weighed along with all of our other interests, values, and goals. We may request the expert's technical knowledge and even seek his or her value judgments, but we do not see such requests as automatically conferring on the professional the right to interfere with our basic interests or to ignore or override our autonomy. (Bayles, 1981)

Balancing the components, needs, and interests at stake in professional-client relationships seems to involve both the client and the professional in both the technical as well as the moral aspects of their interaction. It seems appropriate that the stronger emphasis of the client's role be placed upon evaluation of the professional's technical input in terms of its usefulness for his or her own life goals, while the stronger emphasis of the professional's role be placed upon provision of expert information and means for the client's use. The obligations of the professional involve proficiency in addressing the kinds of problems that clients bring.

Having concluded that he or she can justifiably offer relevant skills and resources to the client, the professional may propose and recommend several courses of action. While it remains the client's prerogative to give or withhold consent to the options presented, the professional also retains the right to withdraw from the relationship if the client insists on objectives or methods that he or she considers to be unworthy or unethical. Under circumstances where agreement is reached, the professional's role would be to work toward the client's goal as efficiently and effectively as possible. The more limited the client's capacities, the more care and responsibility the professional must take and the more stringent the obligations on him or her to protect the client's interests. In all cases, the professional not only offers methodological expertise in pursuit of client's concerns but also attempts to educate clients as much as possible in these methods in order to increase their effectiveness in pursuing their own life goals beyond the conclusion of these relationships.

The power of each participant in the relationship

is more limited than either the therapist or advocate models suggest but not so equal as the contractor model implies. What should we call such a view of the professional-client relationship? Bayles (1981) proposes the inviting term fiduciary, a concept drawn from the legal profession but, nonetheless, appropriate for social workers.

In a fiduciary relationship, both parties are seen as holding power and responsibility, and the interests and judgments of each are given respectful consideration. Because one of them has a more advantageous position, that person incurs special obligations to conduct himself in ways that warrant the trust of the other, who is in a more vulnerable position. The superior knowledge and skill of the professional are recognized, but the power of the client to reach decisions is advanced to a greater extent than in more paternalistic alternatives.

In order to be worthy of the client's trust, the fiduciary perspective places several obligations on the professional. Bayles suggests that the following virtues or norms of conduct by the professional are among the essential ingredients of fiduciary relationships:

1. Honesty: the full disclosure and free flow of all information relevant to the client's concerns, the scrupulous avoidance of lies, manipulations, and misrepresentations.

2. Competence: the obligation to maintain the highest skill and expertise in the areas of practice that the professional offers.

3. Diligence: the energetic and competent pursuit of the client's interests.

4. Integrity: the avoidance of situations that create conflicts of interest or limitations on the professional's exercise of independent judgment on behalf of the client.

5. Discretion: the protection of the client's interest in privacy and avoidance of disclosing information about the client unless consent is given or harm is imminent.

By linking professional practice directly to the traditional moral virtues, the fiduciary model for viewing the role, power, and responsibilities of the social worker appears to offer considerable potential as a framework to guide practice relationships. Social workers do indeed have power to affect the quality of life for their clients and the community. Their specialized training and expertise constitute a strong set of resources that can easily be misused if not guided by clear and consistent principles. The needs and vulnerabilities of clients place workers in the position to use their power to good or bad purposes.

The opportunities to attain such expertise and concomitant power are granted by the society and are not autonomous achievements by the individual or the profession. Hence the professional practitioner has an obligation to the values of the society that sanctioned his role, an obligation to use the resources and power available to him for the well-being of all members of that society.

Pretenses of equality, however nobly motivated, are misrepresentations of the professional-client relationship and serve to obscure relevant differences and moral obligations. Likewise, simplistic separations of technical responsibility from moral responsibility undermine integrity in practice. Both the worker and the client appropriately carry responsibilities for recognizing worthy ends as well as effective means and for weighing their individual preferences in light of the basic values of our cultural heritage.

Confronting Morality

During our psychoanalytic years, social workers tended to assume a form of determinism that made questions of individual choice and responsibility irrelevant. More recently, the field has moved into a form of moral libertarianism that further avoids dealing with our complex ethical responsibilities. While it may be expedient to leave such troublesome areas to individual choice, the inescapable result is to diminish the effectiveness of social workers as mediators between individuals and society and, in the long run, perhaps unwittingly to contribute more to social disintegration than to cohesion. (Siproin, 1983)
We clearly need to give extensive attention to the

ambiguities and inconsistencies in our diverse statements on values and to take seriously our responsibilities for the moral dimensions of practice.

It is time to end our reductionistic efforts to translate moral problems into technical issues. It is time to overcome our tendencies to avoid the moral foundations on which our society rests and from which this profession is derived. The core questions with which social work has struggled for its few generations are fundamental problems for our society as well. Its struggles underlie our own, and our resolutions are contingent upon those of the community. Perhaps our greatest contribution could come in the form of helping our society open up a true dialogue about our unresolved moral conflicts and to work toward a shared understanding of what we really mean by the virtuous life and how we may work together to realize it for us all.

REFERENCES

Bayles, Michael D. Professional Ethics. Belmont, California: Wadsworth Publishing Co., 1981.

Code of Ethics of the National Association of Social Workers. Silver Spring, Md.: NASW, 1980.

Cohen, Nathan E. Social Work in the American Tradition. New York: Dryden Press, 1958.

Felkenes, S.W. The Social Work Professional and His Ethics. Doctoral Dissertation, University of Alabama, 1980.

Hampshire, Stuart. Morality and Conflict. Cambridge, Mass.: Harvard University Press, 1985.

Holland, Thomas P. "Doing Right and Doing Good: Ethical Problems in Practice," Discharge Planning Update, Vol. 4, No.1 (Winter, 1984), 10-14.

Holland, Thomas P. and Cook, Martha A. "Organizations and Values in Human Services." Social Service Review, Vol. 57, No. 1 (March, 1983), 59-77.

Levy, Charles S. Social Work Ethics. New York: Human Sciences Press, 1976.

Lowenberg, Frank and Dolgoff, Ralph. *Ethical Decisions for Social Work Practice.* Itasca, Ill.: F.E. Peacock, 1985.

Reamer, Frederic G. *Ethical Dilemmas in Social Service.* New York: Columbia University Press, 1982.

Reamer, Frederic G. "The Concept of Paternalism in Social Work," *Social Services Review,* Vol. 57, No. 2 (June, 1983), 254-271.

Siporin, Max. "Moral Philosophy in Social Work Today." *Social Service Review,* Vol. 56, No. 4 (December, 1982), 516-538.

Siporin, Max. "Morality and Immorality in Working with Clients." *Social Thought,* Vol. 9, No. 4 (Fall, 1983), 10-28.

Veatch, Robert M. "Models for Ethical Medicine in a Revolutionary Age." *The Hastings Center Report,* (1973), 5-7.

THE SOCIAL WORKER

THE PRACTITIONER:
DEBORAH M. MILLER, M.S.S.A., Ph.D. CANDIDATE

Dr. Holland has presented very compelling reasoning for the place of moral decision-making in social work practice. He has reminded us of principles, critical to our individual practices, no matter the type of setting or level of intervention. I wonder if there are others in the room besides myself who experience both a strong sense of agreement with him while at the same time reacting, that while desirable, such considerations are more likely to occur in "the ivory tower" than "in the trenches."

All too often we do lose sight of moral principles. Not because those principles are unimportant to us in our day-to-day functioning, but because we are faced with constraints that at times make consideration of moral responsibility a near luxury.

My professional practice is with multiple sclerosis patients at the Cleveland Clinic Foundation. It is primarily an outpatient treatment center. I have also worked extensively with dialysis patients. I would like to add at this time that those dialysis patients are insured and often supported through federal money for the receipt of this life-sustaining treatment.

What I would like to do is present a couple of examples of circumstances where moral considerations are very important. These cases are germane because they involve consideration of moral ramifications from, as Dr. Holland has pointed out as is often the case, a number of different perspectives.

In my work with dialysis patients I had to be involved with a couple for whom moral decision-making became an explicit part of our work together. Mrs. D., who was on dialysis, was 42 years old at the time. Her husband was 47. They had no children. Mrs. D. was what could be considered an "ideal dialysis patient." She was gainfully employed, had the respect of her

17

co-workers, participated in a number of social activities, and was generally considered to be compliant with her treatment regime. Her life was meaningful to her and to others in her family. She did quite well on dialysis for several years. Unfortunately she eventually contracted cancer in addition to her renal disease. There was no available treatment for this cancer. Neither was there an effective way to control the pain that she experienced because of the bony metastases to her spine. She nonetheless continued dialysis. Her health continued to decline to the extent that she required ambulance transportation to and from her home for the dialysis. I hate to put dollars and cents into this, but the average cost for each dialysis amounted to about $300 a day, three times a week. As her quality of life declined, and by that I mean her level of comfort, general physical condition, and ability to participate in activities that were important to her, she began to express the desire to discontinue dialysis treatment. This is an issue that the physician, Mrs. D. and I approached with her husband, an emotionally fragile individual, who had always described his wife as "his pillar of strength."

I would like to point out at this time that dialysis is an optional treatment. The decision to continue or discontinue treatment is one that we frequently present to patients and families if they begin to question the benefit of dialysis for an individual who is experiencing an otherwise declining state of health and quality of life.

When we initially attempted to discuss with Mr. D. his wife's questioning of the benefit of continuing dialysis he threatened suicide. He stated that if his wife did not continue dialysis he had no reason to live and he could not tolerate that. Mrs. D.'s physical condition continued to decline. The D.'s became less available to each other for emotional support while Mr. D. continued to maintain this attitude. Long after Mrs. D. wanted to stop we continued dialysis because she felt that her husband's good outweighed her own.

My work with this couple was largely to negotiate between the two of them and to help them to reach their own conclusion about treatment choices. It is in the use of such a treatment approach that we as practitioners begin to find ourselves dealing with many different levels of moral responsibility. Because of the personal contact and the degree of connectedness established with such a couple, their interaction and well-being become a primary concern for the worker.

Nonetheless, as a systems oriented worker, I must say that it is important also to take into consideration the concern and reactions of nurses and physicians on the unit. "How can we continue to dialyze a women in such pain?" "We have other younger people who could be working if Mrs. D. wasn't occupying that dialysis time slot." "Do you know how much it is costing each day to do this?"

These seemingly cold, but equally important, considerations have to be taken into account when discussing ethical concerns of social work practice.

This became a difficult situation to negotiate because of the number of "worthy considerations" involved. There was the physical and emotional pain of this women, the distress of her husband, the reaction of the health care providers, and the allocation of resources. I remember being very aware of the need for moral decisions in this circumstance. I remember the confusion of trying to sort out whose needs and which considerations should be primary. I also remember the intensity and variety of my own feelings and concern that my own "stuff" not get in the way of decision making. Finally I also very clearly remember my confusion about who should be making the decisions and based on what criteria. It is at times like these when it is difficult to act as a moral individual in isolation from other persons who have similar practice orientations but greater emotional distance from the immediate circumstance. There are, I believe, significant components of both societal normative standards and professional standards which constitute an interpretation of "what is ethical." For this reason I believe that consultation with more objective peers is extremely important. With the case in point, such consultation provides help in sorting out appropriate means of intervention; identifying what our responsibilities as "moral agents" are and then assisting us in dealing with feelings about the roles that we play in such circumstances.

My own values were very much in line with Mrs. D.'s desire to discontinue dialysis. I therefore privately had difficulty accepting her struggles about her husband's strengths and weaknesses. I tried to remain as objective as possible in keeping the communication open between them about this very difficult issue. There was an eventual resolution to the circumstance -- it was one without a happy ending. After a time, Mr. D.'s co-workers began to challenge him about how selfish and unfair his behavior was towards his wife. These opinions were ones that many of us at the hospital held but did not feel at liberty to share with him. Fortunately when the issue of fairness was made more explicit, Mr. D. began to look a little more objectively at what was going on. Eventually he did agree to let his wife decide about whether or not to continue her treatment. She did decide to discontinue. Mr. D. remained with his wife and was able to give her a lot of support throughout her final days. As an aside I must speculate that his acceptance of her death was made easier because of the verbal and physical support that he provided to her.

Given that resolution I must once again raise the issue of the moral responsibility we have to consider beyond the individual level. As in the case with Mr. and Mrs. D., there is never one client -- there are always several. It is important to interpret which of those often-conflicting concerns is primary and deserving the highest consideration. In negotiating these moral decisions we are also called upon to be mindful of the institutional and societal needs that both impact upon, and are impacted by, the individuals with which we are directly involved.

There is a significant advantage to recognizing these larger-system issues and making these implicit issues more explicit. To do so informs our practice considerably. Consideration of these larger issues does not complicate the formula which must be involved in making the "right" moral decision because there is never only one "right" decision. The larger-system issues help us not in terms of making decisions but in guiding decisions, in interpreting our practice, and in offering a form for working with clients. As time goes by, and my peers and I are farther away from school and more involved in the daily grind of the work-a-day world, I think we sometimes lose sight of the importance of these issues -- of what it is that we do and why we do it. It is, however, important to keep sight of what it is we do and why we do it so that we can be effective with individuals, their families, and the larger systems with which we work.

There is another case that is on my mind right now because it came up right before I left work to come here. I would like to present this case and perhaps use it as a basis for discussion. I received a phone call this morning from a 72-year-old mother who was extremely distraught. She has a 29-year-old son who is for all practical purposes a quadriplegic, the results of multiple scerosis. He is incontinent of both bowel and bladder. By his choice this young man lives independently of his family in a third floor apartment that is not wheelchair accessible. The only way he can gain access to the outside of this apartment is to be carried by two ambulance attendants. Mr. A. has maintained that it is his right to make his own decisions about his care because he is not dependent on his family or anyone else for maintaining his daily activities. This is correct only to an extent. He has hired a series of attendants to maintain his personal care. Unfortunately he has not demonstrated very sound judgment in hiring these attendants who have, at last accounting, bilked him out of approximately $5000 of his personal money. As a consequence Mr. A. has now become dependent on his 72-year-old mother for providing a considerable amount of his personal care, managing his finances, and, in fact, frequently supplementing his income. Nonetheless he refuses to move back home. He will call his mother three or four times a day because he has soiled his bed or because he is hungry and would like a peanut butter sandwich. For a variety of reasons, too complicated to explicate at this point, and despite her own sense of exhaustion and inability to manage, his mother remains available on this as-called basis. In the meantime Mr. A.'s father is becoming increasingly angry with his wife because of her absence from home. Other siblings have become estranged so that, while they were previously supportive, they no longer are tolerant of either their brother or their mother's compliance with his demands.

The mother called me today to say that she has finally decided that she needs to place her son. Her son refuses to be placed. He is considered to be mentally competent by mental health professionals. He is 29 years old and he is totally dependent upon his mother to manage from one day to the next. She says that she can't do it -- but that it has to happen -- so she will. Her husband is punishing her for doing it. It sounds as if the family is really in a crisis at this point. I am not really certain, however, who is my client? Who is it, in this family full of equally worthy persons, to receive the highest moral considerations? Whose rights become paramount at this point: the mother's, the son's, or the father's? Here are three people having a very difficult time talking to each other. They can't really be effectively involved in problem-solving at this time. The condition is deteriorating to the point that the young man may become a danger to himself. Something has to be done. On the basis of what considerations, and with what priorities, should we proceed?

Chapter 2

THE ENGINEER

THE PRESENTER:
LYNN J. EBERT, Ph.D.

Preamble

At the onset, let me make a few statements, which may sound a bit heretical, to set the framework for what I am about to discuss with you. While this set of conferences deals with professional persons, I personally do not view the engineer as a "professional" person in the same sense as I do an attorney, or a doctor of medicine, or a clergyman.

From my point of view, a professional person is one who acts as an agent in helping men and women carry out their three primary relationships. These relationships are those which concern man's dealings with himself, with other men, and with God. We call these agents, or professional persons, doctors of medicine, attorneys, and clergymen, and the corresponding professions are medicine, law, and religion.

Before you get the idea that I'm "splitting hairs" in making this distinction, let me point out that much of what I will say about the engineer's responsibilities, influence, etc. is the result of this difference between him and the "true" professionals. Let me pursue this concept just a bit more.

There are a number of basic characteristics which set the doctor of medicine, the attorney, and the clergyman apart from other so-called professionals, especially the engineer. The product of the work of the true professionals is usually words -- ideas, concepts, etc. The attorney advises his clients to do certain things; he may represent him in court; he may write instruments for actions, etc. The same is true of the clergyman and for the doctor of medicine. In these actions, tools are involved -- the attorney uses his law library, the physician uses diagnostic tools, etc. -- but the primary or predominant product of the relationship is advice, which the client is free to accept or not, as he chooses. This is generally not true of the bulk of the engineers who practice the profession today.

The second major difference between the engineer and the members of the true professions is the degree of freedom which each has to practice the profession as he sees it. The attorney, the doctor of medicine, and the clergyman sets his or her own hours, sets his or her own fees, operates pretty much as he or she sees fit. This is due largely to the fact that, in their primary function, the true professional does not have to rely on others for the carrying-out of that relationship. This certainly is not the case with the majority of the engineers in practice today. They are dependent upon the close working relationship with many others for the proper execution of their primary functions.

Another difference between the engineer and doctors of medicine, attorneys, and clergymen, and perhaps the last which I should delineate in this discussion, is the degree to which the results of their work are exposed to complete public scrutiny. The relationship between the true professional and his client is usually quite private. The work-product of the engineer is usually open for the entire world to see, to criticize, and to evaluate.

All of these differences, and perhaps several others, set the engineer apart from the true professionals, and constitute constraints upon his actions in carrying out the primary functions of his position. This can be an important point when it comes to assigning responsibility-for-action to the engineer in comparison with other professionals. Most persons are willing to accept responsibility for their actions, if the actions are freely taken, and taken in the absence of constraints. Very often, the engineer is cast in the position of having to accept responsibility for decisions which he has made but which were made under pressure of outside constraints. I hope to clarify these points as I go along.

The Nature of Engineering and Engineers

Having set the framework into which I would like to place the engineer among the so-called "professionals", let's take a closer look at this person, what he or she does, the environment in which he must work, his work product, the impact of his work product on society, his responsibilities, etc.

While almost everyone has some general idea of what engineering is, and what an engineer does, most persons will have a difficult time defining the profession and the practitioner with some degree of precision. This is the result of the fact that the profession is very broad and that it has many kinds of practitioners. Further, the definition will depend upon the definer's point of view and the purpose which the definition must serve. Let me try to give you a definition which will be both general and specific to our purposes here.

The dictionary definition of the engineer is one who practices the profession of engineering, obviously, but it goes on to define engineering in a manner which is relevant to our discussions:

engineering, n: a science by which the properties of matter, and the sources of energy in nature, are made useful to man. (Webster's Seventh New Collegiate Dictionary, G. & C. Merriam Company, Springfield, Mass., 1967, p. 275)

I have another definition of my own for the "engineer" which I would like to set forth because it bears on the responsibility of the engineer.

engineer: one who knows and fully understands the principles of science, and who uses them for a sufficiently large profit.

There are certain parts of the formal dictionary definition which I like and which I think are salient; other parts are not. I think that it is a mistake to define engineering as a "science"; rather, I like to think of it as the utilization of the principles of science -- and I feel sure that the engineer himself views his role as this. However, I do like the concept of using the properties of matter and natural energy for the good of mankind.

I like the second of the definitions because it shows that the engineer must first know the principles of science extremely well, that he further must understand them to the point where he can put them to work profitably, and not only profitably, but for a profit sufficiently large to satisfy shareholders, to provide funds for plant expansion, for increased labor costs, for research and development, etc.

These two definitions, taken together, characterize this person which society today calls the "engineer." In summary, the engineer is the person who, working with scientific principles, takes materials and energy and makes them useful to society, for a sufficiently large profit.

With this concept of the engineer and his profession, let's take a look at the work functions of the engineer:

1. He works with real **things**, with real **materials**.

2. His work-products are things of substance -- machines, devices, systems, and the like. Society calls them automobiles, airplanes, computers, bridges, buildings, roads, microprocessors, and on and on.

3. His relationship to his work-product includes:
   a. developing the concept for the product,
   b. designing the product,
   c. producing the product,
   d. servicing the product, and perhaps,
   e. selling the product, and more frequently in recent years,
   f. analyzing the failure of the product when necessary.

To get some flavor of the scope of the work of the engineer, consider just a few of the functional positions which engineers hold today. They --

- ° design and develop new fuels
- ° produce steel, aluminum and other materials
- ° create new alloys for jet engines
- ° supervise the production of micro-devices for computers
- ° reduce production costs for automobiles
- ° develop new joining processes for ceramics
- ° design and construct nuclear reactors
- ° determine the cause of airplane crashes
- ° develop and build looms for weaving textiles
- ° sell new steels to washing machine manufacturers

Categorically, the engineer's functions fall into (a) research and development, (b) production, and (c) sales and service.

If you get the idea that I am trying to emphasize the fact that the engineer is a very important person, you are quite right. Our entire standard of living, our very way of life, is the result of the efforts of hundreds of thousands of engineers, and as a matter of fact, the improvement of the standard of living of any group of people is paced by the availability of engineering talent and the materials with which the engineer can work. This is the reason that engineers are in such great demand today, as they have been for decades, and will continue to be in the foreseeable future.

I hope that you can see from the nature of the work of the engineer, which I have attempted to describe to you, that the engineer is far different from the doctor of medicine, the attorney and the clergyman, in terms of the manner in which he must carry out this professional function. In addition to working with real materials and producing something akin to hardware, he needs many thousands of dollars worth of equipment, the assistance of many technicians, as well as the cooperative efforts (very often) of other professionals, both technical and otherwise. Very seldom does the engineer work alone. There are some few engineers who operate on a consultive basis, but it is conservatively estimated that these number less than 10% of those persons who are active engineers today. Further, in almost every instance, each of these consultant engineers was a production type of person before becoming a consultant.

Again, let me point out that the fruits of the engineers efforts are available for all to see -- the jet aircraft flies efficiently and comfortably, the computer "spits out" answers faster than the eye can follow, the washing machine lasts 25 years, aluminum becomes so cheap that it can be used for throw-away beer cans. Or conversely, the bridge falls down, the car wears out before the last payments are made, the cost of the computer is so high that the company goes bankrupt. On the other hand, the advice given by the attorney, or the clergyman, or the doctor of medicine is usually held in strict confidence. Only in rare cases is the professional in these fields "called on the carpet" of public scrutiny and criticism for a decision which he has made, either good or bad.

The Power Held by the Engineering Profession

Once it has passed the brute survival stage, society is continually driven forward to bigger and better things by the appropriate motivational forces.

Individuals strive for better standards of living -- more creature comforts, better homes, bigger and faster cars, second and third TV sets, better stereo units, and on and on. Companies are driven ahead by the incentives of greater profits, larger shares of the market, and similar rewards. Nations are driven ahead by the desire for security, favorable balances of trade, increases of spheres of influence, and similar goals. In each of these endeavors, the engineer plays, or can play, an important role.

Since most of the goals of the individual, the company, or the nation, are materialistic in nature, or can be achieved only by materialistic means, and since the engineer deals with the materialistic devices and systems, he is a key component in the quest for the goals of society.

Looking at progress of peoples and nations very objectively, one can say that there are three components to success in progress, assuming that the political and economic environments are favorable. The components are materials (adequate supplies of the proper species), people (sufficient numbers with proper skills), and the proper "know-how" to put the first two together in a directed manner for progress. Of these three, engineering falls into the last category and is a major part of it. Further, of the three categories, the "know-how" is the most important. To illustrate this, one needs only to consider the relative success of the world's powers today.

The United States is recognized as the leading world power, because it has the optimum, or nearly optimum, combination of the three basic requirements. Russia is nearly in the same position, but lags the United States because of its slow start in putting the necessary "know-how" together. Japan must be recognized as a leading power despite its small size, and its relative shortage of basic raw materials, because of its competence and aggressiveness in developing the necessary "know-how." The developing third world countries, especially those in Africa, fall far behind, despite their wealth of raw materials and their large populations, because of their almost complete lack of the necessary "know-how", taken together with the poor basic education of its peoples.

In any event, it seems quite clear that the engineer plays a key role in the achievement of the goals of individual persons, corporate entities, and nations because he embodies the "know-how" which is the "glue" that holds the system together. The importance of the engineer in our society is manifested, among other ways, by the relatively high rate of monetary compensation which he receives for his efforts and his position security.

While the engineer categorically is a key cog in the pursuit of materialistic goals, not all engineers, as individuals, fulfill the role to the same degree. Those engineers who are at the forefront of quest of the goals, about which we have just been talking, are the research and development engineers. They are the persons who are responsible for conceiving the ideas that are both innovative and practical, generally using the existing principles of science, but, on occasion, generating them when they do not exist for specific application. They are, for example, the persons who have succeeded in developing the alloys which made jet aircraft and aerospace flight possible, in creating the devices which we know today as microchips for computers, in conceiving and building the computers and micro-processors which speed up and control production operations, in developing atomic bombs and nuclear reactors, robots, etc., etc., etc.

The engineers who work in production convert the basic developments to viable, working, profitable operations, and produce the final products which, hopefully, will serve the functions for which they are intended for the necessary period of time, trouble-free. The production engineer needs to be innovative in the conduct of his work, but not in the same way as the research and development engineers, nor to the same degree.

In summary, the power of the engineer stems from the fact that he plays a key role in aiding the individual, the company, and, ultimately, the nation, in achieving the materialistic goals which are generally termed "improving standard of living", "progress", "security", etc.

Ethical Considerations Arising From the Work-Power Relationship

There is a whole host of ethical issues associated with the practice of the engineering profession. To a very large degree, the engineer has ignored these issues until the past several decades, and, even today, many are still ignored. Let's try to take a look at the issues and why the engineer has done very little about them.

The issues themselves cover a wide range of topics, and thus it is difficult to place them into convenient categories. They run the gamut from the obvious problems, such as those associated with the ultimate military attack weapons, through considerations of consumer safety and issues of that kind, to the more subtle issues, such as those associated with the welfare of developing third-world nations. The following is a listing of some of the categories into which one might place the issues -- it is somewhat arbitrary, and is probably non-comprehensive, but it will give some idea of the nature and complexities of the issues themselves:

1. Military weaponry
2. Utilization of natural resources
3. Generation of unemployment
4. Environmental effects
5. Product safety and consumer protection
6. Failure analysis

Let's consider each of these to a limited extent, not necessarily with the intent of resolving the ethical issues, but rather with the intent of identifying specific items in the category and their implications.

The arguments surrounding the continued development of more and more military weaponry, both "aggressive" and "defensive", have raged for a very long time. Many thousands of engineers are engaged in these activities. Certainly at one time or other, each must have questioned the ethics, or the morality, of his work. He must have asked himself whether it is better for him to design and create the tools and devices with which to kill or maim thousands of persons, or to use his talent on transportation systems, etc. The fact that the activity still continues means that the answer to questions of this kind is positive and/or that the proper motivations are present.

The reckless utilization of natural resources, particularly those which cannot be replaced, continues unabated by the mature countries of the world, with little or no regard for the rights of the yet-to-be-developed countries for their fair share of them. I believe that most of us are aware of the situation with the petroleum and other fossils fuel reserves, but similar situations exist with materials such as chromium, helium, and others. The concern, in the minds of many, should be not only for our contemporary civilizations, but for the generations to come, both in the mature countries and in the developing countries. Should not efforts be expended presently to find replacement of alternate systems for the production of usable energy, etc., or at least to abate the rate at which these finite supplies of materials are being used? Further, should not the engineers who are presently engaged in the usage of these resources have some obligation to use some of their talent to find conservative and/or regenerative systems? The ethics of the engineer, knowingly depleting the earth's natural resources without putting substantial voluntary efforts into reducing their rate of depletion and/or finding substitute replaceable materials, should certainly be open to scrutiny, if not criticism.

The professional efforts of many engineers results in the unemployment of many craftsmen and production workers. These are the workers who are replaced by the robots and the automated systems developed by one segment of the engineering profession. While the reasons given for the "recession" of the early 1980's included many economic factors, in my opinion, one of the most important, but seldom cited, was the fruition of the efforts of the thousands of engineers and others who worked diligently to develop the robotic and automated systems whose overt goal was the elimination of the hard work of the assembly line workers. There can be little doubt that the goal of these efforts was known by the engineers engaged in this activity. Again, the question can be raised as to whether such activities, necessary though they be, should be carried forward without some consideration of compensatory measures for the workers who will be displaced.

For generations, American and worldwide industry has been willing to ignore the effects of its activities on the quality of the environment in which we must live, and since the engineer has played a major role in the production activities of industry, the results of his efforts have been a major contributor to the pollution of the environment. The purposeful dumping of hazardous waste materials and other pollutants into locations in which their presence was known to be harmful, to both inhabitants and the environment now and for generations to come, is unconscionable. There can be little doubt that the engineer who designs and develops a process that will produce deleterious side products knows the effects of these side products when he engaged in the activity. The fact that it takes major legislation of the Congress to force corrective action certainly points to

32

a lack of ethical responsibility.

The area of product safety and consumer protection is another which involves the ethics of the work of the engineer. Fortunately, it is one in which many problems associated with the lack of ethical regard for possible adverse effects of the work-product of the engineer are readily apparent. In other words, if the brakes on your new car fail, or if the rotary blade on your power lawn mower breaks, or if the picture tube on your television set blacks out the second month that you've had it, it is apparent that something is wrong with its design or manufacture. Because of this, the pressures from the consumer himself, and from consumer advocates, have forced the manufacturer, and his agent, the engineer, to be more careful of their work product in this safety and utility area.

Problems of an ethical nature arise, however, in the more subtle areas of product safety and utility -- those in which product shortcomings are not readily apparent because their effect is indirect, or because it will not be manifest until after long periods of usage. Some of these problems do come to the surface for what they really are. A good case in point for this is the reasonably recent problems associated with the location of the gas tanks in Ford Pinto model cars. Here it was known that the location was potentially dangerous at the time of the manufacture of the car, but the decision was made to keep the tank in that position anyway. There are many other problems relating to questionable ethical decisions of an engineering sense that do not come to the public eye so vividly. Many of these are related to the automotive scene, where cars wear out before they should, busses break down after only a year of service, etc. Similar situations can be found in almost every industry. In all of these cases, it seems quite clear that the product shortcomings were known to the engineer, but that the product was placed on the market anyway.

The area of failure analysis is perhaps the one in which the problem of ethics is most clearly visible. In these situations, the engineer is called upon to render a decision as to the cause of a failure of the product with which he has been associated. In some cases there is a loss of life; in others it may be primarily property loss and injury. Very often the engineer analyst is placed in the position of having to decide whether or not the fault for the failure lies with the company which employs him. If it does, just what is his ethical responsibility to the company, the person making the claim, to society and to himself, in terms of what he reports and how he reports it? In the case where he is convinced that the fault lies with the company or client who employs him, to what extent and how should he reveal the culpability?

The ethical problems arising from the situations described above, and from many others which could be cited, are quite complex for several reasons. They are further attenuated, in some cases, by the circumstances under which the engineer must work. Recall that, as I mentioned in the first part of the talk, the engineer, in most cases, does not operate as an independent professional. He works for a company; he works with others, very often as a member of a team of professionals and non-professionals; his judgments are subject to approval, modification, or rejection by management persons above him. Above all, the primary motivation which dictates the work in which he engages is one of making a sufficiently large profit. These circumstances give him many opportunities to "salve his conscience" in situations where the answers to ethical problems which face him are unsavory.

To illustrate the above, let's consider some of the ethical dilemmas in which the engineer often finds himself. If he worries about making military weapons of destruction, he is told, "They are for defense.", or "If we don't, the enemy will.", or "They will never be used, they are deterrents." If he is told to develop products which involve the extensive use of limited natural resources, he is told, "That's someone else's worry. You just develop what we need.", or, "The government will regulate the supplies when they become critical." If he raises questions about the jobs that will be lost to the automated systems which he is developing, he is told, "Jobs will be created in producing the robots.", or, "If we don't develop them our customers will buy robots from Japan." When he raises questions about the jobs producing the robots being much less in number than those of the persons being displaced, he is told, "That's not our concern. We've got to stay in business."

When the engineer raises issues about the by-products of his efforts polluting the atmosphere, he is told, "We're within the government's specifications for effluents." The fact that the specifications are inadequate, or do not exist, and he knows this, is not a matter for concern. Further, he is usually told, "Don't worry about these side effects, we'll face that problem when it arises."

As I mentioned a few moments ago, the area of product safety and consumer production is one in which ethical considerations have been forced upon the engineer by government regulation, at least to some extent. The longer range and more subtle effects are still in the area of concern.

In the area of failure analysis, the engineer, in many cases, can operate as a true professional -- particularly when he operates as an independent consultant. He must be mindful that he may not become a "gun for hire" by unscrupulous attorneys or other clients, but he must also remember that our courts have ordained that, right or wrong, every man is entitled to his day in court. Thus, if he works on behalf of the culpable party in the problem of the failure, his ethics are set by constraints of serving his client well but still avoiding areas forbidden by law. Very often, this is a fine line which must be walked, but at least it is defined, and the engineer has the opportunity to exercise his judgment without undue interference from third parties.

In summary, the ethical issues arising from the relationships involved in the work of the engineer are quite complex. If one defines "ethics" in terms of setting a proper set of moral values and code of conduct, or as a sense of responsibility to those who are affected by the work of the engineer, the engineer may be able to set these standards properly but may not be able to execute them to any effective degree. This is the result of the fact that he does not have complete control of the total process which involves his work. The process has many inputs in addition to his own, and the final decisive judgments are often completely beyond him. The very best that he can do is to try to influence the decisions in the way that his ethical judgment tells him to, recognizing that the final decision may be completely contrary to his own feelings. Very often he must live with statements such as:

"We can't do that because it will cost us too much money."

"That's not your concern; another department will worry about that."

"If we don't do it, our competition will, and we'll be out of business."

"We meet all existing specifications and standards; don't worry about it."

"We must do it this way to remain competitive."

"If you don't like to do it our way, you can resign; we'll find someone who will."

Because of these repeated frustrative answers, many engineers have developed an insensitivity to issues involving ethics. Many, or perhaps most, of them are seldom aware of the ethical aspects of their daily work.

The Impact of the Profession on Society

By and large, the impact of the profession on society as we know it today has been profoundly good. Those of us who are old enough to remember life in the 1920's and 30's -- days before television, air travel, automatic washers and dryers, air conditioning, super highways and the cars to go on them, transistors, pacemaker implants for cardiac patients, low cost power boats, electric mixers, automatic toasters, electric stoves, and thousands of other conveniences which have become necessities to many -- can attest to the tremendous improvement in the quality of life and its duration. To all of these improvements, the engineering profession has made major, if not critical, inputs. Further, these improvements have come about within the last four or five decades, and they continue to come on to the scene in increasing numbers. Who can guess what even the next 15 years will bring? It is said that 90% of all the scientists and engineers who have ever lived in the history of the world are alive today. Is it no wonder that we have come to expect a continual rise in the quality of our lives?

This almost unbelievable improvement in our standard of living and quality of life has not been achieved without its problems, however. We have already touched on some of them -- unemployment of workers by robots and automated systems, the reckless depletion of the world's finite natural resources, pollution of the environment in which we and our progeny must live, and others. To this list we must add the danger of massive devastation and death from nuclear power plant accidents, repetition of the Union Carbide disaster in India which took thousands of lives, the depletion of the fresh water supplies for many parts of the country, and others.

Despite the gravity of the above problems, there are even more serious problems which have had some root in the work of the engineering profession, or more properly, the globally non-uniform distribution of the fruits of its efforts. It is clear that there are nations which have a high concentration of engineering talent and the resources with which to exploit it, and there are other nations in which this is not true. The former are nations like the United States, Canada, and more recently Japan. The latter are nations such as those in Central America and Africa. This non-uniform distribution has created a spectrum of nations from those which "have" to those which "have not." The struggle of the latter to become the former has led to many global upheavals -- upheavals which have been economic, political, philosophical, and even military in nature. The advent of communism and socialism, and their spread throughout the world, was the result of the rank and file of the members of "have not" nations to better their lot in life. Many of the mini-wars that beset the world today, such as those in Africa, can find at least some root in the desire for members of those countries to improve their way of living.

It has been said that one way to prevent a "have not" nation from becoming a military aggressor is that of giving each of the inhabitants a car, a television set, and other soft-life paraphernalia -- luxuries that would be lost in the advent of an all-out war. As a matter of fact, it can be said that this has happened with the nation which, at one time, was considered to be a major military threat to the United States -- Russia. As the standard of living of the Russians has improved, and believe me it has in the past several decades, they seem to have become less and less of a threat to the United States. Russian citizens now have something to lose in the event of a major military engagement. It is said that the same is happening in mainland China. Many astute observers believe that the same effect could be achieved in Central America.

Implications for the Betterment of Society

On the basis of the key importance of the engineering profession in the continued advancement of our quality of life and standard of living, it is certain that the profession will be with us for a long time and that it will continue to grow and flourish. The demands of society, and the financial gain motivation of the entrepeneurs of the world, will guarantee this. Since this is the case, the shortcomings of the profession must be corrected if the total work-product of the profession is to be optimized. Among other things, this means that considerable attention must be given to all of the ethical aspects of the practice of the profession. It also means that there should be a better distribution of the engineering talent around the world and the necessary support for the utilization of this talent. This latter point is beyond the scope of our present discussion, but the former is not.

Considering the ethical aspects of the practice of the field of engineering, several things are necessary before corrective measures may be implemented. The first of these is the re-creation of an awareness in the mind of the engineer of the ethical overtones which must pervade the profession. The pressures of profit, expediency, management over-ride, and the other factors of which we have spoken before, have constrained the profession for so long that most practitioners in the field have lost sight of many of the moral and ethical aspects of the profession. To illustrate, I doubt if many of the engineers engaged in developing robots and automated production systems give any thought to the fate of the thousands of workers that the fruits of their work will displace. I doubt that many of the engineers developing new pesticides worry about the effects that the new chemicals will have on the streams and lakes into which the run-off of the excess chemical will find its way. So it first becomes necessary to remind the engineers about their responsibilities in maintaining a constant consciousness of all possible spin-off of the work in which they are engaged.

Once the awareness of the ethical and moral responsibilities of the engineer has been reestablished in his consciousness, it becomes necessary for him to have a mechanism by which he can alert the appropriate persons of potential dangers or adverse effects. Further, conditions must be such that he is encouraged to use the mechanisms quickly and completely.

Once having established the awareness and the system for alerting the proper persons of the problem areas, it is encumbent on those making the ultimate decisions in these matters to act upon them promptly and effectively. This is the most difficult part of the solution to the problem. The pressures of profit, market share, and corporate growth that permitted the ethical insensitivity situation to develop in the first place are still there. They must be attenuated to some degree, if not eliminated to a large degree, before the system has a chance of working.

It is highly unlikely that industry, of its own volition or government, of its own initiative in military-related matters, will readily accept the burden of acting in situations of the kind about which we are talking. Compensation or adjustment of some kind must be offered to industry in order for them to cooperate in the matter. Failing to achieve success by such motivating factors, punitive measures might have to be threatened to achieve industrial compliance. In the case of the military, it is not at all clear what types of motivation can be generated to induce positive compliance with the ethical standards for destructive devices and systems. It is quite possible that it will have to be the rising wave of public sentiment that will be necessary to assure compliance, even if standards for weaponry can be established.

THE ENGINEER

THE PRACTITIONER:
EDWARD A. STEIGERWALD, M.S., Ph.D.

Introduction

Thank you for asking me to participate in this conference. The issue of ethics in the engineering profession is one that requires increased focus. When I was in school, considerable emphasis was placed on the integrity of data as the basic ethical concern, but really very little on the broader dilemmas that many engineers and professionals encounter today. Seminars of this type can provide a real contribution in focusing on the ethical issues that continually face engineers and provide a basis for making the proper decisions.

Also, it is always nice to come back to Case Western Reserve University where I have many pleasant undergraduate and graduate school memories.

I still recall a particular incident with Lynn Ebert, who was directing some of the technician and laboratory effort as part of the Case Metals Laboratory in the mid-fifties. I had completed a nice project, had interesting results, and had personally prepared the report and drawn the appropriate figures. Professor Ebert reviewed the report and criticized the figures that I had prepared. He said that our product is both the form and substance of the final report and we should make certain that the report's appearance is totally professional.

In short, he said, "have a real artist do the figures." What does this have to do with ethics? Well, Lynn created a standard -- a norm of performance for the product we were producing in the Case Metals Research Laboratory.

Correspondingly, it is important to create a unit or company standard, a norm of performance, to insure legal and ethical behavior. I will return to this point a little later.

I hope, this afternoon, to provide, as a practitioner, a viewpoint of some of the issues that can occur in real life exposure to engineering practices. I will present some general thoughts on the subject, discuss examples of possible dilemmas and then provide suggestions that can produce a working climate which minimizes the risks of creating serious legal and ethical problems.

General Thoughts

I particularly like Lynn Ebert's inclusion of profit/or cost into the definition of engineering activities. This factor implies the necessity of trade-offs, the review of options, and the selection of the optimum answer when all variables are considered. To evaluate whether we have the right to decide on options, it is important to spend some time distinguishing between legal and ethical issues because often they are entangled and make for confusion.

In principle, there is no debate about legal issues since they are law. We individually and collectively should obey them. If we don't like them, then we should use the appropriate mechanisms for change. This means that proper behavior on issues like price fixing, environmental contamination and clean-up, safety, etc. are established and should be followed. In any organization it is important to reaffirm constantly this position so that the norm is clearly known. It is not an individual matter of judgment, like not completely stopping at a stop sign or going 38 mph in a 35 mph zone; it is a matter of representing the collective company position that the law must be followed.

The matter of professional ethics is more ambiguous since it involves much broader interpretation. The ethics for the engineering profession govern behavior that conforms to accepted professional standards of conduct; therefore, it is determined by engineers. These are not absolute, but can be time dependent, since additional data can often alter the generally accepted conduct.

Within the collective behavior pattern of a profession or group of people, there is also an individual moral position. For example, I remember interviewing a scientist for a job within the Research and Development Laboratory at TRW. We were working on a variety of programs ranging from materials for defense and weapon systems to new alloys for commercial jet engines. The interviewee was very specific, he would not work on a weapon project but would work on a jet engine material program. This was, in reality, a moral or personal ethics decision on his part, not a legal nor a professional engineering ethical problem.

Examples:

When I was in school, the basic ethical tenet that was continually drilled into us was the responsibility to provide accurate and unbiased data. This was extremely important since the data represented the building blocks for continual evolution of theory and practice. However, real life situations are usually not that simple. Let me describe a few generic cases that illustrate possible dilemmas and you can determine whether they represent legal, professional ethical, or individual ethical issues. Placing the problems into one of these categories can often help in deciding on a course of action.

Case #1

A manufacturer of microwave ovens discovers that some of its ovens, during use, leak radiation at levels in excess of the federal standard; however, these levels were markedly below levels identified by health professionals as posing a true hazard. The production problem has been corrected in all subsequent units, but about 25,000 ovens, which could violate the federal standards, were already in the stores. Should the firm institute a recall, keep quiet, or take some other action?

Case #2

A local fisherman noticed a fin deformity in a fish which he caught downstream from a chemical processing plant. He mentioned this to his neighbor, an engineer at that facility. The engineer asked the plant chemist to perform a simple laboratory test on a few bluegills with a specialty chemical which the plant had been producing for some time. The test showed a definite impact on the minnows from the exposed fish.

The plant manager, when confronted with these unofficial test data, informed him that all government regulations had been followed and instructed him not to meddle in amateur science. The chemical had already been widely used throughout the world and the potential mutagenic or reproductive effects of the chemical had not been fully studied since it had been registered long before tests were available or necessary. Indeed the tests that were conducted by the chemist may not be valid. What should the young engineer do now that his boss has told him to mind his own business? This is a very difficult professional ethics issue and a very strong individual moral issue.

Case #3

A machine designer was in the process of finalizing a conveyor design and was about to specify the chain guards. These had to be removable for maintenance, yet fully enclose the moving parts to prevent injury. The customer had asked for quick release fasteners so that maintenance could be performed quickly without tools. However, the design engineer recognized that this would make it easy for anyone to remove the guard and thus increase the likelihood that production workers would oil and maintain the unit while it was running, which would, in turn, increase the chance of worker injury.

Should the designer comply with the customer's request? Should he simply put warning decals around the chain drive to tell workers not to operate the equipment if the guard is absent? Should he install microswitches which would prevent the machine from running if the guards were not in place?

Case #4

An engineer is working in a plant that produces parts to a "frozen" process, i.e., contractually, certain procedures cannot be altered unless the customer formally approves the change. A heat treatment and cleaning operation is shown to be superfluous and has no influence on the final performance of the part. However, contractually it is specified as requiring customer approval for any changes. Should the engineer delete the operation while he is requesting the customer change, which takes 2-3 months, particularly if he has informal indications that the change will be approved? Although there may not be a technical risk, there is the obvious risk of departing from formally agreed upon contractual requirements and creating the possibility of customer relations and legal problems.

Many of the ethical issues stem from engineers and even managers making decisions at a local level that are viewed as acceptable performance. The culture may indicate that changes or decisions can be made as long as, in the judgment of the local unit, everything is technically acceptable or that the trade-offs, or risks, are such that the decision makes sense.

On a higher level, however, such decisions may not be viewed as ethical. For example, in Case #4, the engineer cannot alter a contractually specified process without following agreed upon procedures for such changes. To do otherwise can result in problems for the company (and him) for which he lacks an overall perspective and appreciation.

Problems usually occur when there is not clear congruency between the local culture where many decisions are made and the higher level culture where policy is determined. Unethical conduct is often perceived by the "doer" as ethical -- problems occur when the proper perspective is lost, or when risks are not properly assessed.

Characteristics of Problem Cultures

In most cases, where legal and ethical problems occur, there are some common organizational traits. The following characteristics can provide danger signals that managers can use to minimize potential problems:

- Relatively autocratic managers/engineers or decision makers with strong technical backgrounds and a good product knowledge.

- Weak communication links within the specific organizational unit.

- Relatively closed "society" (The unit strongly objects to outside intervention or audits).

- Dedication to the company (The people involved feel that they are doing the right thing and that they are totally capable of deciding what is right for the business).

- Strong operating and financial pressures to meet short-term financial objectives "at any cost."

The danger signals are not necessarily indicative of a poor performing organization, but, when present, they emphasize the need for closer scrutiny and good communication of expectations.

Aids in Preventing Problems

By way of summary, I would like to present a few recommendations which I feel could minimize the ethical dilemmas that engineers and managers may face. These recommendations essentially create a climate where key professional people can talk about the dilemmas and avoid the common pitfalls.

1. Identify strong top-management support for ethical behavior.

    People respond to what they feel the management really wants to accomplish. Management's actions (not simply words), at all levels, are the primary deterrent to illegal or unethical conduct.

2. Develop good communication and educational programs.

   An educational program, involving case histories and group problem-solving, will create a climate where the proper behavior is known, where ethical problems can be openly discussed, and where proper support is developed for making decisions in complex ethical situations.

3. Establish a strong set of norms and a supporting behavior pattern.

   If the proper culture is developed and open communication available, then expectations at all levels are defined so that decisions are made on a routine basis at all working levels.

4. Conduct selective audits.

   It is helpful to provide a method for conducting audits. Employing self audits, based on a useful audit document or questionnaire, can aid in maintaining the awareness, the systems, and the culture for good decisions without being an excessive burden to an organization.

As a parting comment, in developing an organization which has a high degree of awareness and concern for ethical behavior, we must not develop excessive conservatism so that no one is willing to take a risk or make a decision. A natural organizational reaction, in a unit where a problem has occurred, is to "bump" decisions up to the highest level or make a decision which is the safest from a personal standpoint, rather than one that is totally acceptable from an overall professional or group standpoint. Excellent organizations are able to provide an environment for risk-takers without destroying the awareness for maintaining high levels of conduct.

The issue of proper legal and ethical behavior in engineering is a critical one which only increase in complexity. Seminars such as this one, where we can openly evaluate and define proper approaches, will significantly help future engineers adequately cope with these problems.

THE ENGINEER

THE PRACTITIONER:
BARRY A. ROGERS, M.S.C.E., P.E.

Introduction

Let me begin by giving a little background of my experience as an engineer. I have worked for eight years at a large architectural-engineering company as a structural engineer. As such I have performed calculations, designed, and detailed buildings ranging from a twenty-story office building to an amusement-park structure. I have also worked on various investigations of problems in different structures.

I would like to respond to Dr. Ebert's paper. Basically I disagree with various points and I will explain why as I go along. Part of the disagreement with Dr. Ebert's work is that it is somewhat limited to the material-science field and limited to the University environment as opposed to the so called "real world", that is, the working world outside of the University.

Engineering Defined

In defining "Engineer" I dug back in my resources and came up with an 1891 version of a book entitled How to Become an Engineer. It was a small book, very short and simple. In the introduction it mentions that the title "Engineer" is "assumed by men engaged in many varieties in human industry. From the ambitious plumber's apprentice to the engine driver of a tug boat to he who plans and directs the construction of the most extensive public works." The book continued to define engineering as "the science of employing the physical properties of matter to serve the purposes of mankind, including useful application of different forms of energy." This is almost identical to the dictionary definition quoted by Dr. Ebert.

Let's consider some of the various divisions of engineering. Engineering is a very broad field and engineers are involved in many different types of work. We have talked mainly about materials to this point.

In the construction and design field, other divisions of engineering include civil engineering, transportation, structural, electrical, electronic, mechanical, heating, cooling, plant production, industrial, materials handling, seismic, wind, arctic, naval, space, and the relatively new field of biomedical engineering. And this certainly is not a complete list.

The Engineer's Work

Dr. Ebert's concept of the engineer working for profit is true for one of two major categories of engineers. There is a large category of engineers who work for the public sector -- the government. Certainly the Army Corps of Engineers is a large employer of engineers. And these engineers do work strictly for the good of society: working on the roads, the sanitary systems, the water systems that we have. The remainder of those of us in the private sector do work within the capitalistic system in which companies do try for profit -- the bigger the profit the better.

One final issue in the discussion of the nature of the engineer's work is the term "Professional Engineer" which has a specific legal connotation, particularly as it is directed to building construction. I regret that the designation, "P.E.", was not included after my name in the publicity for this program. The Professional Engineer must meet state-mandated standards for education and experience and pass two exams before being licensed as a registered Professional Engineer. This is identical to the doctor or lawyer who also must pass standards and exams to become licensed by the state. And as such I am proud to be able to attach the designation "P.E." to my name. Many of us engineers do not rigorously utilize the P.E. designation. Why don't we insist on it? I would say perhaps that modesty is one reason; or, more realistically, society as a whole does not understand what a "P.E." is or what the term "Professional Engineer" means. It can also be socially awkward. One can imagine party invitations addressed to "Dr. and Mrs. Jones" and "P.E. and Mrs. Smith." It doesn't have the same connotation. Only a small percentage of engineers do become registered or need to become registered. To design or build any structure, building or public works, a registration is required. This is a legal requirement enacted to protect the public to ensure that the people doing the design have been adequately trained and have sufficient experience.

Engineering Output

Dr. Ebert suggests that the product of an engineer's efforts is an animate object. He refers to the jet aircraft, the throw-away beer can, the automobile that wears out too soon. That, from my experience, is not entirely correct. Many engineers, including myself, produce a set of specifications for a product. In my case it is usually a building. It consists of a set of blue-prints, specifications, and an operating manual for the mechanical engineer. This information is not a physical product but is information comparable to that of the other cited professions of law and medicine. Manufacturing and construction are seperate entities which use the information we engineers produce to create the final product. There are engineers involved in the production of the product, e.g. production engineers and plant engineers. They do work to develop a final product.

The Engineer's Power

I might ask why none of you were afraid to come to this building today? We did not have to worry about the roof falling in or the fact that there wouldn't be sufficient lighting or heat. The reason, I suggest, is the trust in engineers. One of the most important powers of the engineer is the trust of the public. And it is a trust which we as Professional Engineers must work very hard to continue to merit. Every day the public places their very lives in the hands of engineers in the sense that they travel under bridges, they enter buildings, travel in elevators -- these examples can continue. We as engineers are not flawless. In fact our track record of late is slipping a bit and there are various reasons to explain that. Given the responsibility for the welfare of the public one might assume that the engineer would have considerable power. In general that is not necessarily true. There is an old business adage: "he who controls the purse strings -- controls." And in general, engineers are "technicians" who do not control the dollars nor make the decisions. Financial decisions such as the allocations of funds in the public sector is a very political activity. Whether this is good or bad is not for me to say. There is only limited input from the engineer. He will be consulted and provide some input. Likewise in the private sector, decisions made by "management" are often based on short-term profit. The oft-quoted example of the Ford Pinto serves as a case in point. Although I have no proof, I suspect that "engineering" was aware of the problem or became aware of it. Then, per their engineering training, they developed a solution to the problem. In my hypothetical scenario, "management" reviewed the solution, evaluated the associated costs, and opted not to revise the design. Is it fair to blame "engineering" for the Pinto problems?

Before one faults engineers for not making "the big decisions", for serving merely as technicians, consider an analogous situation in the medical profession. In treating a patient the doctor serves as a technician utilizing his tools and training. And when a "big decision" is involved such as removing life support-systems when justified, the doctor, like the engineer, must defer this decision to "management" and society.

The Engineer's Compensation

Engineering is perceived as a "white-collar" profession with associated job security and financial compensation. Beginning with job security, engineering in general is very project-oriented. A company will "staff-up" to have sufficient man-power to complete a stated project. Once that project is completed, unless there is a new project, a company can not afford to retain those engineers and they are usually "released." As such, engineers are often a very mobile group moving from company to company as workloads dictate. In Cleveland there were three main design firms. Engineers would rotate around from company to company depending on who had the large job at a given point in time. It was just accepted and, actually, it worked pretty well from a corporate point of view. For the engineer, it meant minimal seniority, minimal vacation time, minimal pensions, and no security.

As to the monetary compensation, engineers usually don't starve nor do they become what I would call wealthy. Unlike the legal or medical fields, engineering tends not to offer high salaries with time and experience. In fact, every time I go to one of our construction sites and work on solving a problem that has arisen, it bothers me a bit that the people to whom I am giving the solution, people to whom I am giving instructions, are usually earning more money than I am by a fair amount. Yet I must assume all responsibility for the completed structure.

Ethics in Engineering

Dr. Ebert discussed a few ethical issues for engineers, ranging from miltary weaponry, to the so-called "rape of the environment", and unemployment generated by "our" work. As an engineer I think that these issues are ethical issues for society and not just for engineers. It should not be placed on "our" shoulders. Let me discuss some of them in detail, beginning with military weaponry.

I personally have designed a military plant. At that time I never gave a minute's thought to the fact that I was working on a military weapon. At that point in time it was a building. The only reason that I knew that it was a military plant was the title on the drawings. If the owner really wanted to deceive us he could have called it plant "X", which in some cases does happen. As an engineer I was designing a building and there is no significant ethical issue involved with that. In fact, all of us who pay taxes have a stronger role in supporting weaponry than do we engineers who work on a plant or weapon.

Moving on to the utilization of resources, let me ask about the synthetic-fuels project which is one that I was interested in personally. Dr. Ebert suggests that engineers have a responsibility to develop other fuels in order to preserve fuels for future generations. It certainly wasn't the engineers who canceled the synthetic fuels project. There were many engineers who depended on that project for their livelihood. It was canceled by society, if you will; politicians, if you want to point a finger. It was canceled by a society which feels that the current oil glut is such that we needn't worry about the future. I don't think it is fair to blame this decision on engineers in any way, shape, or form.

53

Unemployment of workers due to automation, interestingly enough, finds engineers to be one of the groups that are being influenced by automation. In many companies over the last five years an increasing amount of work is being done with fewer engineers. There is a reliance on automation, on computer drafting, and on computerized design. So to say that we engineers are at fault for jobs lost to automation is somewhat ironic in that we are suffering from mechanization along with the rest of society. Certainly one must look at the broader scope, or at least look at it from a different angle. We as consumers are always looking for a better product, a more reliable product, at a lower cost. I believe that it has been shown clearly that one way to achieve lower costs is through automation. We as engineers are serving society by introducing automation to manufacturing firms.

Let me move on to some ethical issues of my own. The first one that always seems to appear in any discussion of ethics is money. The construction industry in which I work is one that is notorious for what can politely be called a lot of things but what comes down to bribery in most instances. This is, unfortunately, known to occur in the construction business, though not necessarily in the engineering business. Several years ago as a young naive engineer working as a structural designer on a local job, I was having discussions with a sub-contractor who wanted to take what I thought to be a short cut on a particular part of his work. He suggested at one point that I should perhaps join him on his sailboat for the weekend. I happen to love sailing but couldn't ethically allow myself to be involved in that. This is only a minor issue, but it did certainly register a point with me and emphasizes the fact that we all must make these ethical decisions.

Computers are, oddly enough, one of the biggest ethical issues that I find in the engineering profession at this time. Several months ago I had a discussion with an engineer who had developed and was marketing a series of computer programs to design steel beams, wood beams, and the like, to be used in apartment complexes and small industrial commercial projects. When the engineer/programmer had first developed the programs he refused to sell them to several architectural firms that had ordered them. His thinking was that these architects would use the programs to replace the engineer because the engineer would no longer be needed to size the members for the project. Secondly, he was concerned that the architects who didn't understand the structural engineering involved could easily make a mistake and misuse the programs, misinterpret the results, or not understand when the programs couldn't solve the problems. He wrestled with that decision for several months before concluding: "If they don't buy them from me they are going to buy them from someone else. Mine are probably better than the other ones they are going to buy. I might as well sell them mine and hope that they get the better job out of it."

A second issue which arises with computers is illustrated by the following: Two or three years ago on the West Coast a large computer program had been used to design a nuclear power plant. After the plant had been constructed and was in the process of going on line there was a flaw discovered in the computer program. There was an error in the logic. At that time they did shut the plant down completely and did a thorough investigation to determine what, if anything, needed to be done to the plant to make it safe. But it brings up an issue that I wrestle with almost daily. In today's world we can't avoid using computers. We are not serving our clients well if we don't use computers. They are so much more efficient time-wise and can do a more detailed analysis. No longer can we as engineers review the computer programs in detail to make sure we understand the logic. Ten or fifteen years ago most of the programs were written by engineers in-house and we knew exactly what was in the program. Now programs are getting too big and too complex for us to spend the time to go through them. We have to blindly assume -- it could be argued that we should blindly assume -- that the answers from the program are right. If that is true, and an error is discovered, who is responsible? Is it the engineer that uses the answers or the programmer who wrote the program? Basically the profession at this point has said that it is clearly the engineer's responsibility. He is the one who has decided to use the program. He must use the program properly and must investigate the result to make certain that it has a valid result.

As the last topic in the area of ethics, consider the involvement of the public. The following is a story that I'm still thinking about. I heard the story third-hand and cannot vouch for its accuracy. Also, I must emphasize that my company was not involved in the project. An engineer was retained to investigate the structural soundness of several existing office buildings. An insurance company was going to buy these as an investment. The structural engineer-consultant was retained to make sure that the buildings were in good shape before the company spent the money. In reviewing the original design the structural engineer quickly realized that the lateral bracing in the building, the "X" bracing that many of us see in buildings, was almost non-existent. This was in the Gulf Coast area which is subject to many hurricanes. When one considered a hurricane loading on this building there was just no way the that building was structurally adequate. The engineer went back to the original designer and said, "Something is not right here. What am I missing? I don't understand." The explanation given was that the developer had determined that he wanted it built that way. He had told the engineer, "Ignore hurricanes, pretend that they don't exist. Design that building without that extra strength and extra cost." The developer's logic was simply that, if a significant hurricane occurs and causes damage to the building, even knocks the building down, there would be plenty of government money available to rebuild. He was going to use that government money at low loan rates to rebuild. The developer felt that it was economically better for him to operate in that way. It is a frightening scenario, and I repeat, one whose accuracy I cannot vouch for.

Engineering and Society

Moving on to the impact of engineering on society, we all recognize engineering is very important in improving our standard of living. But I might suggest that engineering may also have done a disservice to society along the way. This is a personal comment; I don't know that I have seen it in print before. Over the past decade the engineer working in the big dark room has always been able to come up with bigger, better, faster products of some sort. Society has come to rely on the engineer to do that. In today's society, perhaps even in past societies, technology and the engineer cannot solve the problems that we currently face. Engineers can't do that and it is unfair to expect us to solve the problems of society. One specific example is that of air bags in automobiles, a debate which has been kicking around for a lot of years now. Should we, as engineers, make the decision that you, the consumer, must pay the additional money and face the risk that this air bag would blow out as you were driving down the road? That may not be an engineering decision. It is a decision that you individually should make when you purchase a car, or which should be dictated by a government agency. Having engineers make the decisions may be somewhat akin to a dictatorship where there is not representation nor a chance for the consumer to elect an engineer, or effectively change the engineer's judgment.

Certainly another issue like air bags is genetic research. How are we as engineers to make the decision whether genetic research should continue. There has been great controversy in past years as to whether genetic research should be allowed because of the dangers of some mutant escaping. Several communities have actually enacted local bans against genetic research. The entire concept of genetic research has great possible rewards but also certain risks. Are we as engineers qualified to make, and should we make, these decisions in a local community or indeed globally?

Along with looking at the impact of engineering on society, I would like to look for a moment at the impact of society on engineering. I have noticed in our profession that engineering has been demoted in the eyes of the public both in status and in financial compensation. Many of the better talents coming out of schools these days are headed for more glamorous fields -- into the legal field or in the field of financial consulting. Many companies are having some problems finding new and talented people in the engineering field. If this is to continue, we could end up with a definite shortage of well-qualified engineers in the future.

Another devastating effect of society on engineering is the legal aspect. We have read of the great malpractice insurance rate increases for doctors.

In engineering we have a similar program which has increased at the same alarming rate that malpractice insurance has increased. In some areas of engineering, particularly in geo-technical engineering, it is not possible to get malpractice insurance. Therefore the geo-technical people have formed their own insurance company. But, as this leads into lawsuits, engineers will have to become more conservative, as Edward Steigerwald has mentioned, which would be a dangerous thing and a negative thing for engineering. We will have to protect ourselves more and more in the future and this is not good.

Allow me to close by citing the oath that I pledged when I became a registered Professional Engineer:

> I pledge to give the utmost performance; to participate in none but honest enterprise; to live and work according to the laws of man and the highest standards of professional conduct; to place service before profit; to place the honor and the standing of the profession before any personal advantage; to place the public welfare above all other considerations. In humility, and with the need for Divine Guidance, I make this pledge.

Chapter 3

THE NURSE

THE PRESENTER:
VIOLET MALINSKI, Ph.D., R.N.

The purpose of this paper is to explore the ethical issues arising from the practice of nursing and the power inherent in the profession of nursing. Five areas will be explored:

- ° The nature of the work
- ° The nature of the power
- ° The relationship between work and power and the ethical issues arising from this relationship
- ° The positive and negative impact of nursing on the welfare of society
- ° The implications for nursing which could lead to a more humane society.

The Nature of the Work

The phenomenon of concern to nurses is people in their wholeness as they interact with their environment. Nurses provide a range of services to clients, which may be individuals, families, groups, or communities, whose needs range from health maintenance and promotion to restoration and support. They may provide this range of services as employees of organizations such as hospitals, health clinics, community mental health centers, or birthing centers; as solo practitioners engaged in private practice or as partners in group practices designed to provide services to a general or select population, such as home health care services to clients discharged from the hospital to the community. Other nurses are engaged in the education and professional socialization of students in basic and advanced nursing programs designed to prepare both generalists and specialists in the various fields of nursing. Others are generating the research needed to validate the practice of the art of nursing and to test or generate new theories in the science of nursing. Still others are involved in health policy and planning initiatives.

Nightingale viewed the nurse as having charge of someone's health. She offered the following distinction between nursing and medicine in her 1859 book, Notes on Nursing: What It Is and What It Is Not:

> We know nothing of the principle of health , the positive of which pathology is the negative, except from observation and experience. And nothing but observation and experience will teach us the ways to maintain or to bring back the state of health. It is often thought that medicine is the curative process. It is no such thing; medicine is the surgery of functions, as surgery proper is that of limbs and organs....the function of an organ becomes obstructed; medicine, so far as we know, assists nature to remove the obstruction, but does nothing more. And what nursing has to do is put the patient in the best condition for nature to act upon him. (p. 133)

Nightingale recognized the importance of the person's environment and described nursing as "the proper use of fresh air, light, warmth, cleanliness, quiet, and the proper selection and administration of diet -- all at the least expense of vital power to the patient." (p. 8)

From Nightingale on, nurses have been concerned with the health of their clients. Although precise definitions of nursing have changed over the years, a consistent theme among them has been the welfare and well being of other human beings, with recognition given to the context in which they live, including family and physical environment.

In 1980 the American Nurses Association published a document describing the social context of nursing, the nature and scope of practice, and specialization in nursing. Nursing, A Social Policy Statement, reflected the ideas of the Congress for Nursing Practice, the structural unit of the A.N.A. charged with activities related to practice, legal aspects, implications for practice of evolving health care trends, and public recognition of the importance of nursing to health care. The Social Policy Statement (1980, p. 5) defines health as "a dynamic state of being in which the developmental and behavioral potential of an individual is realized to the fullest extent possible." This definition recognizes the uniqueness of experience and personal being of the client. For example, the person with a chronic disease still has the potential for health. Someone who is dying can be assisted to achieve a healthy death. The definition of nursing presented in the Social Policy Statement (1980) is consistent with Nightingale's and is the definition of nursing offered here for discussion: "Nursing is the diagnosis and treatment of human responses to actual or potential health problems." (p. 9)

The focus of nursing, therefore, is clearly on the person experiencing a disease state or condition, not on a medical diagnostic category. For example, human responses might consist of disrupted sleep patterns; self image changes accompanying pregnancy or loss of a body part; problematic affiliative relationships, such as dysfunctional family communications; or the experience of pain.

In this definition, nursing encompasses services to both the sick and the well, providing a comprehensive approach to health care for individuals and families across the life span as well as for groups and communities. Nurses might focus on activities directed toward health maintenance and health promotion or toward restoration and support.

A nurse makes a diagnosis within the context of the nursing process, a deliberate, systematic method utilizing observational and problem-solving techniques to identify actual or potential problems, implement appropriate interventions, and evaluate their effectiveness. (Carpenito, 1983) Within this framework, Carpenito (1983) defined nursing diagnosis as:

> a statement that describes a health state or an actual or potential alteration in one's life processes.... The nurse uses the nursing process to identify and synthesize clinical data and to order nursing interviews to reduce, eliminate, or prevent (health promotion) health

alterations which are in the legal and
educational domain of nursing. (p. 4)

The National Group for the Classification of
Nursing Diagnosis is composed of nurses from the United
States and Canada who represent practice, education,
and research. They have been meeting since 1973 to
develop a nursing diagnosis classification system, now
numbering 50 diagnoses.

The Nature of the Power

Nursing involves a process of interpersonal
relationships. For example, the nursing process
represents shared decision-making and action between
nurse and client. The A.N.A. Standards of Nursing
Practice (1973) describe this process as a
collaborative one between nurse and client, with mutual
responsibility for decision-making. The Social Policy
Statement and the A.N.A. Code for Nurses (1985) further
elaborate on the nurse's role in providing information
to clients, enabling them to exercise their autonomy or
freedom, one expression of which is choice among
treatment options.

The Code for Nurses states clearly that the
dignity and uniqueness of the client are to be
respected. Thus, "truth telling and the process of
reaching informed choice underlie the exercise of
self-determination, which is basic to respect for
persons." (p. 2)

By emphasizing information, autonomy, and choice
we affirm that individuals have their own unique ways
of being and creative potentials. They need to become
attuned to their own rhythms, not disconnected from
them once they assume the role of "patient." Clients
have self knowledge to share and contribute to the
helping process.

The interpersonal nature of nursing entails
recognition of nursing as a social phenomenon. (Ashley,
1973) According to Ashley, nursing's power "derives
from society's recognition of nursing as an essential
service." (p. 638)

A similar point is made in The Social Policy

Statement. Professions are part of, and evolve from, society and can be said to be owned by society in the sense that they acquire recognition and relevance in relation to the needs, conditions, and traditions of the society and its members. (Page, 1975) The authority for nursing practice, therefore, derives from this social base and constitutes a social contract between the profession and society. Inherent in this contract is the need for self-regulatory activities. One such activity is the formulation of state nurse practice acts, which constitute the legal authority to practice and which stem from the social contract between nursing and society. (A.N.A., 1980) The Code of Ethics and the Standards for Practice, formulated by the American Nurses Association, further specify aspects of the social contract.

According to Fiesta (1983, p. 1), "autonomy operationally is power." There are many definitions of power, and they usually entail the idea of power over, power to use against someone, or power to make someone do something. Within nursing, a more appropriate concept is that of empowerment, a process of mutually shared power which acknowledges clients as equal partners in the health care system. Rather than trying to exercise power of authority over clients and trying to make them comply with what health care providers want, nurses need to provide health teaching and other tools that enable clients to choose knowledgeably.

For nurses, autonomy entails the freedom and authority to exercise informed judgment and implement nursing actions. Within the context of the nursing process, this means, for example, making an assessment, formulating a nursing diagnosis, implementing and evaluating nursing actions designed to promote, maintain, restore, or support clients' health.

Moral and legal accountability for one's own actions go hand-in-hand with autonomy. The Code of Ethics charges the nurse to assume responsibility and accountability for nursing actions, maintain competence in nursing, participate in the profession's efforts to implement and improve standards of nursing, and participate in efforts to establish and maintain employment conditions conducive to high quality nursing care. (A.N.A., 1985, p. 1)

Work and Power: Ethical Issues

Two major conceptualizations of "the nurse" in the last decade have been nurse as change agent and client advocate. For the purpose of this paper, I will focus on the role of the nurse as advocate. According to statement #3 of the Code of Ethics (A.N.A., 1985, p. 6), "The nurse acts to safeguard the client and the public when health care and safety are affected by incompetent, unethical, or illegal practice by any person." The accompanying interpretive statement explicates this as the need to be alert to any instances of incompetent, unethical, or illegal practice by any member of the health care team or the health care system, or any action that places the client's best interests in jeopardy. Furthermore, in the role of client advocate, the nurse is charged with taking appropriate action in such cases.

This view of advocacy puts the emphasis on the nurses' role as protector of the client. For the nurse to act in other than an adversarial role with one or more members of the health care team, good collaborative working relationships are essential. For example, the nurse needs to be a participant in the decision-making process, as the client should, also. Often such collaboration is missing, and the only recourse the nurse sees is that of whistle-blowing.

In a 1981 issue of the American Journal of Nursing, for example, Murphy described an incident observed by a nurse. A surgical resident severed a client's carotid artery during tracheotomy, and the person bled to death. When the nurse tried to report the incident, the medical director cautioned her not to pursue the matter without an attorney. "Dr. X kills the patient and I need the lawyer." (p. 1691)

When cast in the role of coordinator or facilitator of comprehensive care, the nurse, as client advocate, often functions as a mediator among members of the health care team, between team and client and between client and family. This may be one of the most common approaches to advocacy, yet one with many pitfalls. For example, the client and family often do not see the nurse in such a role, holding a more traditional view of the nurse's place in the health care setting. One or both may resist the nurse's efforts to serve as mediator. Depending on the setting, other members of the health care team may not see the appropriate role for the nurse. Social workers often see client advocacy as an essential part of their role in the health care setting. If the nurse and social worker together engage the client in the process of shared decision-making that may work very well. If the two health care workers are not in accord, the client will be stuck in the middle.

Another problem lies in the definition of client -- individual or entire family. If both parties favor different courses of treatment, for example, they may find her-/himself trying to mediate between two sets of conflicting wishes.

Often nurses "forget" the object of their advocacy and serve as mediators between the health care system and clients in support of the former. As Ashley (1973) put it, "To the degree that they function as the system's or the physician's advocate, they fail to effect change in the provision of health services to society." (p. 640)

Kohnke (1982) defined advocacy as a two-fold process: informing and supporting a person, enabling the client to make the best possible decision for him-/herself. The process of informing means having or obtaining the necessary knowledge, to communicate to the client, presenting it in such a way that the person is able to hear what is being said, and explaining possible outcomes of each course of action discussed. Next, the nurse must support the client once the choice has been made. This entails respect for the person and belief in the client's ability to make an informed choice. This may mean supporting the client against the wishes of family members and/or other members of the health care team. The family may ask the nurse to "talk to the patient." The physician may ask the nurse to dissuade the client from a selected course or to obtain the client's signature on a consent form for a treatment which the client has already rejected. In supporting the client, the nurse may be placed in a position where her/his actions will be perceived within the institutional setting as disobeying orders.

Nonaction may be an important part of the support process. (Kohnke, 1982) For example, the nurse must be sensitive to one's own values and beliefs about what is and is not appropriate. Nonaction involves keeping oneself from undermining or influencing the client's choice, as well as refusing to cooperate with others' requests to help change the client's decision. Within this view of advocacy, the nurse is careful not to assume the role of rescuer, stepping in to act and do for the client. Keeping this in mind can help the nurse stay out of the family system in the sense of being sucked in between client and family. For example, part of the informing and supporting process is assisting the client to explore possible ways of presenting the decision reached to family members and how to cope with anticipated responses. The nurse can support the client through this process yet not take on the responsibility for dealing with the family as the client's surrogate.

Such a view of advocacy can be very difficult to implement, given the traditional roles ascribed to patient and nurse within the ethos of the hospital culture. Jo Ann Ashley's (1976) historical study of nursing's development, published in book form as Hospitals, Paternalism, and the Role of the Nurse, documented the legacy of the hospital apprenticeship system. Nurses (women) cared for the hospital family. Policies and procedures to guide management of this institutional household were formulated in the best interests of the hospital and were designed to make it look good and preserve its reputation.

> For 24 hours a day, nurses were expected to be versatile in their skills, to demonstrate their ability to take care of whatever needs might arise, whether in the area of patient care, medical treatment, housekeeping, dispensing drugs, or supervising the diet and the kitchen. Like mothers in a household, nurses were responsible for meeting the needs of all members of the hospital family -- from patients to physicians....
> In addition, women (nurses) were expected to look out for the needs of men (physicians) in the hospital family who, for the most part, did not reside in the household, but were free to come and go.

> In the absence of men, women were expected to assume full responsibility for their decision-making functions...this role was, of course, relinquished upon the return of the men. (Ashley 1976, p. 17)

The nurse served as wife and mother in this hospital family, the physician as husband and father, and the patients as the children.

Many nurses and clients have not been able to relinquish the roles of surrogate mother and surrogate children perpetuated over the years. Clients often expect to be taken care of and have the onus of decision-making removed from them once they assume the role of patient. This surrogate mother-child relationship provokes a slide into paternalism, with the nurse making decisions for the client because of expert knowledge or experience.

The A.N.A. Code, with its emphasis on the nurse's role as protector of the client, may inadvertently provoke paternalistic action when it becomes a matter of who decides what is harmful to the client. For example, members of the health care team agree to respect the wishes of a comatose patient as outlined in a living will despite objections from the nurse. The nurse truly believes that other members of the team are acting in a way injurious to the person. On whose behalf is she/he acting by "blowing the whistle?"

Nursing and the Welfare of Society

Historically nursing has served the public good. Nightingale was instrumental in effecting needed changes in sanitation and other health measures in the hospitals of her day. Public health nursing flourished in this country in the first quarter of the 20th century. Lillian Wald and Mary Brewster opened the Henry Street Settlement House in 1893 to serve the needs of the poor on New York's Lower East Side. The Frontier Nursing Service has delivered midwifery services to the poor in Appalachia since 1925.

Nursing has attempted to deal with issues of autonomy, responsibility, and the legal and moral bases for practice by formulating a Code of Ethics in 1950, periodically revising it, and setting standards for generalist and specialist practice. The <u>Society Policy Statement</u>, published in 1980, can be seen as a statement affirming nursing's social responsibility and the essence of the social contract between the profession and society. As such, it represents a starting point for continuing dialogue. Clients have not always been able to articulate what they want from nurses, and nurses have not always been able to explain what they have to offer that is different from the other health professionals.

Nurses learn to cooperate and collaborate with other health care workers and this often serves to maintain the status quo rather than to effect change in the delivery of health services to clients. When nurses place their allegiance with the health care setting rather than clients, the greatest potential for harm exists. This may consist of covering up an error committed by another nurse or other professional or collaborating to withhold information. In the early 1970's, for example, the women's self help movement received impetus from the trend to withhold information from women about their own bodies, whether it was basics of physiological functioning or complete information about birth control measures. For example, it was common practice in one birth control clinic, and probably many more, to remove all manufacturer-supplied information from packets of birth control pills and tell the clients, poor, black, often unemployed and unmarried, that there were no problems associated with taking the pills. The ones removing the information and doing this "counseling" were all nurses. This was clearly a misuse of the nurses' power.

Ashley (1972) discussed the problem of misused power in terms of the traditional roles of nursing supervisors. Supervisors often identify with the "powers that be" in the institution, those in medical and hospital management, usually men, rather than with the nursing staff group, usually women. This isn't an unusual pattern in a society that traditionally confers direct power on men and only indirect power on women. A couple years ago I lived in another state where the Nurse Practice Act was up for revision. The largest medical center in the area issued a gag rule forbidding nurses employed there to engage in any activities, even on their own time, to promote passage of a revised act.

Anyone caught doing so was to be fired on the spot. The Director of Nursing supported hospital and medical management in this, not the staff nurses.

The historical development of nursing reflects the continual strivings of its leaders to achieve recognition, with moves to upgrade the educational base and to institute mechanisms for licensure and certification. One outcome, however, has been the formation of a caste system to the exclusion of a collective consciousness among nurses. Nursing, as a profession dominated by women, is inextricably linked to gender issues because women, as nurses and as clients in the health care system, face the same pressures, attitudes, and stereotypes. Higher education for nurses means higher [education] for women. Only a hundred years ago "medical authorities" warned that providing a young woman with a college education would lead to atrophy of her uterus. In 1909 Lavinia Dock (in Nutting, 1912, p. 27), put the issue in perspective: "the thing of real importance is not that nurses should be taught less, but that all women should be taught more." In adopting an essentially male paradigm of professionalism, nurses have often lost sight of the implications for a predominantly female group. I offer this as a point for discussion as it impacts on the welfare of society.

Implications for Nursing -- Toward a More Humane Society

The A.N.A. Code recognizes health care as a universal need, irrespective of racial, ethnic, economic, religious, political, educational, and sexual differences. The nurse respects the worth and dignity of the client regardless of the nature of the health problem. The Code's emphasis on client self-determination provokes a re-examination about beliefs regarding the independent and dependent roles of client and nurse, hopefully encouraging movement toward a mutually interdependent view of the nurse-client relationship.

Curtin presents the basic human rights introduced earlier in this paper -- independence, freedom of action, and ability to choose -- as essential components of the advocacy process. They provide a framework for discussion of the implications for nursing which could lead to a more humane society.

Curtin (1979) has suggested that the philosophical foundation of nursing is advocacy. "We must -- as human advocates -- assist patients to find meaning or purpose in their living or in their dying....Whatever patients define as their goal, it is their meaning and not ours, their values and not ours, and their living or dying and not ours." (Curtin, 1979, p. 7) This philosophical ideal is based on recognition of our shared humanity. It recognizes the integral unity and uniqueness of individuals as well as their interdependence and interrelationships within the world. Nurses can assist clients to maintain this unity and integrity. (Curtin, 1979)

People are not objects to be acted upon, the kidney in bed 3 or the hysterectomy in bed 10, the arm from which the technician draws blood without any explanation. Nurses may not be in control of the settings in which they work, but nurses can control their own actions. Because nurses are the only health care workers who are present in a hospital 24 hours a day, 7 days a week, nurses can and do control the environment of the unit. Working together and with clients and their families, nurses can structure an environment that is responsive to threats to the client's independence, freedom of action, and ability to choose. Providing information in a way that is manageable and allows the client to hear and question what is being said helps to maintain the mutuality of the nursing process. The goal is to extend such collaboration to all members of the health care team, client, and family, whenever possible.

An important facet of freedom in Curtin's view is the freedom to define for oneself what one should be, what one's own image of self entails. To illustrate, she gave the example of a 22-year-old male patient diagnosed with primary cancer of the testes. He had a wife and two sons and worked as a jockey. He and his wife discussed the diagnosis and the need for an orchiectomy and elected to have the surgery. They had been told the effect the operation would have on their relationship. What the young man had not been told, however, was that he would develop breasts and a feminine voice and lose his facial hair. He committed suicide nine months after the surgery. Curtin pointed out that, having been given this information, he still might have had the surgery. However, by not giving him the complete information that would have allowed him to come to terms with his own self image, what was and was not important, health professionals violated his authenticity.

Self image and authenticity fall within the domain of nursing because of nurses' concerns with client responses to actual or potential health problems. Nurses focus on ability to cope, social supports, interaction patterns, functional ability, lifesyle, and quality of life. Physicians, on the other hand, tend to focus on the disease process, how to ameliorate/eradicate/control it. Both perspectives are essential. Combined with a third, the client's view of his/her health patterns and responses and rights to autonomy, freedom, and choice, the potential exists for more humanistic health care. Nursing advocacy will be an important step in this process.

REFERENCES

American Nurses Association (1973). Standards for Practice. Kansas City, MO: A.N.A.

American Nurses Association (1980). Nursing: A Social Policy Statement. Kansas City, MO: A.N.A.

American Nurses Association (1985). Code for Nurses with Interpretive Statements (revised). Kansas City, MO: A.N.A.

Ashley, J. A. (1973). This I Believe About Power in Nursing. Nursing Outlook, 21, 637-641.

Ashley, J. A. (1976). Hospitals, Paternalism, and the Role of the Nurse. New York: Teachers College Press.

Carpenito, L. J. (1983). Nursing Diagnosis: Application to Clinical Practice. Philadelphia: J. B. Lippincott.

Curtin, L. (1979). The Nurse as Advocate: A Philosophical Foundation for Nursing. Advances in Nursing Science, 1:3, 1-10.

Fiesta, J. (1983). The Law and Liability: A Guide for Nurses. New York: John Wiley and Sons.

Kohnke, M. (1982). The Nurse as Advocate. In E. C. Hein, & M. J. Nicholson (Eds.), Contemporary Leadership Behavior: Selected Readings. Boston: Little, Brown, and Company.

Murphy, P. (1981). Deciding to Blow the Whistle. American Journal Of Nursing, 81, 1691-1692.

Nightingale, F. (1969). Notes on Nursing: What It Is and What It Is Not. New York: Dover Publications.

Nutting, A. (1912). Educational Status of Nursing. Bulletin 7, No. 475, U.S. Bureau of Education, Washington, D.C.: G.P.O.

Page, B.B. (1975). Who Owns the Professions? Hastings Center Report, 5:5, 7-8.

DICTA
os6.5
11/11/85

THE NURSE

THE PRACTITIONER:
GAIL E. BROMLEY, B.S.N., M.S.N., R.N.

"What is nursing? What is the power of nursing?"

I'm quoting from one of Liv Ullman's chapters in her book Choices and it reads as follows: "I'm learning about compassion. I find its gesture in old people and in little children. In relationships and solitude I look for it in myself. When most deprived, some show the ultimate compassion." I think the power of professionalism in nursing is derived from society's recognition of nursing as an essential service -- a human service which shows compassion. Over the years, there have been many changes in nursing; namely, the nature of the work, which has changed due to the change in technology. That which remains unchanged is the caring aspect of nursing.

Historically, as we look at nursing, there are several metaphors that are associated with nursing. One such metaphor is the traditional mother-substitute role for the patient who is in a child/dependent role. The nurse follows the orders of the physician, who typically is in the father-role. Several recent research studies investigated roles of health care professionals in neonatal intensive care units and described in a dynamic way how the roles were played out. Nursing had a very powerful role within the settings. Nurses were viewed as maternal individuals. While they were regarded by others as being in a power role, the nurses did not necessarily acknowledge the power role which they had.

Another metaphor associated with nursing is the professional contractor. This is probably one with which many of us are more familiar. In this role the patient and nurse negotiate a plan of care for the patient and the nurse consults with other health care professionals to develop a contract that meets the patient's needs. Historically, loyalties in nursing were primarily with physicians. Nursing was available to the patients and to family to provide reassurance and uphold confidence in the physician. The ultimate goal was to instill hope to aid the patient's progress.

The confidence in the authority figure -- the doctor -- was instilled by the nurse. The loyalties of the past with physicians are no longer as strong. Currently, the loyalties observed within nursing have been realigned to focus on patients.

As times have changed, so too has the role of the nurse as a patient advocate, the legal metaphor now recognized as a prominent role within nursing. This change in role relationships required more courage from the nurse. The nurse's involvement in defending the rights of the patient occurred in a powerful way. Within the institution nurses have sometimes assumed the role of "whistle blower", or as the health care professional who would refuse to follow through on a physician's orders - all of this done with the patient's rights in mind as well as the nurse's freedom of choice.

A nurse provides a range of service to people. The choices are innumerable in terms of how a nurse can be involved: the nurse may assist a family in problem-solving with a family member or patient who must make choices regarding care. Patients and families are faced with economic as well as quality-of-care issues. I believe that the nature of the work in nursing practice is evolving. Because of that, there is a range of possibilities and a range of problems and dilemmas with which nursing must cope. A major factor facing health care institutions is the DRG system. The change in reimbursement rate means fewer dollars for the institution, which leads to, and the demand for, greater productivity and continuous monitoring of manpower costs. The nursing staff members in institutions across the country are faced with the dilemma which you may have read about in articles in "Working Mother" and/or "The New York Times." The articles relate that nursing is no longer the profession that nurses and non-nurses once thought it was. The job strains are great and the nurse-patient ratio has changed, causing adjustments and readjustments in delivering nursing care. The dilemma then is what services the nurse will provide to the patient and to the family. In any given situation there are X dollars and X number of staff nurses who can be allocated to a given unit; therefore, priorities must be addressed as to what cannot be compromised. In many instances nurses are leaving nursing because they and the needs of the patient. As a result, the nurses feel that they cannot express the intensity of the aggression that they have. Oftentimes the aggression gets displaced on to the patient, which only serves to make the patient less able to progress in his/her treatment regime.

One of the most prominent choices which a nurse can make in a health care institution is deciding how and when the patient and the family will be physically and psychologically prepared to go home. The choice to prepare patients and families must occur early-on in the admission. Many of you probably know that preparation for discharge begins as the person is hospitalized, since resources must be identified early. Post-hospital preparations are most important and, if not adequately planned, the patient and his/her future in terms of health status can be negatively impacted.

In nursing-educational circles, the nursing educators are perceived as not keeping up to speed with the problems in clinical practice. At the present time, nurses need to function in a pro-active position more than ever before. We, as professional nurses, need to demonstrate our power and use the choices that we can, educating other nurses and educating patients and families so they understand their choices. The practical world is much harder than most nursing educators are willing to describe. I think that if we are going to stay together as nurses and use our power to make certain that patients are provided the best care, then we need to be prepared for the adversarial relationships and learn how to best handle them.

Another area where power of the professional nurse is displayed is in the professional nurse-physician relationship. There is the potential for misuse of power with organ-harvesting. If there is a need or desire to make money and a nurse chooses to share distorted information, altered data, with other professionals, organs could potentially be harvested for other than ethical purposes. As nurses, we have a Code of Ethics, but a Code of Ethics can be similar to policy and procedure manuals, lining nursing station shelves. Within the conscience of the nurse, he/she has the power to choose right from wrong. The power of the nurse is vital in situations where a nurse should question unethical behavior. Patients, families and nurses rely on the professional Code of Ethics, the fate of which is determined by individual integrity. While we can read the Code of Ethics and the Standards of Care from A.N.A, how can we actually deal with the dilemmas in that Code.

As nurses interact with homicidal or suicidal patients, they are in a powerful position to maintain safe environments for patients. I was intrigued recently by an incident that was portrayed on the television show "St. Elsewhere" in which the nurse working in the Emergency Room assessed an adolescent as potentially homicidal. The nurse communicated her concern to the physician, who said, "You just remember that I have more education than you do and my status is up here and your status is down here." The nurse responded, "I think you are wrong." The patient ultimately killed someone and, in soap opera manner, the physician came back and apologized to the nurse. The portrayal was irritating from the standpoint that a highly-viewed program minimized the power and knowledge of the nurse and did not portray her pro-active option of interceding with the physician. The nurse had clearly more power than she chose to exert in that situation. It was a real life situation. I think many of us in nursing have been in that situation where a patient was homicidal or suicidal and we conveyed that to a physician, who made a choice not to listen. There are additional concerns in the portrayal of this incident on "St. Elsewhere." The portrayal of the nurse as the patient advocate was absent in the program. The nurse had other choices to exert her power; namely, go to the Vice President of Nursing, go to the C.E.O., go to the Board of Directors with the intent of assuring that the adolescent was properly cared for. Perhaps "St. Elsewhere" displayed real life, or possibly wished to convey a demeaning role for the nurse. I would hate to think that this was an acceptable manner for a nurse to be portrayed to the public. It demonstrated a lack of power to make judgments which were in the patient's interest. I thought it cause for concern.

As Violet Malinski mentioned, I think that the nurse is in a role to decide which information is appropriately provided to a patient. There are instances in our society where a patient has sought an abortion, but health professionals did not regard abortion as an option and therefore the patient did not have informed consent. A physician may have decided that an abortion was not the women's right to choose. Such information, therefore, was not shared with the patient.

As we face the fact that many nurses are unwilling to continue careers in nursing, those of us who remain in the profession must stay powerful to promote patient welfare and prevent the profession from losing credibility and confidence. In our hearts we all know it can be unbearable to live in a cognitive dissonant state where our value system and the value system of the system in which we work are not the same. I think in the next five to ten years with the prospective payment system we are going to be facing even more difficult decisions. Concerns will largely be related to the elderly population and related also to the decreased availability of certain treatments and procedures. What will these changes mean to us in nursing? There is the possibly that at some point there will be an age cut-off for dialysis, or an age cut-off for cardiac surgery and other procedures. How will we cope with these issues?

Nurses need to consider how the public views the profession and each of us individually. Whether it is in the media, or in a discussion group, or in our day-to-day lives, how do people view us as a group of professionals? We have power and I think people can look to nurses for power to help make decisions. Many of us are in positions where the question, "What are our choices?" is being asked by individuals who regard health care as being anti-people. Neighbors, friends and relatives regard nurses as possessing power in that nurses are capable educators and generally know the politics of the health care bureaucracy. We will need to continue our roles as patient advocates.

In the future, nurses will make choices as to whether or not they will care for AIDS patients and other patients who are regarded as "undesirable patients." Another ethical dilemma will involve hiring practices which, due to downsizing, may violate EEO standards. I think you are seeing this situation in institutions where there is a closed hiring practice. This hiring method provides a mechanism with the potential to prevent classes of minorities from having opportunities to enter the system.

Another cause for concern, as Violet Malinski stated, is the "gag order" -- where nurses are terminated for questioning certain practices where there are cover-ups in an institutuion, or cover-ups of problems in an environment, in which they are prevented from acting as patient advocates. Nurses do have the power in their numbers alone to fight unacceptable practices. In some instances, rather than an institution dealing with those problems and the nurse having the power to be able to make the change, that nurse may be terminated from the system. A bureaucracy can easily avoid the patient's problem.

There is the "dumping syndrome" of patients who are unable to pay. How many nurses in emergency rooms of private institutions were present when a patient was told that he/she had to be shipped to a county hospital where indigents can receive care? What is the role of the nurse in those instances where there is a life or death issue? I'm certain that practice will continue.

Societal welfare, as it is affected by professional nursing, will hopefully be positive. I think the fact that Medicare and insurance companies are changing what they will reimburse will affect nursing. Where nursing is viewed as a second-class citizen in an institution, there is the potential for future dilemmas. Will a nurse who has a sound Code of Ethics and believes in a value system wish to remain in nursing during this transition, this time of crisis? Will the person be able to tolerate the system or will the individual have to leave the system in order to cope on a day-to-day basis? Or does the individual become a crusader and stay in the system in hopes of maintaining good standards and fighting the good fight and working with political process so patient care standards are upheld?

How does a nurse cope with an institution or environment where the elderly really are not valued? I find it ironic that the literature is glutted with articles regarding geriatric care being the wave of the future and the elderly are being more valued. There are more courses about the elderly than ever before -- yet Medicare has cut the health care benefits. Now the elderly are going to be paying at least $100 more in

1986 for their deductibles than they have in the past. How does that affect a person on a fixed income? From what part of their budget do they get $100? Probably their food budget, or some other necessity. How can the elderly maintain their emotional and physical well being with these types of changes?

Another dilemma nursing is facing in Ohio is the Nurse Practice Act. The Practice Act has become very controversial. The purpose of the Act is to protect the public. The real issues are, as all of us who have been a part of this Practice Act know, political, territorial, and, of course, an issue of economics. How is the Nurse Practice Act going to impinge on the practice of medicine if we are able to prescribe, if we are able to get involved in nursing diagnosis? It has become an enormous threat to physicians and the bottom line becomes the bottom line -- an oversupply of physicians.

In considering the metaphors of roles in nursing, surrogate mother and patient advocate, I see it as a very difficult kind of marriage. We have health care systems dedicated to patient's rights, standards of care, and providing choices interfacing with a business mentality. In order for nurses to remain powerful, they must understand the politics and the economics without giving up the caring, nurturing role. Nursing has been socialized to believe in humanity, in helping people and believing people should have freedom of choice. We are socialized to believe that nursing assists a person to become more independent.

I think the implications for nursing are to try to help create a more humane society. With the large numbers of nurses in the United States, it intrigues me that we can't get it together enough to take a stand to support the elderly, to support health care issues more than we have. We can all come up with excuses regarding all of these issues, but the fact remains. Strength in numbers can make the difference. We can make the difference.

So, in summary, we have a number of dilemmas. We have the power, we have the choices, we have the knowledge of the choices, and we can translate those choices to the patient and the family; but the dilemmas will include dealing with the cost constraints, and whether we choose to be in power in the health care institutions. Another dilemma relative to power is whether we take a pro-active stance for ourselves and for our colleagues in nursing. When nurses are dismissed because they "blew the whistle," and we probably would have reacted the same or want to react in the same way, how often do we take a stand? The single major question we must ask is, "What is our commitment to quality patient care?"

THE NURSE

THE CONSUMER:
CAROL J. ROTTMAN, Ph.D.

My only credentials for being here is that I'm a consumer of the product that many of you dispense or are learning to dispense. You might even call me a conspicuous consumer because within the experience of my lifetime I have repeatedly been in the situation where I had to accept help from nurses. For my own self as a patient, I went through three deliveries, several surgeries, and later a bout of internal bleeding which put me in the hospital for over two months. With my family, I was a consumer of nursing via one of my children who had a serious accident four years ago. He was paralyzed by a spinal cord injury in a diving accident and was hospitalized for a year and a month, and has subsequently been hospitalized for surgery. In addition, after all those experiences, I elected to do my doctoral dissertation on parents of low birthweight infants, who were hospitalized in a neonatal intensive care unit. For seven months I interacted with families within the hospital setting. Parents and their children are great consumers of nursing.

I am pleased to be asked to represent consumers because I come from a very medical family and have always cared about care-givers. My father and my brother-in-law are Obstetricians, two sisters and one brother are Registered Nurses. All of my life I resisted, against great pressure, joining the medical profession but instead became a teacher of blind infants. Within my work I have had my share of exposure to medicine in many ways and was always able to see medical care from the side of the consumer and the provider.

When I read Violet Malinski's paper, I realized how hard it is to be a nurse when you have a Florence Nightingale to live up to. You look back 100 years, and she already said the profound things that you might think are so new today. When I think that 100 years ago Florence Nightingale was already saying that "as an

83

astute observer you can do what medical marvels and technological gagetry cannot do -- <u>restore the human spirit.</u>" Essentially that's what I want to talk about today. This is a very experiential talk about "restoration" taken from my experience. Some of my story may encourage you in the profession of nursing.

I know something about the work of nurses, because I received so much from them. My first experience came when I was growing up and was nurtured at times by my father's faithful nurses. All of them happened to be single and they happened to be very nurturing individuals. They were our nannies; they became part of our extended family.

Another experience I had with a nurse came once when I was hospitalized for surgery and there was a shortage of nurses on the unit. I needed to take a shower but my blood lines and I.V. lines were getting in the way. They had to call a free nurse in from the baby nursery to help me because there were no others available. I will never forget the shower I had that day. Never were my toes or fingers better washed than they were that day, and never will they be again!

One of my dearest memories of the kind of extra mile that nurses go is when our son was hospitalized. Many of you know about the striker frame, which is the bed that you put a paralyzed person on so that you don't have to turn the patient but you turn the bed instead. He was on one striker frame for about four weeks. When he was on the down rotation, it was extremely boring just looking down at the floor. One of his young nurses, who was also trying to encourage him to look at life a little more positively, got under the bed and talked up to him for most of the rotation.

Another nurse I will always remember was the primary nurse for a baby who eventually died after nine months of struggling for life in the Neonate Intensive Care Unit. She and I met again at the child's funeral. She was the only one of his caregivers who was willing to walk the extra mile with the child's family.

So I have seen nurses as nurses, as companions, as compassionate friends, but I've also seen the converse.

I've seen nurses as gate keepers, as puppets, and some in my experience, especially rehabilitation nurses, as aloof professionals -- the "Don't call me by my first name" kind of nurses. The dividing line for me, as well as for my family, has always been, "how does this nurse make me feel?"

My son, who was 17 when he was hurt, is now 22. As a frequent consumer of nursing, he knows exactly what he likes and doesn't like. He feels he should be in charge of his own care which some nurses don't like too well. I remember when he was only a month into hospitalization, he would say to me some nights, "I certainly hope I don't get ----- as my nurse tomorrow. She makes me feel ashamed to be in this situation." I knew after awhile what that meant to him.

I also know something about the power of nurses through experiences like I've been mentioning. Nursing involves the process of interpersonal relationships and I believe therein lies the power. For example, there was a young woman who was a nurse on the unit which our son came to just a few days before his 18th birthday. Not many of the nurses had gotten to know him very well but this nurse could quickly sense his need to have something to celebrate. At this point he wasn't eating very well and nothing tasted good; he was battling infection and was still coping with what it was like to be paralyzed. She went out and smuggled a can of Coors beer and a pizza into the hospital. The pizza one doesn't have to smuggle, but she said, "You know I could get dismissed for this can of beer." Even though he could not drink the beer, nor could he eat the pizza, he can always look back and know that somebody cared enough to celebrate his birthday. Turning 18 is a rite of passage that doesn't happen again. She rallied all the other nurses around to enjoy the festivities so they really did make a celebration of it.

I also see this interpersonal relationship when a patient or a family of a patient is having trouble with the new role that they are in. In the neonatal ward, as many of you know, there are many young, inexperienced parents who never in the world thought they would have a premature baby, especially a baby under 2 pounds that was struggling for life, having many special procedures being done to it daily and hourly. The parents ask the question, "How am I ever going to take care of this baby?" There was a very young mother, I think she was under 18 when she had her baby, who watched and waited before her baby could be touched or handled. But she was eager to try to see what she could do. Nurse after nurse gave her the feeling that she might not be able to handle her child's care. One night a nurse simply said, "I know you can do it." From that point on the mother saw herself as very much involved in the baby's recovery. She told the nurse later, "If you hadn't believed in me I don't know if I would have believed in myself."

I have also had negative experiences with a nurse's power. One incident happened just this summer when my son had surgery. His was an unusual operation where the doctor had to remove some plastic that was initially put in his neck to stablize it, the kind of operation that doesn't happen very often. The neurosurgeon had to actually drill the plastic out of his neck. My husband and I were there at the hospital at 7:00 a.m. and we waited for over 7 hours during the surgery. The neurosurgeon came to talk to us and his hands were red from the physical pounding of the drill to get the plastic out. I began to be very nervous about what my son was going to be like after having this abuse to his neck. I saw him being wheeled in from surgery into his room, I waited a few minutes until they transferred him into his bed, and then I wanted to go to make sure he was okay. The nurse met me at the door and said, "Don't you know this is the step-down unit and we have visiting hours only 15 minutes every 3 hours?" I walked past her as if she hadn't spoken to me. I said, "I waited for 7 hours to make sure he was alright. I won't stay long." In defense of this nurse, she also became a very dear friend before the hospitalization was over. But at that point she wanted to defend the territorial rights that she felt were her domain.

We are talking about power. From a consumer's point of view I think that your power is a combination of what you have to do and the way you do it. This combination is caring. I think it is made up of three parts: caring for, caring about, and caring with. Now certainly you don't come to nursing school just to find out how to be nice to people. There are a whole lot of skills you must learn and if you don't know those, you really don't have a right to be in there working with patients. So you need the medical skills to work with patients and then you need to care about them as persons.

Violet Malinski mentioned the wholistic approach, caring for the whole person. You have to try to see the whole person and the whole family and what the whole experience is meaning to them. But some people can stay at a distance and they can say, "My goodness that is an interesting family situation." They get involved in the intellectual thinking about it but they never get involved with the family or the patient. I think that is the special component of caring with, and that's what I see as the role of advocate: involvement and empathy. Now I suppose there are some patients who don't want you involved in their lives. But I would say, especially with the long term patients or the patients that have a great deal of uncertainty in their lives, they certainly hope that someone is going to get involved in their lives. It is kind of a lonely business there in hospitals.

About two years ago, I heard Sue Norris, a clinic specialist at Rainbow Babies & Childrens Hospital, talk about ethics in nursing. She concluded by describing the nurse as the advocate.

I thought to myself -- of course, right on, that is what a nurse ought to be. I picked up a book in the library by another nurse, Barbara Huttman, called The Patient Advocate, which I thought would say that nurses should be the advocates for patients. But all she said was, "the patient really needs an advocate, find one." Why does a patient need an advocate anyway? I believe that as consumers of health care we stand to lose our personhood when we go into a hospital care setting. Surrounded by all the lifesaving machines, the technicians who man those machines, and our own temporary stance of dependence and vulnerablity -- at times we do need somebody to speak on our behalf. We do need an advocate.

I had a profound experience when I was ill, which may have started me on this whole road of wanting to speak for the consumer. I was one of those classic or seasonal G.I. bleeders but nobody knew why I was bleeding nor how to stop me from bleeding. After several weeks in a local hospital I was transferred to the Mayo Clinic where they are supposed to know everything. Days and weeks passed and I was very lonely. My husband did come with me, but together we were without our kids and our friends to support us. Every day we hoped for news about my condition which would lead to an end of this ordeal.

At the Mayo Clinic there are metal covers on the patient's records so you can hear the clicking as the doctors moved down the hall on their daily "rounds." My husband and I had a system; we felt that if we could "nab" these doctors every time they came down the hall to visit, we could get our questions answered. So, as soon as I heard the clicking, I would call him in the library where he was trying to get some work done. He would appear magically just as the doctors came in. I could hear the doctors outside the door describe me as a "super interesting case," but inside my room I was desperately trying to get them to regard me as a real person. After two months and 47 units of blood, the bleeding stopped for no apparent reason. My case remains an unsolved mystery; six years later I am wondering if I might have to go through it all again.

A person has an awful lot of adjusting to do to become a patient. Both my husband and I, usually competent professionals, felt very weak and vulnerable in the hospital situation. We needed an advocate. Before you have to be hospitalized, you feel confident. You are somewhat in control of your life; you have work to do; you have responsibilities; you have people depending on you. In moments, all of that is stripped away. You are forced to become as dependent as a small child. I believe a nurse can offer strength, or power, if you will, through <u>caring</u>.

I would like to describe that special power of the profession of nursing. Each of us has a motivation for doing what we do and going into the profession that we do. When I was trying to decide what I wanted to do feel they simply cannot cope with the demands and they are unwilling to readjust to the altered levels of productivity.

The other dilemma in an institution involves nursing administrators. There are many pressures placed on nursing administration by physicians and administrators. One must take a hard look at exactly what gets compromised along the way and what gets prioritized in terms of delivering patient care. As a result of the pressures, adversarial relationships are occurring more frequently in health care institutions. We frequently hear staff nurses say, "I'm being 'sold down the river' because I don't have enough people on the unit to take care of the patients. The acuity of the patients is far greater than it used to be, the technology is more complex. I just can't do it anymore. I will no longer compromise my professional career in order to go along with these DRG/cost reimbursement standards."

As professional nurses, we need to determine how patient care is being affected by the reimbursement changes. As I observe fatigued, frustrated nurses reacting to the effects of the DRG system, I also observe how the nurses' fatigue affects his/her interactions with patients and family members. Their interactions with their colleagues, with the physicians and health care professionals in an institution are likewise affected.

Nursing administrative decisions that are made, based on the choices available, directly impact on the nursing staff members in an institution. These choices made at the power level in nursing get translated into how a professional nurse can interact with a patient and family. One must rely on the integrity of the professional nursing leaders as they make choices, decisions, as it is conceivable that an angry nurse could feel put upon and could allow his/her anger to affect patient care. I think we all have seen this happen. Because of our roles as nurses, the expressed anger is a powerful message, however undesirable. Nurses have a powerful impact on patients and family, such that their inability to provide the energy to care has a negative impact, which may not promote health or wellness. What happens is that many staff nurses feel sandwiched between the nursing administrative decisions with my life, a lot of my friends were going into nursing. At that point in history, the only honorable things for women to do were to be nurses or teachers. They were very womanly things to do. The mediator role, which both of the nurses have described today, fits perfectly with the kind of role that society approved for women. The role was like the very traditional role of mother: one who looks out for everybody and who cares about everything; the one who does 101 things at the same time; the peace maker. To be an advocate, as Violet Malinski pointed out, the mediator role can be a very slippery position. In fact, I don't really accept it as the role of advocate at all. For example, I found in the Neonatal Unit that doctors are not talking to the parents about their infants nearly as much as they should. Some nurses try to serve as go-betweens when they really should tell doctors to talk to the parents -- not be the mediator between the two. Parents suffer because there is no direct communication with doctors and the choices about treatment are unknown. The advocate role in this case is to bring the doctor and family together.

A second part of the advocate role arises naturally from the caring profession of nursing. Nurses have always been trained to <u>care for</u> patients, from the lowliest of jobs, like the bath I described earlier, to the intensive monitoring of fragile infants. More recently nurses have been urged to wholistically <u>care about</u>, not only their patient, but also his or her family or support group. However, a nurse can still remain detached and separate from the patient until he or she learns to <u>care with</u> each patient. "Caring with" requires the <u>ability</u> to so empathize with the patient that one seeks to compensate for the temporary weakness and become strong for them within the complex health care system. When the work of nursing and the power of nursing combine it is in the form of <u>caring with</u>.

There are several barriers to that kind of a role for nurses. One is the horrible power structure within the hospital spectrum. I was surprised when I started my study to discover the power structure in nursing, although I was well aware of the hierarchy in medicine. When I saw that the two of them fed together I realized that it is really hard to change the system. There is so much deceit that goes on when you try to maintain a system. So much energy goes into working through a power structure in order to get things done. Open communication is curtailed, which harms both the nurse and the patient.

Another reason that might be considered a barrier is that nurses cannot advocate for someone else if they are afraid to advocate for themselves. I feel that very strongly. You must have a sense of your own professional duties and responsibilities. You have to know what you are good at and why the patient needs you so badly.

A third barrier to the advocacy role is the fear of involvement. As Gail Bromley has said, she is tired of seeing tired nurses. But I have seen nurses energized when getting involved with families and staying involved with families. I have seen them find a new purpose in their work. One of the practices of nursing that I have never understood, which seems to thwart involvement, is the practice of rotating between patients. In some long term situations, like that of my son, a relationship is formed that contributes to healing. During his early hospitalization he became fond of a young nurse. The supervisor apparently thought it was an unhealthy situation, and rotated her to work with other patients. That relationship was broken and it was never established again. This also happens in the neonatal unit. A family looking for support and comfort latches onto a helpful nurse only to have her assigned elsewhere. I feel this is unfair to the patient.

Another barrier to advocacy is the nurse's own vulnerability. A nurse also needs support in order to do the caring job that he or she has to do. I would like to suggest something radical that I have observed in my life as a nursing consumer. Nurses can get support outside their profession from the very people that they are helping. Those families and patients you have been instrumental in helping may be your biggest allies, your friends, and your shoulders to cry on. Nurses and families need mutual support.

I don't see the advocate role as something that is optional. There is great power in caring: caring with, caring for, caring about people. At this point, I believe that only through the nursing profession can we humanize the whole medical profession. This puts great weight on the nursing profession, but from my point of view that is where it is going to have to be. The nurse advocate has a quiet kind of power. To borrow and expand a quote about mother-power -- "The hand that rocks the cradle... or starts the I.V.'s; or writes the endless progress notes; or reaches out and comforts a patient... can rule the world."

Chapter 4

THE MANAGER

THE PRESENTER:
DR. JOHN D. ARAM

Most discussions of managerial ethics focus on the age-old issues of understanding the nature of ethical standards and determining if they have been violated. Analysis of these problems often leads to related issues, such as the role of interests and consequences and the importance of ends and means, but discussion usually remains confined to the same basic question: what is right and wrong managerial behavior?

While this is a valid and important question, I will argue in this paper with those that see a second critical dimension to the problem of management ethics. This question involves what "is" versus "what might be" -- let's call it the ethic of "possibility." This second dimension is more difficult to talk about than the ethics of right and wrong; in fact, rather vague, inexact, and possibly embarrassing terms -- "excellence", "aspiration", and "perfection" -- are used to convey this concept.

Identification of these two dimensions of moral conduct is not a recent discovery. As early as 1759 the moral philosopher Adam Smith made an intriguing analogy.[1] The rules of justice (right and wrong), according to Smith, can be compared to the rules of grammar which are "precise, accurate, and indispensable." Smith wrote, "If I owe a man ten pounds, justice requires that I should precisely pay him ten pounds, whether at the time agreed upon, or when he demands it."

Some may be surprised to know that other virtues, such as prudence, magnamity, and beneficence were also of major interest to Adam Smith. He compared these values to achieving an outstanding composition where "there are no rules whose observance will infallibly lead us to the attainment of elegance and sublimity..." At best, he wrote, our notions about how to achieve these virtues are like the knowledge of writing

93

excellence -- "loose, vague, and indeterminate."

Business ethics follow a similar distinction. Considerable attention is devoted to searching for appropriate "rules" for business behavior -- rules that, like basic grammar, establish minimal conditions for human conduct. Many of today's ethical controversies in business center on minimal obligations of corporations to various stakeholders, for example, employees, customers, or members of the public.

Interest in attaining higher values also exists today as it did for Adam Smith, but, unfortunately, this concept appears less well understood and receives relatively little attention. James MacGregor Burns' acclaimed book, Leadership, may best illustrate Smith's second concept in today's literature.[2] While the search for ethical rules to govern business conduct is extremely important today, the ability to understand and realize Burns' rather vague and indeterminate concept of moral leadership also holds significance for managers and for the future of our economic system.

In this presentation I will discuss each of these approaches to business ethics and outline their implications for managers. Subsequently, I will address the specific questions posed by the Center for Professional Ethics pertaining to the work and power of the manager.

The Ethics of Duty

The requirement for minimal rules is a well established principle in our society. People generally recognize that they cannot go around, say, whimsically bashing heads. Most people realize that if others were to do similarly, everyone's safety and security would be threatened. Giving up limited individual freedom for the benefit of collective interests is well established in Western political philosophy and is written into our Constitution.

Legal philosopher Lon Fuller termed agreements about minimal responsibilities the "ethics of duty."[3] Duties are the essence of the Golden Rule; they represent conditions to which persons concede as they recognize a community of interests among themselves and others. Minimal responsibilities are, everyone realizes, best sought by understanding the law.

The law, however, provides only a starting point for identifying the ethics of duty in today's business environment. As much as we try to identify clear statements of management duties from the law, we are more likely to find changing concepts. Note the following areas which appear to be affected by changing views of corporate duties:

- The liability of manufacturers for injury to product users has evolved dramatically over the last half century away from a principle of negligence where the burden of proof was on the injured party to show manufacturer liability. Today, a doctrine of strict liability generally applies in which a producer is liable for injury caused by a defective product regardless of the measures the producer may have taken to prevent defects.

- A serious weakening of the traditional employment-at-will doctrine governing employee-employer relationships appears to be in process. Previously based on the concept that either party was free to terminate the employment relationship at will, a doctrine of "wrongful discharge" appears to be gaining support in the nation's courts. As with strict liability for product injury, this movement represents greater restrictions on the freedom of managerial action and implies considerable tightening of corporate duties.

- Corporate takeover attempts and the high frequency of mergers, divestitures, and buyouts today have generated a substantial amount of litigation that may ultimately place a higher standard of fiduciary responsibility to shareholders on corporate managers. The court's recent blocking of Revlon management's attempt to choose a friendly purchaser called for a higher standard of management duty to shareholders. Other cases suggest possible movement toward greater shareholder suffrage.

The above trends in the common law usually result from hundreds of decisions in a fragmented and decentralized judicial system. As such, however, these emerging responsibilities of business may represent sustaining public expectations. Many other issues and topics could be added to a discussion about the legal obligations of managers, but an inescapable conclusion is that "minimal condition" rules governing business practice will be increasingly more numerous and more restrictive.

What does this information tell us about the business environment in general? I suggest several conclusions.

First, widely accepted obligations of managers are continually evolving, making the ethics of duty a moving target. Social, economic, and technological changes in the society alter expectations for corporate action and redefine the minimal rules that are widely accepted.

Recognizing that ethical judgments are relative to particular times and situations, one writer declares that, "The morality of an act is defined by the situation of which it is a part."[4] Product injury implies certain obligations when product technology is relatively easily understood, distribution channels are simple, and a strong norm of self-reliance prevails in society. Change these situational characteristics, as they have changed over the past century, and product injury will be seen quite differently by plaintiffs, juries, and the public at large.

Managers may not agree with these changes, but in order to cope more effectively with today's business environment, they might best assume that minimal rules and ethical duties will inevitably change. An ability to adapt firm practices in light of shifting minimal rules will be a most useful capability.

A second conclusion is that dispute will always be

present about the legitimacy of the stakes and expectations of interested parties. Rather than a linear process, the evolution of common law consists of tens, if not hundreds and thousands, of contested situations. Valid, fiercely defended, and incompatible arguments about the duties of business are present at any one time, and clear and widely accepted definitions of minimal rules are usually attained only over decades. These debates and delays are necessary, for no other process is capable of fairly determining the rules by which society as a whole wants to live.

This conclusion means that managers will be continually working in ambiguous and disputed environments. I believe that successful managers in this environment are capable of a dual awareness -- on one level they may be active advocates and protagonists for a particular point of view or interest. On another level, however, they perceive that larger and long-term issues are decided by society and managers prevent themselves from getting locked into treating specifics as the ultimate stakes. Again, effective managers will not allow their strongly felt positions on the issues to block constructive adaptation to a wider process.

I have argued that society establishes minimal rules for business behavior -- rules that can be called an "ethics of duty." The social expectations implied in various duties may often be experienced as "no win" situations by managers -- at best they may avoid violating a perceived rule and may avoid being labeled "unethical."

I have also argued that these rules are not stable. Because society is dynamic, the situation of business changes and expectations for business behavior change. There is always a fairly large zone of dispute about the ethics of duty for business, and clarification comes slowly. Moreover, increasing awareness of business-society interdependence leads to numerous challenges to existing definitions of minimal duties for managers and corporations.

What can managers do about ethical duties in a sea of ambiguity and conflict where any action may be subject to challenge and criticism? When the definition of duty is in dispute, standards of conduct are unclear, and external interests groups are aggressive and visable, what guidelines might a manager adopt? Simply complying with established law may stimulate more clamor, risk ignoring legitimate issues expressed in public sentiment, and fail to further the image the firm wishes to portray. The following are two suggestions for managing the ethics of duty in this complex and unforgiving world.

The Wall Street Journal Rule

The first suggestion is based on an "as if" exercise. Before making a decision, a manager might imagine that all parties possibly affected by the decision have knowledge of the fact that a choice is being made. If the manager's action is sufficiently consistent with general norms of fairness, as experienced by affected parties, one can have confidence that the decision most likely falls into acceptable ethical behavior. If uncertainty about the reactions of others is high, or if some troubling issues remain, the decision may need further review. Carl Madden, economist, professor and former business school dean, puts the issue this way, "Unethical behavior, at its root, takes the form of some attempt to suppress the truth."[5]

I call this principle the Wall Street Journal rule. If I wouldn't be happy to have the nature and consequences of my decision described in full detail on the front page of the Journal, perhaps I should reconsider it. This principle takes its cue from the English statesman, Gladstone, who stated, "publicity breeds responsibility"[6] and from an elaboration of this thought, "Sunlight is the best disinfectant, electric light the best policeman."

Internal Environment As a Lever

Anticipating responses to disclosure of one's decision may avoid wrongdoing when the ethics of duty are unclear or in contention, as they often are. Another common issue today, however, is not the manager's conduct, but the conduct of subordinates. Senior managers in firms accused of fraudulent reporting of expenses on government contracts, including General Electric, Rockwell, General Dynamics, and others, have had a problem recently of how to get the whole organization, and this often means a very large organization, to conform to desired minimal standards of conduct.

The famous social psychologist, Kurt Lewin, developed a classic formula: Behavior = f(Person + Environment). Employees may commit acts that company leaders, as well as society, find objectionable. And yet, the same senior managers cannot be absolved from responsibility for these actions; managers are responsible for the internal environment in which the action occurred.

To paraphrase a comment attributed to Immanuel Kant, "We must not expect a good organization because those who make it are moral men. Rather it is because of a good organization that we may expect it to be composed of moral men."[7] In other words, the norms, values, and standards of the organization have an important and controllable influence on personal conduct.

Handles for creating a good organization are well-known: clarity of goals, quality of communication, development of people, presence of internal control. Recall a dominant theme of Greek tragedies in which the errors of one generation appear to create insoluable dilemmas for the children of the next. Similarily, the errors of upper managers in failing to clarify goals and standards of evaluation can allow the personal ambitions of managers to run against the broader interests of the organization. The presence of unchanneled personal ambitions by some managers may often present their subordinates with difficult choices: is it better to object to a particular corporate practice at the risk to one's own job or career interests or to maintain strict loyalty to one's boss, even though the interests of the organization risk being violated? The quality of the internal environment in a firm can be called an "entropic" process -- it needs a constant input of new energy to maintain a given level of performance.

A second suggestion for conforming to the ethics of duty today is to fully understand and persistently seek to develop a high quality among those factors comprising the internal organizational environment.

The Ethics of Possibility

Lon Fuller refers to a second type of ethical conduct as the morality of aspiration. While this perspective is rooted in an ancient concept of the highest fulfillment of personal capabilities, it has expression in the world today. The entry of "excellence" into the language of management may represent more than a catchy phrase of some pop writers and may correspond to a deeper awareness of something needed in our institutions.

I call your attention to a speech by Kazuo Inamori, Chairman and Chief Executive Officer of Kyocera Corporation, a firm that must be judged as one of the most innovative and successful in the last quarter century.[8] The title of Mr. Inamori's speech was "The Perfect Company." His talk presented philosophies, policies, and performance to back up this extreme aspiration. Contrary to widely prevailing practices in the U.S., the competition appears to be dead serious about putting this business of excellence into practice.

Economic markets have what I would call an "enhancement" effect -- numerous individual transactions lead to a common benefit. Unfortuately, our institutions have no such invisible hand that leads individuals' actions naturally to a collective benefit. Rather, their functioning appears much more vulnerable to the influence of personal and limited group interests. Our institutions need the same enhancement effect as our markets provide. Unfortuately, large organizations rarely function consistently this way.

Let us look at several apparent paradoxical, but not unfamiliar, situations in U.S. corporations. Why is it possible for workers to lose their jobs against their desires when the job could have been maintained by negotiation wage concessions and changes in work rules? We know it is possible that members of a group might define their interests as not "giving in" to the other side. But isn't this interest definition irrational when such a stance may cost the member's jobs? Isn't this a case of "shooting oneself in the foot?"

It is not infrequent for individuals' or groups'

immediate perceptions and assumption to lead to short-term actions that contradict their long-term, and what would appear to be their truer interests? Trade protectionism has a similar characteristic in that actions by one party designed to increase its advantage may lead to a series of responses by others that result in suffering for all parties. What may appear rational in a narrow and short-term perspective seems irrational and paradoxical in a broader and long-term context.

We are all familiar with debilitating conflicts within an organization where negative perceptions of others' motives and "winning" become more important than achieving organizational goals. A recent study described how one CEO's closed and possessive attitude toward the board of directors led to foregone opportunities to increase the company's wealth and the personal wealth of the CEO as well.[9] Why would that CEO apparently act against his own interests? Such paradoxical behavior seems to involve people trapped in a set of narrow and short-term assumptions or perceptions.

In a perfect market, prices incorporate future uncertainties. There is no debate about self-interest in a perfect market; self-interest is always economic and always immediate. An institutional context, however, imbues self-interest with ambiguity and choice, and we speculate that people's immediate actions may occasionally take them further from their long-term and more basic goals.

What happens for a person or group when winning becomes less important than attaining a common goal? What allows or encourages one to shift perceptions, assumptions, and actions to broad from narrow interests? Most people have seen the ambiguous drawing that can be seen as a haggard old witch or as a beautiful young woman. A shift in one's definition of self-interest is similar to the shift in one's perceptions that occurs in that experiment. I always perceive my self-interest in some context; change the context and I may be more likely to change my definition of my self-interest.

What does this have to do with management? A great deal of corporate success depends on whether people throughout the firm share the same purpose, goals, or, what might be called, "context." Without a common context it is likely that differing definitions and expressions of self-interest held in the organization will collide. We've all been witness to work instances resulting in substantial losses of efficiency, effectiveness, and creativity for this reason.

Establishing context is the responsibility of general management. The position of CEO embodies the broadest understanding of the organization. What good are goals and visions at this level if they have no presence in the perceptions that others utilize to affect their decisions and actions?

Tom Peters reported an intriguing statement of the CEO of a successful company in Silicon Valley.[10] "Do you know who my best marketing person is in this company?" asked the CEO. Answering his own question, he replied, "It's that man or woman on the loading dock who decides NOT to DROP the box into the back of the truck." The loading dock worker who does not drop the box has a different context for his actions than the worker who lets it drop and most likely damages its contents. Who, other than the CEO, ultimately has the responsibility to act to create this context and to affect the premises of action far below in the organization?

Earlier I mentioned Burns' writing on moral leadership. "Leadership", according to Burns, "is a triggering or inciting force in the conversion of conflicting demands, values, and goals into significant behavior."[11] Does this leadership process occur in today's large organizations? Yes would be a fair answer, but at what level of significant behavior? Do not managers today have the potential for achieving higher levels of integration of both individual and institutional fulfillment than is often the case? Realizing that potential constitutes the ethics of aspiration or of possibility.

Moral Leadership

The Work of the Manager

My purpose is not to attempt to catalogue all the dimensions of work and power of the corporate manager, but rather to focus attention on those aspects of general management I feel are most relevant to the future prosperity of our enterprise system. I believe that creation of a shared purpose and integration of individual efforts toward this purpose are most critical tasks for general managers.

There is good reason for the spate of writing and the intense interest in leadership today. Unfortunately, much of the discussion appears directed either to the personal qualities of the leader or to the process of leadership and influence in the context of direct face-to-face relationships in the firm.

The central issue of executive work in a large organization is how to affect the assumptions of decision making and the premises of action of those not in direct contact with the executive. Programs need to be developed, systems built, and institutions improved. These responsibilities, which result in the context for realizing goals and interests of organizational members, constitute the work of the general manager.

The general manager has the broadest and most comprehensive responsibility for this work. Every manager, however, carries a parallel responsibility, albeit within a more limited sphere. The tasks of establishing coherence of direction and integration of effort reside in varying degrees throughout the management structure. Naturally, the extent to which lower level managers understand these tasks and are prepared to perform them is, in good measure, a function of the broader managerial environment of the firm induced from above.

The Power of the Manager

None of the conventional concepts of power fully describe executive influence in these tasks. The traditional authority of the executive with its customary ability to reward and punish others' behavior may be of some use but is limited in pursuing this work. Similarly, both expert and charismatic power have roles to play but fail to describe adequately the needed influence process.

The distinction between transactional and transformational leadership articulated by James

MacGregor Burns constitutes a better point of departure for our purposes. Many individuals show leadership by initiating mutually beneficial transactions -- economic, political, or psychological -- with others. The purposes of each party are interrelated and each purpose is advanced by interaction of the parties. They have no sustaining joint purpose, however, as each person seeks succession of other similarly fruitful transactions. The executive as allocator of resourses, rewards and penalties, motivator of associates, spokesperson, mediator, and decision maker is a transactional leader.

In contrast, by emphasizing values and purposes, transformational leadership fuses the purposes of leaders and followers and raises both to higher levels of motivation and human conduct. In short, the perceptions and assumptions of members are altered, a new consciousness arises, and new possibilities emerge. Concluding her acclaimed study of corporate change masters, Rosabeth Moss Kanter writes, "The architects of change have to operate on a symbolic as well as a practical level...They have to operate integratively, bringing other people in, bridging new realities, and reconceptualizing activities to take account of this new, shared reality."[12]

This fall a class of M.B.A. students was asked to identify such a person and to write a paper on this person's impact on an organization for the society. Their choices were not surprising: Gandhi, Ataturk, Cromwell, F.D.R., Friedan. Organizational psychologist, Bernard Bass, says that leaders such as these are capable of generating performance in their subordinates beyond expectations. In addition to several other factors, Bass argues a quality called "intellectual stimulation" is an aspect of transformational leadership. Such leaders may consist of "prime movers...oriented toward growth, adaptation, learning, cognitive goals, variety, and creativity....They do particularly well in envisioning change and acquiring resources."[13] The content of their ideas are often the thoughts that galvanize and direct an organization strategically.

In sum, many of our traditional concepts of power may not be adequate to understand what is termed "moral leadership." Our clearest models come from social movements and leaders of large scale religious and political change. However, a close examination of modern business may reveal serious nominations among corporate leaders, such as Lee Iacocca, Ross Perot, or Kazuo Inamori. While undoubtedly more measured in business, the process of moral leadership is relevant to today's corporate setting.

Relationship of Work and Power to Ethical Issues in Management

I argue that there is a correspondence between the ethical issues management faces and the way in which work and power are defined in the executive role. Executive work may continue to be defined primarily in the context of traditional activities -- planning, organizing, deciding, supervising and controlling. Managerial power may be seen primarily in conventional terms of formal authority, expertise, and identification. Under these views of work and power, however, corporations will continue to face a series of challenges about the ethics of duty. Our contentious and litigious society is based on these concepts and their derivative practices. Adhering to the ethics of duty as the solution to difference and conflict within employment organizations, and between corporations and its external stakeholders, is to infer a future comprised of increasing levels of debilitating conflict.

Managers of organizations are capable of higher aspirations. Corporate leaders have the capacity to raise the level of interaction above zero-sum processes and endless debates on whose definition of legal rights will prevail. Furthermore, the plain facts of global competition suggest a high likelihood that some firms, in any particular industry, will achieve a high level of integration that serves as a source of innovation, efficiency and adaptive ability. The United States economy requires equally or more productive organizations in a global context. However, reliance on concepts of leadership, executive work, and power prevalent today may not successfully meet the competition.

This concept implies a change from corporate managemant to institutional leadership, from transactional to transformational leadership, and from a mindset of duty to a vision of possibility. Managers can assume fuller responsibility for the context of work throughout their organizations and seek more deliberately to affect the premises of action throughout the firm. Values and purposes need to be utilized more explicitly as instruments of power. Integration of differences can be attained, and interests can be elevated to long-term, positive-sum relationships.

Impact on the Welfare of Society

The presence or absence of corporate moral leadership on the welfare of society will be immense. While the market system must be relied upon as the primary mechanism for allocating resources and gaining economic efficiency, the size, scale, and complexity of society rarely allow managers to divorce economic effects from the social and political effects of decisions. Given a high level of sophistication and a strong investigative ability in society, virtually every corporate action is subject to close, public examination, any group perceiving a stake in the issue appears willing to extend itself an invitation to the party.

This situation will continue to make the ethics of duty a hotly contested battleground for addressing conflicting claims on corporate action. Yet, managers have considerable leadership influence in determining what issues are shaped, how they are expressed, and how flexible or inflexible positions become. By creating different contexts for work, managers can influence the definition and expression of interests and attain higher levels of both individual and institutional objectives.

Implications for Professional Practice

I have suggested a variety of prescriptions for managers in the business of business ethics. First, managers must accept working in a changing, disputed and ambiguous environment concerning minimal standards for corporate conduct. I have recommended an ability to work persistently in pursuit of immediate interests while being willing to compromise for broader and long-term objectives. Principles involving "as if" disclosure and the development of high quality internal environment have been suggested as guidelines to ethical behavior, in the presence of ambiguity about the ethics of duty.

These ideas pertain to the objective of avoiding charges of illegal or unethical behavior. I have argued that a second dimension, the ethics of possibility and moral leadership, is also relevant to managers and to the success of our economic system. Rather than avoiding charges of unethical behavior, this concept seems to bring about positive, productive relations that would not have otherwise existed without executive leadership. Managers need to realize and act upon the latitude for defining perceptions and creating contexts in corporate behavior. Not only will moral leadership in our corporations lead to a more humane society, but it may also be a necessary condition for maintaining a competitive and prosperous economy.

Managers will be required to articulate ideas and ideals that elevate others' aspirations and result in higher levels of personal and institutional fulfillment. Oliver Wendell Holmes is reported to have spoken to this point, saying, "There are one-story intellects, two-story intellects, three-story intellects with skylights. All fact collectors who have no aim behind their facts are one-story persons; two-story persons compare reasons, generalize, using the labors of the fact collectors as well as their own. Three-story persons idealize, imagine, predict. Their best illumination comes from above through the skylight."[14]

NOTES

[1] Adam Smith, The Theory of Moral Sentiments. D.D. Raphael and A.L. Macfie, eds., (Oxford: Clarendon Press, 1976) pp. 175-176.

[2] James MacGregor Burns, Leadership. (New York: Harper and Row, Publishers, 1978).

[3] Lon L. Fuller, The Morality of the Law. (New Haven: Yale University Press, 1964).

[4] J. Fletcher, Situation Ethics. (Philadelphia:

Westminister, 1966).

[5] Carl Madden, "Forces Which Influence Ethical Behavior", in Clarence C. Walton, ed., The Ethics of Corporate Conduct. (Englewood Cliffs: Prentice Hall, Inc., 1977) p. 73.

[6] Felix Frankfurter, "The Federal Securities Act II", Fortune, (August, 1933) pp. 53.

[7] Fuller, p. 152.

[8] Kazuo Inamori, "THE PERFECT COMPANY: Goal for Productivity", speech presented to Case Western Reserve University, June 5, 1985.

[9] John D. Aram and Scott S. Cowen, Information and Corporate Directors: The Board and the Process of Management. (New York: National Association of Accountants, 1983).

[10] Thomas J. Peters, "Developing Distinctive Skills", California Management Review, Vol. XXVi, No. 3, Spring, 1984, p. 120.

[11] Burns, p. 38.

[12] Rosabeth Moss Kanter, The Change Masters: Innovations for Productivity in the American Corporation. (New York: Simon and Schuster, 1984) p. 305.

[13] Bernard M. Bass, Leadership and Performance Beyond Expectations. (New York: The Free Press, 1985) p. 111-12.

[14] Robert K. Mueller, "Leading-Edge Leadership", in Contemporary Issues in Leadership, eds., William E. Rosenbach and Robert L. Taylor (Boulder : Westview Press, 1984) p. 341.

THE MANAGER

THE PRACTITIONER: ROBERT LALLY

I have been asked to participate in this program and my role particularly is that of the manager in a small business. Included in my introduction was the fact that Norton Brothers has been around in this Northern Ohio area since 1888. It is the oldest contractor, roofing and sheet metal contractor in the area. We employ seasonally -- 20 people in the winter time and about 50-55 people in the summer time -- in the field. We are a very seasonal organization. We have a gross of about $3 million. The government defines small business, in the contracting field, at least by 5 million dollar gross and up to 250 employees. We are definitely small business.

I suppose, as I talk about business management for the most part, I believe I was selected because so much of the theory in school is directed toward the large corporations, the national organizations, and the general dynamics of multinationals. These theories can be applied to small business, I am sure. As a practitioner, the practical aspect of my work is more direct and more immediate in the day-to-day operations. The small business manager is dealing daily with suppliers, change-over, employees, and customers. He wants to do the right thing and have the right things done to him. This time of year, Christmas time, you get into the question of purchasers receiving gifts from suppliers and salesmen. In the past few days I have received letters from Lincoln Electric, and from LTV Steel Company, which state their positions. They point out very dramatically that giving gifts to purchasing people is not in the best interest of the organization. Even LTV Steel Company put a dollar amount on the gift: $20.00. Presumably, anything up to $20.00 in value was permissible without disciplinary action by upper-management. So apparently they look at it as a difference in degree but not in kind. A purchasing agent told me one time that the most important gift to him was the fact that the supplier is available on the other end of the telephone to answer his questions, respond to his needs and to advise about a delivery. That was the best gift that purchasing agent could ever receive. This enabled him to perform his job much better.

The responsibility I have to an employee is to provide a safe environment for work. This is done by union contracts. The employee can very well be careless about safty practices, yet strict liability is imposed upon the employer. This responsibility I have is the "ethic of duty", of which Dr. Aram spoke, and not an ethic of choice. The customer that I deal with is protecting his building from the weather. All that customer really wants is to have his building protected from the elements. He does not want the roof to leak. Put on one-ply, put on two-plies, put on three-plies -- he really doesn't care. It doesn't matter to him. The ethics of duty is taken into context by contracting with him. I can put a two-ply on and it's not going to leak but my contract with him says three-plies. So therefore, the ethic of duty is to put on three plies.

In the past half-a-dozen years, sophisticated specifications came into being because of the concern about the contractor cheating -- cheating on the job, cheating the owner -- that there now has been created built-in standards and protections. Sometimes I think that these specifications are dictated by the self-interest of the owner's representative, or the architect, or whomever compiles those specifications, because they are given out in quantity, presumably impressing the owner that his dollar for the inspection service, or for the specification-writer, has been well spent. These types of things are expensive to prepare, it takes a lot of money to prepare these standards and presumably they're not really acted upon very closely in the field. Really this expense is unnecessary if we would deal properly with each other, if the contractor was not always thought of as cheating the owner or trying to shave the job. This then becomes a matter of attitude. When we provide these standards and inspections we are trying to force ethical conduct -- ethical conduct that shouldn't have to be forced -- and in so doing it becomes very expensive. It is an expense that someone must pay.

Business ethics is no different than personal ethics. We are only operating in a different theatre. We all want to do the right thing. So defining the right thing becomes the problem based upon our own moral standards of righteousness. Our system of free enterprise has a great deal of self-interest. In my experience in business, I have found how easy it is for people to rationalize, to rationalize their actions very subtly to support their self-interest. Self-interest, of course, can be expressed by groups. And this is often done by single interest groups.

Our society puts a great deal of emphasis on success. We don't hear much about integrity. Success, as materialistic, is a concept that has been spawned by the Industrial Revolutuion. That is fairly recent. Integrity has always been revered by men and women. It now becomes for us a matter of emphasis how we deal with, and how we define, success.

The Christian concept is not so much about being born again but being forgiven again, and again, and again. There is a story of the construction worker going to confession, baring his soul to the priest because he has spent a very long lifetime stealing. He stole from the job sites: the mortar, the bricks, the lumber and the nails. The priest, recognizing the reformation in the man said, "Can you make restitution?" "Oh, certainly Father, certainly. If you have the blue prints, I really have the lumber!" Restitution is most important when we start thinking of ethics; restitution is the essence of forgiveness. Restitution must be made to the party of whom we have taken unjust advantage. The contribution to the collection plate on Sunday is no substitution for dealing with the party that we have offended. There is a quotation attributed to Benjamin Franklin and he referenced the Quakers that they pray for each other on Sunday and then prey on each other during the week. Now there is certainly a certain contradiction in that type of attitude. Think about it. We should really opt for integrity as the mark of success.

Technology has progressed to such an extent that our standards of living have improved tremendously. Yet technology has revealed that we are polluting our streams, our lakes, and our atmosphere. New decisions now are forced upon our managers by law. This then is expanding the ethic of duty. It now becomes the duty by public law and not by choice.

The ethics of possibility stated by Dr. Aram is

an excellant concept of the manager taking the positive steps towards excellence in his or her organization by forming the moral and ethical attitude of other decision-makers. Too often there is a void in corporate management. There is a lack of concern for society, for the environment, and for saftey; because of the dilution of the bottom line. The cry from the public then causes government to intervene with a multitude of regulations for the "protection of society." And then we are be set with the bureaucratic excesses of an E.P.A., the Environmental Protection Agency or the Occupational Safety and Health Administration. Instead of acting positively earlier, management now only has the right to complain as the government comes in and takes over. Similar is the old question in construction, "Why is it that there is never enough time to do the job right the first time, when there is always plenty of time to come back the second time and fix it?" It is always more expensive, too!

I do not view my personal role as a manager as a power position. That, of course, is subjective. In my limited dealings with big industry, I can understand managing as a power tool. It can be a career-enhancement position or, for the smaller mind, of self-aggrandizement. The effectiveness of a manager is always judged by his superiors and very often by his subordinates. The most non-productive aspect of middle management, as I see it, is the "CYA syndrome." More time is spent doing that than in managing productively. There is little time for the "CYA syndrome" in small business. In small business the manager is always exposed. There is little barrier of a middle-management condition.

To be able to do good is extremely satisfying. To have the power to do good is awesome. With this power comes responsibility. As a young manager skills are being developed leading to, hopefully, becoming a manager with greater responsibility. Your superior's management ethics may well be different than yours. The question of running contrary to his directives, or being an "in-house whistle blower", may well affect your career. You may not be around long enough to effectuate the good, ethical principles that you espouse and that would be good for the competitive position of your employer. Do you antagonize at that point? Do you go along? Do you compromise? There really are no pat answers to these questions. And each situation needs a lot of questioning. This is not to define situational ethics depending on the circumstances -- I can do this and I can do that -- as was referred to by Dr. Aram. Fundamental justice is demanded at all times whether by law or by our moral code. A moral code is essential or we have subtracted from ourselves the content of our life, the content essential to genuine quality of our life -- our inner being.

With business ethics it is necessary to guard against rationalization. We all rationalize our actions. Be aware of that as well as the rationalization of others. What responsibility do I have for the pollution of the environment? I have to control the emissions of the smelly, dirty tar kettle. Do I have that responsibility? Many tests, pro and con, have been made about carcinogens in tar. Different materials are being developed. Question: "Will the marketplace pay for these additional costs? What is my duty toward the workmen as we remove all the asbestos roofs?" Asbestos was used for many years in roofing before technology cried out against its use. It is very difficult for me to be concerned about a workman who has been smoking for years and years. But wherein lies my duty? Relative to this is the manager's responsibility to protect the consumer from himself. The self-interest of the consumer is often economically motivated. Get the most for the least and impose strict liability on the manufactuter or contractor. What about the responsibility of the consumer to educate himself? Maybe pay a little more for a safer or better product.

The "Wall Street Journal principle" as expressed by Dr. Aram was certainly well founded. And this applies to a small business manager as well as the large business manager. Not being published on the Wall Street Journal, of course, the small business manager utilizing this principle provides the awareness that, even though there is no high visibility media exposure, there is always the contradictory position of the media regarding the right of the people to know. The business decisions that are made with genuine ethical integrity, and incidentally consistent with the bottom line, can be second guessed by the self-interest of others. Thus the published results can be very biased. Then enters the Public Relations man for big industry. I have no experience in this field, so no further comment.

Personal integrity along with your continuing development of a moral code, because you do know right from wrong, is the basis of professional ethics. This is not always an easy task. Thus a positive perception of ethics is more beneficial to you, to your customer, and to the entire business community, than a fear of being labeled unethical. Once the positive steps are taken, the following steps become easier.

I'm pleased to be here. I didn't really have any idea of the make-up of your group. I had the idea we were coming to college students and I guess we are all learning. But I appreciate the fact that you people obviously are already in the field. You know what it is and we are not talking to a group of idealistically motivated people. You have seen the problems in the field, I'm sure. I hope we are able to contribute a little bit to your recognition of ethical concepts and recognition of the fact that Dr. Aram pointed out, namely, this field is a moving target. It doesn't mean that it makes it loose for all of us. It means that we as managers have a great deal more responsibility to make it work.

THE MANAGER

THE CONSUMER:
SUSAN COVERDALE

I speak today as a consumer of management. My qualifications are simply my experience in the work force in companies where I have been working under, or managed by, some other person or persons. My training is in computer programming and systems analysis, therefore most of my work has been on or around computers. I draw the majority of my thoughts for this talk from three work situations: 1) I worked for an international company which sold computer equipment and accounting software to go along with the computers. 2) I worked as an independent consultant for a manufacturing company developing software and helping them to decide on, and install, accounting and manufacturing software. 3) I am currently (1985) working at Hawken School where I am responsible for computer curriculum at the high school level as well as overseeing all educational and administrative hardware and software located on two different campuses.

There are many ideas in John Aram's paper that I can directly relate to but on a different level. I will address these ideas as a consumer of management in four basic areas.

I. Short-Term VS. Long Range Goals

When I was working for the company selling computer equipment and software, one of my biggest problems was when a salesman would sell a computer with certain promises. I call this the "no problem" syndrome. A customer buys a computer and wants it to print on 5-part carbon invoices..."no problem." The customer wants to use ledger cards..."no problem", or the customer needs to set up 10,000 customers on one data disk..."no problem." Well, some, or all of these, items might be impossible, depending on the equipment sold. The "no problem" became my problem but only after the customer had signed a contract and made a down payment. I then gently had to tell the customer about a better way to handle his data. "Ledger cards? Don't you know that no one uses ledger cards anymore? It's old fashioned. Five-part invoices? State-of-the-art calls for carbonless invoices and

115

3-part will certainly do for you. We're all trying to conserve, you know", and so on. The end result was a customer that is not really happy, a salesman that reaches his quota this month, and a variety of stress related problems for me. Eventually the Cleveland branch of this company closed. If you don't have satisfied customers your product doesn't continue to sell. A short-term goal was reached but the long-range possibilities were non-existent.

This general attitude is common in the computer industry. In the past five years computer companies have come and gone, and the only ones that have survived are the ones with the long-term goals. These are companies who took their time to develop a quality piece of hardware and the solid, easy to use, software to go with it. They took a back seat initially because their prices were higher in order to cover their developmental stage, but they are the only companies that are still alive today.

The incentive to produce quality items has to come from management. An employee must be given the time, training and materials to do a job properly. This leads into point #2, clarity of goals, quality of communication, development of people, and presence of internal control, which are handles for creating a good organization.

II. Clarity of Goals, Quality of Communication, Development of People, and Presence of Internal Control

Unreasonable deadlines frequently seem to be a problem of management. The computer field is particularly bad in this area. It seems that once a person or company decides to purchase a computer, they want it running TODAY. I can understand their excitement and enthusiasm, but this is not always possible and certainly not when programming has to be done. My experience has been that when a programmer is working on more than one project the squeaky wheel gets priority. I cannot tell you the number of times I have been taken off of one project and put exclusively on another without being asked ANYTHING about the status of each project. This "transactional" form of management can be counter-productive.

Direct communication, especially in my field, is a must. Often times, decisions about what equipment should be purchased is made by a person who is not currently doing the task the new equipment will assist. The end result can be a product that cannot be used and/or has to be reordered. This leads to greater expense and a lack of confidence in the equipment as well as management. My first suggestion, when consulting with a company about computers, is to get the people who will be using the computer involved in the decision about the computer. Aren't they more likely to cooperate with a decision they helped to make?

Another way to aid in the development of people is to invest in employee training. I have seen so many people come back from a seminar or course with new energy, which boosts the morale of all the people around them.

III. Common Context

Franklin Delano Roosevelt, in his second inaugural address, states, "We have always known that heedless self-interest was bad morals; we know now that it is bad economics." Common context is very important to the working environment. I feel this goes hand-in-hand with delegating responsibility. Many of my situations have involved responsibility with no authority. This can be extremely frustrating as a consumer of management. One of my responsibilities on the job has been to evaluate, purchase, and maintain computer equipment. I will never forget the day when I was asked to help someone in his office because he was having trouble hooking up a cable. When I got to the office, I discovered a whole new computer system. I was shocked. I had never been consulted, or even informed, of this purchase, which amounted to about half of our computer budget for the year. You note who was expected to help out with this equipment when it couldn't be set up properly!

Asking someone to do a task and then not respecting or following his suggestions is a direct blow to his self-esteem and is certainly not an example of working towards a common context. Each and every employee is an expert in his own area. Use these experts to assist you. Give them the freedom to utilize their expertise. A common context gives each employee a sense of self-worth.

Applying common context on a larger scale, think of how much further along we would be in the development of computers if companies had tried to work together rather than work exclusively for their own betterment. Initially, each computer company did things just enough different so that no computer was compatible with any other. If you purchased a computer from one company, you had to use their service, their software, and their additional equipment if you wanted any. If corporate interests were for the betterment of society, no company would try to limit the consumer in this way.

IV. Finally, Norms, Values and Standards of the Organization Have an Important Influence on Personal Conduct

I have always found that my manager's ethical stance directly influenced my ethical response. It is very difficult for an employee to go on a business trip with a group of people from his company and try to stay within reasonable limits of an expense account when he sees his manager going all out and abusing these privileges. Managers who ask employees to snitch on each other don't make their workers feel very comfortable when they are behind closed doors. These may seem like minor points but they can really lead to an unhealthy working environment. Honest, ethical behavior by a manager is the best way to encourage the same behavior in his employees.

You as a manager are the ones to bring out the best in your employees. You need to lead by example. Transactional management takes a small step towards a narrowly defined goal. Transformational leadership provides for a giant leap for society.

Chapter 5

THE PHYSICIAN

THE PRESENTER:
MARY B. MAHOWALD, Ph.D.

Power is a term that is rarely neutral in its impact. For some it connotes a basic value to be pursued and upheld, a good in itself. When we talk about Black Power or Women Power, we are affirming a positive right for a group of people, a good to be promoted by others besides blacks and women. In medicine, a positive understanding is the power to heal, to save lives, and to relieve human suffering; in other words, the basic goals of medicine as a profession.

For others, the term power has negative connotations suggesting a division between the empowered and the powerless or less powerful, providing opportunities for exploitation, and disvalues as inequality or injustice. Crimes of violence, after all, are an expression of power, and we attempt to reduce the incidence of such acts by withdrawing power from people through imprisonment or denial of liberty in other ways. In medicine, abuse of power may lead to denial of its legitimate use through forfeiture of one's license to practice. The entire system of certification of professionals, whether by the government or by the professions themselves, is a means of insuring that their power is exercised positively rather than negatively.

My purpose in this paper is to clarify and critique the power of the physician, as a specific example on the part of the professional person. To that end I (1) develop a concept of power as itself morally neutral; (2) propose and defend a criterion by which the uses of power as moral, immoral, or amoral; (3) discuss the power that physicians of the past have had, and the power they have today professionally, personally, and politically; and (4) describe a model of the physician's role which is consistent with (2) and with basic ethical principles. It remains the task of individual practitioners to apply this framework to the unique cases which they encounter.

I. Power in General

Preliminarily, consider a basic definition of power as ability or capability with regard to someone or something. The ability may be intellectual, physical, or psychological; it may be innate or instrumental. Intelligence, for example, is an innate power; income is an instrumental power. Either of these is a power whether exercised or not. Moreover, the very perception of power implies psychological power over the perceiver, whether or not the perception is correctly founded. Obviously, power is a correlative term because it necessarily connotes another over whom the power may be exercised. The one who has power is superior to the other, at least in respect to the power that may be exerted. An inequality between them is thus inevitable, and at times at least, morally problematic. It becomes especially problematic when we consider degrees of power as possibilities for increasing inequalities, and for obstructing the autonomy of people. On one end of the spectrum power means outright coercion or force; at the other end it means minimal and often subtle influence, such as education or dissemination of information. Between these are various degrees of power, such as the power to persuade or to manipulate others. The lives of physicians are filled with opportunities for expressing the full range of degrees of power.

The sources of power are in some ways mysterious. Undoubtedly there is an element of luck or divine gratuity, and probably an element of desert. Physicians are typically gifted by nature with ability and opportunity to learn the art and science of medicine; most of their patients are not similarly, or as extensively, gifted. But most physicians invest a great deal of time and effort in developing and maintaining their professional competence; the power derived is thereby earned. So power is at times a function of chance or inborn abilities, and, at other times, it is developed over time through specific efforts. Rarely, if ever, can we know for sure whether our own or others' power is deserved or gratuitous. Nonetheless, there seems to be a prevalent human tendency to consider our own successes as earned, and our failures as inevitable.

To understand power as it applies to the professional person, we must consider, at least briefly, the meaning of a profession. From different accounts three traits are usually mentioned: an intellectualy based expertise, independence in exercising that expertise, and a humanitarian or human service orientation. (Bayles, 1981; Flexner, 1975; Metzger, 1975) The first two characteristics are forms of power in themselves; but it is the third mark of a profession, its service feature, that distinguishes a profession from a business, strictly speaking. The purpose of business is profit to oneself (or to one's shareholders) (Friedman, 1962); the purpose of a profession is service to others. Obviously these purposes are often mixed in the same individual, regardless of his or her occupation. It needs to be recognized, however, that the purposes are in fact at times at odds. To the extent that professionals reap personal profit through the exercise of their professional power, the profit and service motives appear to be more at odds.

II. Criterion for Moral Assessment

Accordingly, I want to propose a criterion by which to assess whether a given occupation truly fulfills the third essential mark of a profession, despite the fact that the person engaging in that occupation accrues profit and/or prestige from the activity. The criterion looks to a crucial link between the moral neutrality of power and its moral or immoral uses. Professional power, I believe, is morally exercised only to the extent that it empowers the individual or group of individuals it affects. To the extent that it dismantles their power it is immoral; to the extent that it does neither (if possible) it is amoral. This criterion is consistent with the moral theory by Kurt Baier in The Moral Point of View (1985). Professional power, then, is power for empowerment; it fulfills its essential purpose only to the extent that its exercise enhances the lives of those on behalf of whom the profession is practiced. If an individual professional enhances ONLY his or her own life through professional practice, an essential feature of the profession is betrayed.

Given that criterion for assessing the uses of professional power, let us review the profession of medicine as according special powers to physicians and evaluate those powers in light of the proposed criterion. Our evaluation must also take account of the specific tasks of the profession, as ways in which its service function is fulfilled. (Freidson, 1970) Specific tasks of medicine as a profession are those of healing, saving lives, and alleviating human suffering. The power of the physician for accomplishing these tasks is somewhat different for the different specialties within medicine; e.g., in reproductive medicine, the physician has the power to bring human lives into existence where this would not otherwise occur, through advances in treatment of high risk pregnancies, and infertility treatments such as artificial insemination, in vitro fertilization, and embryo transfer. Neonatologists have power to maintain the lives of very premature or extremely disabled newborns, or to allow their death by declining to treat them, with or without parental consent. Gynecologists and obstetricians have power to cut off the possibility of new life, and to prevent birth, through sterilization and abortion procedures. Today's surgeons have power to remove organs from a brain dead patient, and use these to save, prolong, or improve the life of another. Intensive care specialists have power to prolong life or allow patients to die, through use or refusal of resuscitation procedures.

The ordinary practice of medicine represents legitimization of power over people to an immense degree. Consider, for example, the violation of bodily integrity which surgery in all its forms represents; consider the assault upon natural body functions which drug management entails; consider the ways in which psychopharmacology or psychosurgery can transform the human psyche; and consider the intrusions on time and privacy that routine medical examination and hospitalization involve. In the name of therapeutic privilege, physicians are empowered to withhold information from the very source of that information, and to undertake treatment without the patient's consent.

Beyond these powers which apply to the practice of medicine and its different specialties are powers which accrue to most physicians as common accouterments of their profession. Personal income is generally well above average, even after high malpractice premiums are paid. A certain level of prestige is another common feature, as attested by the fact that physicians, more than any other group which earns a doctor's degree, generally use and expect to be referred to by their title. (Gorovitz, 1982) The title itself envokes respect, the rendering of which is acknowledgment of power.

As physicians increasingly recognize their power to influence the public at large, some are attracted to political roles as ways of more effectively fulfilling their therapeutic goal. Recent close examples of this recognition include Otis Bohen, family physician and former govenor of Indiana, who succeeded Margaret Heckler as Secretary of the Department of Health and Human Services; and David Jackson, neurologist and former director of the medical intensive care unit at University Hospitals, Cleveland, who became Director of Health for the State of Ohio and is currently (1986) seeking a seat in Congress. Other physicians see their lobbying efforts on behalf of health related bills as part of their responsibility to present and future patients; e.g., Jerome Paulson, pediatrician at Rainbow Babies and Childrens Hospital, helped to enact child seat belt legislation in Ohio; William Moir, cardiologist at University Hospitals, Cleveland, who has been actively promoting in Columbus "living will" legislation through publications and testimony in the state capital. The political power of effectiveness of these individuals obviously derives from their status as physicians. But perhaps the most striking recent example of social or political power of physicians is the influence of the organization called Physicians for Social Responsibility (PSR). Two years ago, the American founder of this organization and recent Nobel prize winner, Bernard Lown, a Harvard cardiologist, told the medical students at Case Western Reserve University that it was their responsibility as physicians to use the power of the profession on behalf of the most important therapeutic goal of our time, the prevention of nuclear holocaust. Worldwide membership in this organization of physicians has increased with the recognition that physicians have greater power and responsibility in this regard than do other professions.

III. The Social Power of American Medicine

The social power of American physicians has recently been chronicled by the sociologist Paul Starr (1982) as reflecting a complex relationship between prestige, or public image, and economic status. According to Starr, back in the early 19th century when America was mostly rural and sparsely populated and non-scientific views of illness prevailed, claims of medical competence were largely disregarded. Health problems were mainly dealt with in the home by family members. During the latter part of the century, as transportation and communication improved, and medicine became more scientific, both the prestige and the income of the physician escalated. Education became more standardized and physicians developed "mechanisms of dependency" such as control over access to drugs, hospitalization, entry into medical schools, and their own fees. In effect, they assumed the dominant role in the health care industry while nurses and other health care professionals were subordinate. The subordination of other health care professionals is evidenced by the fact that they remained salaried employees while the AMA insisted on maintaining power or control over the profits of physicians. Then, as now, the vast majority of subordinate positions within the health care industry were occupied by women. Starr attributes this to the fact that male physicians thought they might thus maintain control of the industry.

During the middle part of the 20th century, the ascendancy of power of American medicine was accompanied (and probably incremented) by its success in avoiding government intervention, while nonetheless drawing government funding for its institutions and research programs. Although private health insurance expanded, physicians' fees continued to be set by the profession itself. Despite a shortage of physicians, there was increased recognition of unmet health care needs of the poor, and increased suspicion of those who held positions of authority and high income. Personal, professional, and political power of physicians continued, but the power generated by their prestige diminished. Concomitantly, the power of the AMA declined through decreased membership, infighting and factional argument within the organization. A greater number of physicians were politically radicalized to speak out against "the system," and the women's movement articulated criticisms of the ways in which female patients were treated. (Arms, 1975; Scully, 1980) Ivan Illich wrote his iconoclastic critique of medicine as causing more medical problems than it solves. (1976) The rise of the wholistic health movement de-emphasized the physician's role by stressing the role played by patients themselves as well as the role of other health care practitioners. (Guttmacher, 1979)

During the 1980's we have seen a continuation of the complex relationship between the public image and economic status of physicians. Starr points to two factors which have further limited the power of physicians: a rapidly increasing supply of physicians and continued efforts by government and business to control medical costs. Abortion laws, dialysis funding, and Baby Doe regulations are but a few examples of govermental interventions which have affected medical practice. Although DRG's (Diagnostic-Related Groups, a prospective method of federal reimbursement) are directed towards hospital costs rather than physician's fees, they have clearly had an impact on the way physicians manage patients' care, and soon the impact will be more directly felt through establishment of set fees for physicians' services. (Dolenc and Dougherty, 1985; Morreim, 1985) No doubt the desire to avoid both government interventions and the litigation occasioned by malpractice claims have reduced the level of independence of physicians. The fact that malpractice claims have been escalating at a rate of 12% a year (Danzon, 1985) encourages physicians to choose modes of treatment which will reduce the likelihood of suit. Generally this means prolonging treatment, even in cases where the physician believes it is no longer in the patient's own interests. As one physician observed, "I never write a DNR order (i.e., an order not to resuscitate a patient) even when I know that a patient is dying, because I'm more likely to be sued for that than for continuing treatment." The climate of litigation has thus resulted in the practice of defensive medicine, a situation which is costly and unfortunate for everyone involved, except perhaps for some attorneys. It has also prompted the departure of highly qualified and needed individuals in subspecialties such as obstetrics and intensive care to specialties less likely to provoke litigation.

It seems clear, then, that in many respects the power of American medicine has diminished over the last few decades, even while the expertise of medicine has developed to an incredible degree. The diminishment may be inevitable because increased specializations have brought about dependencies within the profession itself and on the service of non-physician specialists. An important benefit of this type of "decentralization" of medical power is that increased specializations promote a higher quality of care, at least in situations where the experts collaborate to effect optimum integrated decisions. Another reason for decreased power is that decisions about patients have extended beyond the medical area, from questions about how to treat a patient to whether treatment ought to be provided. Fortunately, or unfortunately, each new advance in medical science answers the question of whether something can be done affirmatively but simultaneously raises the question of whether it should be done. Since the latter is a moral rather than medical question, medical expertise alone is simply not adequate to answer it. An adequate answer requires moral considerations available to patient and physician alike, as well as to others involved in the moral dilemma.

IV. Models of the Physician's Role

If physicians interpret their professional power as encompassing the right to make moral decisions for competent patients, they thus exemplify a paternalistic model of medicine. Hippocrates himself endorsed this model when he advised physicians not to discuss diseases with patients so as not to confuse or anguish them. (Reiser et al., 1977) The ethical principle he thus appealed to is the principle of beneficence, which entails the obligation to do good, and even more importantly, to avoid harm. (Beauchamp and McCullough, 1984) Doing good and avoiding harm becomes paternalistic when it violates the autonomy of individuals. A paternalist model, then, is one where the physician may overrule the wishes of a competent patient in order to promote a benefit which the physician defines. Certain specialties within medicine present greater likelihood of decisions by physicians without the consent of patients, e.g., intensive, emergency, and pediatric care, where patients are often not competent to make their own decisions. However, so long as the patient is not competent, beneficence may be practiced without impugning autonomy, and therefore without paternalism. We cannot violate autonomy if autonomy is not present; and in the case of temporarily unconscious patients, we are more likely to be violating their wishes by not treating than by treating them. Moreover, where there is no time to ascertain a patient's wishes in a situation where delay is life threatening, beneficence requires that treatment be provided even in the absence of explicit consent.

A second more contemporary model of the physician's role reverses the emphasis on the professional's power and places this in the hands of the patient. Thomasma (1983) refers to this as a patient autonomy model of the physician-patient relationship. It is, in fact, an instrumentalist view of the physician's own role. Through the modern doctrine of informed consent, patients have power to withhold consent for treatment, even lifesaving treatment, so long as they are competent and fully informed of the implications of refusal. To the extent that the physician undertakes to fulfill the patient's will, he or she is an instrument of the patient's power. In a pluralist society such as ours, this model is especially appealing to those who would like to avoid the controversy, ambiguity and emotional burden that often accompanies moral dilemmas in medicine. For example, obstetricians and gynecologists may opt to follow a women's wishes regarding fertility enhancement or curtailment, regardless of how her wishes affect others, and regardless of how they perceive their moral responsibility. The obvious flaw of the instrumentalist model is that recognition of the patient's responsibility does not obviate the need for the physicians to come to terms with the moral dimensions of the case. The physician remains responsible for what he or she does or doesn't do.

Since paternalist and instrumentalist models both suffer serious flaws by imputing power to just one or the other side of the physician-patient relationship, I'd like to propose a model which distributes power more equitably. I call this a collaborative model; it is one which recognizes that power is shared by all of the autonomous individuals involved in medico-moral dilemmas. Among physicians themselves, the collaborative model has long been effective in the practice of obtaining consults or making referrals. The team model of health care decision making has increasingly been followed in many settings, evidencing broader recognition of the usefulness of multidisciplinary input. The same model is applicable, and in fact preferable, for ethical decisions. Recently, hospitals have been strongly encouraged by the government to extend their decision base yet further through establishment of hospital ethics review committees. These committees include non-health care professionals in their membership. The reason for extending the decision base is twofold: to acknowledge the fact that others besides physicians and patients are responsible for ethical decisions in health care, and to improve the quality of those decisions. Obviously, shared decisions mean shared power. Besides the principles of beneficence and respect for autonomy, which are crucial considerations in evaluating the power of physicians, there is a third princlple with which an adequate moral assessment must be concerned, and that is justice. (Beauchamp and Childress, 1982) This principle is best expressed in the collaborative model of the physician's role, because justice entails an equitable distribution of power. Insofar as either of the other models focuses exclusively on the physician's or patient's power, it does not adequately address the principle of justice.

Unlike paternalist or instrumental models of the physician-patient relationship, the collaborative model takes account of a crucial difference between ethical and strictly clinical dilemmas, viz., that our ethical responsibilites extend beyond the patient to all of those affected by our decisions. Another difference between moral and clinical obligations is also acknowledged, viz., that every agent involved in a moral dilemma has a distinctive responsibility stemming from the degree of power which the agent actually possesses and the role which the agent plays in the situation. (Role and power are related but not identical either morally or factually.) These distinctive responsibilities yield different answers to the question "What should I do?" In other words, in each specific case, the moral responsibility of the physician is different from that of the nurse, and different from that of the patient and from that of a family member. The moral decision of each must be based on a unique role and power. At times these moral decisions are in conflict, but this does not imply that one is right and another is wrong. However, one who denies power over others by claiming that he or she was simply following another's orders is guilty of what Sartre calls "bad faith." (1956)

Although different moral positions may be valid, individuals still face conflicts in settling their own moral questions. A rule of thumb to be followed in cases of conflict is that the power of the one most affected should count most. Ordinarily, this means that the autonomy of the competent patient is paramount. The physician empowers the patient by respecting his or her choice. For the non-autonomous patient, however, the principle of beneficence is paramount. The physician empowers that patient by attempting to optimize his or her interests. Occasionally, this may mean allowing (and allowing is a kind of empowering) the patient to die.

Although the patient's power as autonomous, and the physician's obligation to empower the patient, are primary considerations, neither implies that the power of patient or physician is absolute. Harms and benefits accrue to colleagues and family members and even to others in society, as well as to patients. Respect for autonomy extends to all of these individuals too, even though legally we may only be required to obtain the informed consent of the patient. Justice, and a collaborative model of practice, requires that we advert to applications of beneficence and respect for autonomy beyond their relevance to patients and physicians. It demands that we recognize power as inevitably and desirably shared. To return to the criterion discussed earlier by which we may assess the moral, immoral or amoral uses of power, justice demands that power be exercised in an empowering manner that applies to all of those affected by our decisions. We only act justly with regard to all of those involved in moral dilemmas to the extent that our professional power empowers them to empower others. When this occurs we act collaboratively.

To summarize then, the impressive power of modern medicine is itself morally neutral. It remains neutral if its exercise leaves others unaffected either positively or negatively, which may be impossible. Its exercise is immoral if it reduces the power of others, by doing them harm of denying their choices. The power of medicine is morally exercised when it empowers others by restoring their health and affirming their freedom. It thus fulfills the specific goals of medicine and the essential purpose of any profession.

References

Arms, Suzanne. Immaculate Deception. New York: Bantam Books, 1975.

Baier, Kurt. The Moral Point of View. New York: Cornell University Press, 1958.

Bayles, Michael. Professional Ethics. Belmont, Ca.: Wadsworth Publishing Company, 1981.

Beauchamp, Tom and Childress, James. Principles of Biomedical Ethics. New York: Oxford University Press, 1983.

Beauchamp, Tom and McCullough, Laurence. Medical Ethics. Englewood Cliffs, N.J.: Prentice-Hall, Inc., 1964.

Danzon, Patricia M. Medical Malpractice. Cambridge: Harvard University Press, 1985.

Dolenc, Danielle and Dougherty, Charles. "DRG's: The Counterrevolution in Financing Health Care," Hastings Center Report. 15, 3 (June 1985).

Flexner, Abraham. "Is Social Work a Profession?" Proceedings of the Natural Conference of Charities and Corrections. Chicago: Hildman Printing, 1915.

Freidson, Eliot. Profession of Medicine. New York: Dodd, Mead, 1970.

Friedman, Milton. Capitalism and Freedom. Chicago: University of Chicago Press, 1962.

Gorovitz, Samuel. Doctor's Dilemmas. New York: Macmillan Publishing Company, 1982.

Guttmacher, Sally. "Whole in Body, Mind and Spirit: Holistic Health and the Limits of Medicine," Hastings Center Report 9, 2 (April 1979).

Illich, Ivan. Medical Nemesis. New York: Pantheon Books, 1976.

Metzger, Walter. "What Is a Profession?", Seminar Reports 3, 1, Program of General and Continuing Education, Columbia University, 1975.

Morreim, E. Haavi. "The MD and the DRG," Hastings Center Report 15, 3, (June 1985).

Reiser, Stanley et al. (eds.). "Selections from the Hippocratic Corpus," Ethics in Medicine. Cambridge: MIT Press, 1977.

Sartre, Jean-Paul. Being and Nothingness. Trans. by Hazel Barnes. New York: Philosophical Library, 1956.

Scully, Diane. Men Who Control Women's Health. Boston: Houghton-Mifflin, 1980.

Starr, Paul. The Social Transformation of American Medicine. New York: Basic Books, Inc., 1982.

Thomasma, David. "Beyond Medical Paternalism and Patient Autonomy: A Model of Physician Conscience for the Physician-Patient Relationship, Annals of Internal Medicine 98, 2 (February, 1983).

THE PHYSICIAN

THE PRACTITIONER:
HUGH J. LESLIE, JR. M.D.

When I was asked to speak as "the practitioner" in this "The Physician Conference" as part of "The Power of the Professional Person" conferences, I expressed my concern about the word "power". As Mary Mahowald has pointed out, "power" to me has an immediate negative connotation, and I was reluctant to be involved. But after brief conversation and elaboration with Bob, I agreed to participate -- and, therefore, I am here.

I certainly want to thank Mary Mahowald for the excellent presentation. I think it is important to mention again the three criteria she stated in the definition of a profession:

1) An intellectually-based expertise
2) Independance in expressing that expertise
3) A humanitarian or human-service orientation.

As interpreted by many non-medical persons, the medical professional would be an individual aspiring "to heal, to save lives, to relieve human suffering." But this is a non-realistic, a hero-worshipping type of approach to the practice of medicine. A physician in his practice of medicine is attempting to improve the quality of life for his various patients. As a general pediatrician my endeavor is to maintain the best possible mental and physical health of the children under my care -- and to teach the parents the normal phases of growth and development. These measures allow parents to have confidence in their role -- allowing an improved quality of life as a nuclear family.

Pediatricians use similies that are child-oriented rather than adult-oriented. We talk "child language" more readily than "adult language." Therefore as I elaborate about the "spectrum of power", let us assume it to be a teeter-totter. One end of the teeter-totter is the outright coercion of force of power; the other is the subtle influence -- the teaching and presenting of positive things. In every walk of life -- the medical profession included -- persons sitting at the upward end of the teeter-totter will be the exploiters, using their "power" negatively. But, as the teeter-totter tips, I believe that most of us, as we sit at the upper end of the incline, are humanly interested in teaching people how to cope better with their daily lives and problems -- the subtle influence.

Unlike the "3-R's" of elementary school, the "3-R's" of the medical profession are responsibility, respect, and righteousness.

Let us consider first, "responsibility." Maybe an individual has to have innate nature to become a physician. But of major importance is dedication -- dedication to years of study, perhaps 13 to 14 years beyond high school; dedication and perseverance sufficiently strong to allow one to overlook the early accomplishments of his peers; dedication of one's family, not only frequently providing the financial opportunity for study but also the often-needed emotional support.

It is also the responsibility of the physician to continue to accumulate his expertise, the first item of the definition of a profession. Not only does he acquire this expertise during his medical school years and his residency years, but continually during the years of medical practice. This involves constant study -- participation in the teaching of students and residents, participation in continuing medical education programs, as well as stimulating study done individually. Again, I emphasize that this is a responsibility that a physician owes to his patients. Parenthetically, I want to add that one of the privileges of the medical profession is that as one enters retirement he still is encouraged to participate in continuing medical education courses to allow him the personal satisfaction of maintaining his individual expertise. This privilege is sharply in contrast to the "exit" that much of the business world gives to an individual upon retirement.

Another aspect of responsibility is that responsibility given to the physician by the patient, or in pediatrics by the parents of the pediatric patient. One of the best examples of such responsibility is illustrated by the following, frequently repeated, experience. A young couple, expecting their first child, will visit with me in my office for a prenatal conference. The scheduling of a prenatal conference is relatively new. During the past five to seven years, instructors of Lamaze classes and many obstetricians have advised such conferences before parents select the pediatrician for their child or children. The interview is initially stifled by first appearance contact, but this is broken by the mother beginning to read general questions from a legal-size paper, i.e., washing clothes, changing diapers, feeding the baby, etc. But what they are silently saying is, "Are you the person that, as a parent, I want to assume the pediatric care of my child? Will you be responsible, not only after birth but throughout all of those 18 years that you will be our pediatrician? Are you the very responsible person that will enter our family?" Being on the upper end of the teeter-totter and having the strongest desire to educate parents and subtly influence them, I reply that 90% of my role as pediatrician is to teach Moms and Dads the phases of normal mental and physical growth and development. Ten percent of my role is the care of the child -- not only as the child is enjoying good health, but also during the periods of illness. I believe that it is the responsibility of the physician -- and it should be a primary desire -- to teach the patient sufficiently that the patient has an adequate understanding about oneself and one's medical problems. This can and should be done in all types of medical practice.

A physician is frequently asked to assume the responsibility of immediate decision-making -- a process that he should readily be able to accomplish by exercising his accumulated expertise. As in pediatrics, a frequent phone call at 3 a.m. is that of a 3-year-old with sudden fever of 104° F. The parents ask what they do to control the fever. But the real question requiring immediate decision-making is whether measures for diagnosis should immediately be undertaken or whether procrastination for six hours would be more enlightening. This is true responsibility -- assumed by the physician.

The second of the "3-R's" is "respect." The physician must respect the patient, and in turn the patient must respect the physician. We all experience about us a pro-prioceptive ring -- a barrier of independence, or a ring of intimacy. A sudden disruption of the ring can lead to fright, loss of respect for the transgressor, or at the very least discomfort. Regardless, whether an individual's barrier extends six inches or three feet, the physician must obtain the respect of the patient to allow this barrier to be broken since the physician-patient relationship is generally a touch contact. A child of 2½ years on the pediatric examining table is frightened but is able to communicate. To break this barrier of independence and establish touch contact, I tell the child to place his hand onto my warm hand -- and I count his fingers with him, which he can too readily follow. When I care for adolescents, I initiate the examination by talking about school activities and extra-curricular activities. Similar approaches can be used in practice of adult medicine. The physician must respect the patient's individuality and establish an air of comfort -- not just brashly look into the ears, place a stethoscope onto the chest or palpate the abdomen of a naked object.

The patient must have proper respect for the physician. The patient must be willing to give an accurate history as his physician carefully listens with keen ears. Diagnosis is so often dependent upon obtaining a good history.

It is needless to mention that the parent-patient-physician relationship commands the greatest of confidentiality.

In the previous paper there was reference to "physical assault on the human body" -- a negative connotation of power. I will take exception to this expression in daily pediatric practice. After a sufficient period of persuasion, physical examination of the uncooperative child should be performed to diagnose the disease and to readily allow the parents to again comfort the child -- even though holding to restrict combative activity is mandatory. "Physical assault" in reference to surgery is an inappropriate comment. If one has appendicitis, an appendectomy should be performed, such procedures not implying negative power by the physician. Indeed, I agree that proper explanation of the procedure to be performed should be given to the patient and parents -- again, teaching, as I have mentioned earlier.

The third of the "3-R's" is "righteousness." I will use the term synonymously with "justness." This is a two-way street. The patient, or perhaps parents of the patient, must be just with the physician -- not, as is too often the case, assuming that he is "too busy" or has "too many patients." A physician does worry about his patient -- and too often a physician is not kept informed because of the assumptions that I just mentioned. Pediatric examples of such fairness, or righteousness, that frequently are breached are:

    1) The phone call that is placed about the sick child, and when the phone reply is made, there is no answer. I will dial repeatedly until I get an answer even up to five to six hours later. Occasionally I will dial the emergency rooms.

    2) A phone call placed in the middle of the night and I have advised what to do. I not uncommonly am wakeful through the rest of the night.

So we do worry about our patients and righteously want to hear back from our patients. Every specialty of medicine has its particular worries -- the cardiologist performing the coronary angioplasty, the obstetrician the delivery, the psychiatrist counseling the depressed patient.

Complicated medical problems are now handled by a team approch -- the physician, the consultant, the nurse, the patient, the family, the clergy, and the ethecist. Such team approach in major medical centers is now the standard and will continue as such. Although at times the outcome may not be the most righteous for improved quality of life, at least the decision-making has been shared.

Lastly, I will counter by stating that I do not think that the medical profession is losing any esteem over the past few decades. The physician is no longer the stereotype person of the twenties or thirties -- the person wearing the dark blue suit, white shirt with stiff collar, and black wing-tipped shoes -- and saying, "Do as I say!" But today the physician practices with an in-depth fund of knowledge, with readily-available knowledgeable colleagues with whom to consult, and frequently is in a multi-disciplinary medical center where a holistic approach to patient-care can be rendered. He indeed is able to fulfill the definition of a professional.

Chapter 6

THE PROFESSOR

THE PRESENTER:
SANDRA W. RUSS, Ph.D.

The nature of the work of the professor involves three primary areas -- the professor as teacher, as researcher, and as university citizen. Each of these areas will be discussed separately, with a focus on the types of ethical dilemmas that arise.

Professor as Teacher

As a teacher, the role of the professor is to impart information, teach students to think critically and problem solve, and to encourage student personal and intellectual development.

One of the first questions that arises is what information to cover and emphasize in a course. The professor is very influential in choosing texts with particular orientations and in stressing some topics over others in lectures and on tests. We all have a tendency to talk about what we know and think is important and to give short shrift to what we don't know or think is unimportant. How do we fight that tendency? Makosky (1986) gives some guidelines about choosing the content to be covered. Although she focuses on psychology courses, these criteria appear to be widely applicable. Content should: (1) have broad relevance to the field, (2) cover basic concepts that will not be quickly dated, (3) be empirically well supported, and (4) cover information which is useful outside the field and relevant to other disciplines. I have also found that using texts with broad coverage of material and theoretical approaches is useful. If that is not possible, then using a text with an orientation different from one's own gives a more balanced presentation to students. For example, when teaching an undergraduate Abnormal Psychology class I have used a text with a behavioral bent. My own psychodynamic orientation came through in the lecture material. Bringing in outside lecturers with different areas of expertise and different points of view is also helpful. In this time of specialization, it is important that one identify one's areas of expertise and areas of relative ignorance to students, so they can weigh the information they are receiving.

It is also crucial that the professor identify his or her biases and values, if relevant to the course material. Finding the balance between conveying one's own conclusions enthusiastically, but not in a dogmatic fashion, and encouraging other points of view, is a constant challenge. To give 'just the facts,' in a totally neutral fashion would, it seems to me, dampen the instructor's enthusiasm for the subject matter and the process of teaching. What is important is to give the rationale for one's own conclusions and interpretations. This involves presenting the rules of problem solving approaches and interpretation of data unique to the discipline. In this way, the professor is modeling the process of problem solving, critical thinking, and data interpretation which is the key to understanding a particular discipline. Students are free to accept or reject the conclusions, but they are learning the process of developing hypotheses, testing them, collecting and interpreting data, and reaching intelligent conclusions in a systematic fashion. A professor of mine once referred to the need to identify the "productive units" of any culture which should be passed on to younger members. (Moore, 1966) "Productive units" exist in disciplines as well and include the fundamentals of current knowledge and the basic rules of problem solving and inference. Teaching these fundamentals should enable students to continue learning on their own and master more specialized areas. Teaching specialized content information becomes a secondary consideration using this framework. (see Russ, 1980) Also, one's own opinions and conclusions assume less weight. What is important is teaching the process of collecting, weighing, and interpreting information.

Another important consideration in teaching is the need to be aware of the impact of what one is saying. One goal of teaching is to help the student consider alternative points of view of the world and different value systems. This process should make students uncomfortable. In the field of psychology, where so many of the topics are relevant to daily life, students may begin questioning long-held values and opinions. The professor needs to be aware of this process and be sensitive to the problems which may arise for individual students.

Another area of influence of the professor is that of career choice. The professor can be very influential through career advising. It is natural that one is enthusiastic about one's own discipline and would want to interest students in that area as a career. However, the career advisor must help students decide for themselves by giving information about career opportunities, discussing the pros and cons of the profession, and by encouraging students to talk with others.

In the area of student development, the professor has to find the right balance between evaluating performance and encouraging development. In large classes with rather rigid grading criteria, this is a difficult task. Often, a student needs a successful positive experience, is truly trying, but, based on objective grading criteria, must receive a mediocre grade. The professor needs to find other ways of encouraging this student. It is easier to facilitate and encourage student growth in small seminars where there is more time for professor-student contact and more room for the student to pursue the subject matter in an individual fashion. In a small seminar, it is also easier for the professor to get to know and appreciate the unique abilities of the individual student.

The teacher-student relationship is a crucial factor in student development. The relationship is powerful in enhancing intellectual and personal growth and can be inspiring. It can also be misused in a variety of ways. Students can be exploited, and faculty and the university community need to be vigilant about the variety of forms of exploitation that can occur. Certainly, sexual harassment and exploitation is a topic about which there has been much consciousness-raising and, hopefully, we are making progress in that area. There are other, more subtle forms of exploitation about which we could use more discussion. Over-using students as research assistants or teaching assistants is one example. Another is unfairly granting favors to some students and discriminating against other, perhaps more "difficult" students.

Professor as Researcher-Scholar

One of the main functions of the professor as research-scholar is to convey the ethical values of the discipline. One excellent review of ethical issues in science is Jackson's Honor in Science (1986), sponsored by Sigma Xi. Jackson stresses that the professor communicates these values not only through direct teaching but also through day-to-day functioning. In this regard, the professor is truly a role model. Students learn not only from what one says, but from what one does. Jackson also points to the importance of an esprit de corps within a research laboratory or institution. He uses Webster's dictionary definition of esprit de corps as "the common spirit existing in the members of a group and inspiring enthusiasm, devotion, and strong regard for the honor of the group." Jackson implies that it is this kind of spirit within a group that will enable the kind of values and communication to occur which is necessary to maintain a healthy competition as well as high ethical standards. The professor has a responsibility to maintain and teach these values but also to try to develop such an esprit de corps within his or her own research group.

One commonly held myth is that there is a conflict between the functions of teaching and research; i.e., one can be a good teacher or researcher but can't do both. I say myth because in most of the discussions I have had with my colleagues there is a consensus that carrying out research improves the quality of teaching and creative teaching contributes to one's scholarly endeavors. Teaching and research are not only compatible functions, but each enhances the other. There is a conflict between teaching and research, but it is not inherent in the functions, it is because of the time demands on faculty. Professors are always choosing between putting in more time on a lecture, or on a chapter that is overdue, or spending an extra 20 minutes with a student. These are difficult choices and here is where the ethical dilemmas arise. It is very difficult to give students optimal amounts of individual time. Once again, small seminars provide optimal amounts of individual time. Once again, small seminars provide a better arena for teacher-student contact. Professors develop their own ways of juggling all these time demands and deciding how much time a particular student needs. Discussion groups of faculty around this sort of topic might prove useful.

Professor as University Citizen

The professor can be very influential within the university community and has a responsibility to contribute. One has a responsibility to try to develop an atmosphere which will: (a) keep academic standards high, (b) ensure faculty development and focus on issues of faculty morale, (c) develop a sense of collegiality within the university, and (d) enhance a sense of ethics within the university community. It is also important for faculty to participate as much as possible in university planning. This model of administration and faculty working together in planning activities is becoming increasingly important in a modern university. (Keller, 1983) Task-focused committees can be very effective ways of tackling difficult problems within the university. Evolving guidelines for a variety of complex issues can also provide a framework for individual ethical conduct.

Impact of the Professor

Clearly, the professor can be very influential in effecting students, contributing to the knowledge base in his or her own discipline, and in enhancing the university community. Ideally, the professor would help students to become intelligent decision-makers, prepare for a career, develop a love of learning which would improve their quality of life, and create a tolerance of, and interest in, different cultures, ideas, and values. Professors need to be aware of their influence on students' lives, to self-monitor their own teaching and interaction with students, and to consult continually with colleagues about problems that arise.

When I think back on the professors who most influenced me and my development, they were individuals who loved their disciplines and also who conveyed some appreciation of my abilities. These are important characteristics to develop in oneself and to value in one's colleagues. In many ways, professors could choose to be more powerful than they are in their interaction with students and in their participation in the university community.

References

Jackson, C.I., Honor in Science. New Haven: Sigma Xi, The Scientific Research Society, 1986.

Keller, G., Academic Stategy: The Management Revolution in American Higher Education. Baltimore: John Hopkins University Press, 1983.

Makosky, V., "How To Survive the Information Avalanche." APA Monitor, 47., January, 1986.

Moore, O., (Lecture presentation, Fall, 1966).

Russ, S. "Graduate Training in Clinical Psychology: Quality and Beyond." American Psychologist, 35, 766-767., 1980.

THE PROFESSOR

THE PRACTITIONER:
ELDON JAY EPP, S.T.M., Ph.D.

When I was approached about responding to Dr. Sandra Russ's presentation I confess that I thought first in terms of what one would perhaps think of as negative aspects of ethics. I thought about the case of alleged plagiarism by one of our faculty members, or fraud in travel expenses that we uncovered in the Dean's Office, or reports that were filed about the misuse of the WATS line. Every case of telephone misuse that I recall ended up at $900 before we discovered it. Or I thought about the professor who, when he moved to another position, moved all of his office furniture with him, even though not a stick of it belonged to him. Or I thought about a professor who accidentally received two pay checks and we had a year or two of struggle before we could persuade him to return the mistakenly sent pay check -- those sorts of things. Well, when I received from Dr. Russ the outline of what she was going to discuss, I felt ashamed of myself because I had thought in these negative, petty terms rather than at the more noble and grand level of ethics addressed in the presentation that she has just given to you.

I confess that shame, because by all means we should start with the positive. Certainly we shall get down to some of the other, more negative, issues as time goes along, but I think the real emphasis ought to be on the professor's responsibilities and goals that lie in the area of teaching and research. The ethical issues, therefore, must be viewed within these particular contexts. In teaching and research, faculty members, faculty colleagues, and students all have various values, various responsibilities, and of course various rights. And these need to be respected. That, I suppose, forms the basis for any discussion of ethics in the professional field of the university or college professor.

Ethics consists, as you will all recognize, not merely of rules and certainly not of rules that are arbitrarily imposed by administrators, or by department chairmen, or by groups of faculty, or groups of

145

students. Rather, I would hope, we have certain policies that relate to ethical behavior that result from reflection on the implications that various paths of action or various kinds of behavior will have for both faculty and student. These policies develop, I suspect, from social interaction; they develop from our collective perspectives on the implications of, or the consequences that will flow from, any action, or lack of action. And so, whereas rules or guidelines may often result from those reflections on the implications of what we do or do not do, ethics is never as simple as a collection of rules.

I am not an ethicist nor am I an attorney, though at times -- especially in the Dean's Office -- I have wished that I were both. Hence, I do not come with the statement of an ethical theorist. Rather, I thought I would take the same approach that Sandra Russ has taken in general and try to reflect both upon some of the things she has said and also to add a few cases and a few incidents that might highlight some of ethical issues that we all face.

Perhaps I may begin by responding to some of the issues that she raised, for example, in the area of teaching. The choice of the content of a course, as she discussed it, and the communication of values are all things that every professor thinks about. This is particularly the case in fields like Political Science, Religion, Psychology, and Education, where people have very strong opinions and very strong convictions. I suppose that those of us in the field of Religion are much more sensitive to these issues than some other professors are in other fields.

I agree completely with Dr. Russ's emphasis that method is the all important thing within the teaching context. This not only avoids a lot of problems, but it places the emphasis where the emphasis ought to be. And in my field certainly this is the case. We stress method. How does one learn about antiquity? How does one approach issues in the philosophy of religion? Or what historical methods are used for dealing with the very many historical issues that arise? And so method, I think, is exceptionally important and must be dominant.

In religion, as Dr. Russ implied concerning her

own field, we try to be objective as well as enthusiastic. And there is some potential conflict there. But the dominant guideline in our discipline for many years has been that we must be objective in the presentation of our material. In our field the key word is "empathy." We eschew in principle any view that says only a Christian can teach Christianity or only a Jew can teach Judaism or only a Muslim can teach Islam. Rather, we emphasize that anyone who is properly, that is competently, trained can teach these areas; but we do expect empathy. We do expect the person, so to speak, to "get inside" that other person's religious view -- to feel it, to understand it as best one can in that empathetic sense, and then teach it with some enthusiasm. It may not be one's own view, but one is honestly trying nonetheless to "live" it, to "experience" it, and is presenting it in that way.

The 1963 Supreme Court decision against prayer in public education, which now unfortunatly has become a live issue again, is what really opened the way for the so-called objective study of religion in the public institutions in this country. Beginning about that time there has been a large and steady development of programs in the study of religion. The University of Iowa had one for a long time and it was the only state institution that had a graduate school of religion that I know of. The director of that program, shortly after 1963, was hired by the University of California to head up its pilot program in the study of religion which was to be centered in Santa Barbara. Being in the biblical and religious field everyone was envious and we all said to him, "Remember me when thou cometh into thy kingdom." We wanted to be employed by the state of California in any one of these new state programs because that is where we thought the future lay. Well, one point is simply that there is an ethical issue there -- professional jealousy -- which I will not pursue. But the larger point here is to say that as my discipline moved into the public university it faced these kinds of questions far more immediatly and perhaps far more sharply than other fields, because religion was not to be identified with the state. So we had to lean over backwards -- a practice we already had followed before 1963 in the teaching of religion -- so that we would be presenting an objective case. We are quite familiar, therefore, with these kinds of issues, and I think that any conflict there between objectivity and one's own convictions can be quite easily overcome and can be successfully overcome in all fields if one only keeps in mind a few simple goals: objectivity, fairness and empathy.

On the subject of teaching effectiveness, an area of faculty responsibility that Dr. Russ was addressing, permit me simply to make a comment or two. I experienced, in back-to-back classes in graduate school, the epitome of the poorest kind of teaching and the paragon of the finest. I am sure you all had these kinds of experiences. What I considered a very poor teacher was a man who had been trained in what at that time was the best institution for the field of history. He had the best degree in the country and what did he do? He sat at the desk in a class of 50-70 students with his class notes from his distinguished graduate school in front of him and, as he turned the pages, he read them to us. When the time was up, he closed his notebook and walked out of the room. And if someone dare ask a question he would reluctantly acknowledge the person and say, "Look it up and report next time." And no one, of course, ever asked a question after that. That kind of teaching raises an ethical issue. His rationale may have been, "I have the best training in the world, so it is good enough for my students as well and I will simply give it to them out of my notebook."

The class that followed was taught by a brilliant young man who had earned doctorates from both Harvard and Boston University. He came into class at the precise beginning moment, with only a 3x5 card in his hand with a few notes jotted on it. He would open up a subject in a brilliant, lucid lecture, extemporaneously, although, of course, he would have studied hours to prepare it. When the bell rang the lecture would have rounded out to a perfect conclusion. Now, this didn't happen everytime; but sometimes there was spontaneous applause at the conclusion of his lecture.

This sort of contrast raises, I think, some very interesting questions of faculty responsibility. What are the responsibilities in conveying material, in organizing material, in presenting material? I was glad that Dr. Russ raised those issues because I think they are extremely important and issues we do not think about sufficiently when we consider professional ethics in the teaching field.

Permit me now to refer to a couple of other cases simply to raise some additional issues. I am going to take some real cases. I have looked over the audience very carefully and I do not think anyone will be able to identify those involved, and anyway in most cases those in the examples are people who have long departed from the University. A trustee once reported to me, as I recall, that a neice or nephew of her's was in a class in which the professor had announced on the very first session of his Monday/Wednesday/Friday class that during the semester there would be no classes on Friday afternoon -- ever. That was a bit of a shock to us. In another case a parent, as I recall, reported to us that her son or daughter had taken a number of courses with a professor in one of our departments and had taken courses at three levels: introductory, intermediate, and advanced. The complaint was that there was virtually no difference between and among these three courses. In other words there was an enormous amount of overlap in the material presented. Now I think every one in this room would say that in both these cases there is "something wrong here." Others might at least say, "something ought to be done here." There might be a few of you who would say, "There is no problem -- academic freedom." Conceivably the person who dismissed all Friday afternoon classes may have had very good reason for doing so -- that may have been a pedagogical mode. But I dare not identify the person any further. It was conceivable that there were outside class activities that may have been substituted, or something of that nature. In any case, I think that most people would have responded to the preceding two cases that there is "something wrong" or "something should be done about this." Now those two cases are, it seems to me, very simple, at least to one who is not an ethicist (of which I keep reminding myself and you). I think they are very simple when you begin to ask the question, "What is determinative for any action that might be called for in those two cases? Is academic freedom the determinative thing, and if so, what sort of solution, or answer, would you have for either of those two situations, or is faculty responsibility the basic consideration that might dictate some kind of action?" Obviously, I opt for faculty responsibility.

I am reminded of another faculty member who was very prominent, very active. He was the chairman of the department and had all kinds of outside activities and had grant money coming in. Conversing with that person at one point, someone in the office mentioned his teaching and he said, "Where does it say that I have to teach?" That sent us running to the Faculty Handbook. If you look in the Faculty Handbook, it says,

> Faculty members of the University are scholars whose responsibilities within the University are to the students, to their colleagues, and to the adminsistration. Their responsibilities beyond the University are to their profession, and to the communities, etc. The manner of meeting these responsibilites is almost as varied as are the members of the University community.

It does not really mention teaching, at least not specifically. Well, a little later in the handbook, there is a discussion of faculty responsibilities, one of which is teaching, and one of which is research, and one of which is something else. So at least there is an implication that a person hired as a faculty member has to teach. But it appears that there might be other ways to fulfill faculty responsibility than through teaching; we all can cite examples. So, even if the governing principle in these cases were to be faculty responsibility, one still might not be able to solve the matter. Actually, in the first two cases I find the solution simple because the determining principle is a legal one. There are sanctions because there are legal expectations based on student's payment of tuition. Therefore, if the parent or a trustee who is an aunt of a student is excited about something that seems not quite right, then a potentially actionable situation exists -- a legally actionable situation. So that sends the administration or the department chairman running very quickly to straighten out such a situation. The contact hours in the classroom must meet the general expectations of the three-hour course and, if they do not, then you have a potentially actionable case on the part of the parent who says I am paying all this money and I am not getting my money's worth. Or in the case of overlapping material, I am paying money for three courses when I should have paid for only one. In such questions, if there is a legal sanction or a legal constraint, the action is quite easily dictated. In so many other cases it is not that simple. The area of faculty responsibility becomes a very tricky one, especially when it is combined with that very difficult and sometimes troublesome, but always praiseworthy, phrase: "academic freedom." There has to be a balance in all this.

I want to comment on the other ethical dilemma -- I suppose it is ethical -- that Dr. Russ referred to, namely the research versus teaching aspect of a faculty member's role. There is real conflict here. Each of us will have his or her own judgment as to how this conflict or dilemma should be resolved. The view that I have always taken is that of President Bok of Harvard University -- and it has been said by many others -- that a person who is an excellent teacher but does no research will burn out in about 10 years. His strongly-presented view was that professors must be on the cutting edge of scholarship or eventually they will have nothing to teach, or if they do have something to teach it will be neither up-to-date nor relevant. I think many of us will come out on that side of the dilemma. Yet there is a tremendous conflict between teaching, research, and all the other things that a faculty member has to do. I was once asked to describe to one of the College Visiting Committees the responsibilities of a faculty member in terms of tenure and promotion. On that occasion they invited all the new faculty from that year to attend. I made a presentation which I called "The Faculty Member as Actor", or something like that. I portrayed the faculty member as a juggler, who has to juggle at least four balls in the air: teacher, scholar, researcher, and community and university servant. At least those four. And for a young faculty member coming into her or his first position and coming up for tenure at the beginning of the sixth year this is an extraordinarily difficult task. It is almost impossible in view of preparing courses and meeting all the other demands. All sorts of ethical questions begin to arise within that faculty member. "What do I do with this class? I'm not ready for it!" "How am I going to produce the publications?" And so one begins to think of ways in which one can pull it all off and pull it all together.

I suppose what one ends up doing, primarily, is to work from strength. And this relates to something that was said earlier, namely, "What do I do in my courses? I am basically an ancient historian and expected to provide a survey of 19th century history and I had only three weeks on the 19th century in my history course. Yet I happen to be an expert on some prominent feature that recurs in the 19th century, and I happened to study that feature over 12 centuries. What I will do in this lecture is take that area I know and apply it to what little I know about the 19th century." Is that an ethical response? Is that a proper response to the content of a course, especially if it happens time and time again? So questions of that type will arise. But I think that one has to realize that being a faculty member is an extraordinarily difficult task under the kinds of conditions that we impose upon young faculty.

Finally, I would like to run down a short list of things, some of which have been covered and some of which have not. There is an area that very little has been said about and that is confidentiality and rights of privacy. What are the implications for this subject when faculty members put the final examination papers on a chair in the hall outside their office and they sit there for three months, six months, and even nine months? Most students do not pick up final exams from the preceeding semester. One faculty member staples the exams all around three sides and puts them outside his door. Posting grades with names, though I see very little of that, raises another ethical isssue about rights of privacy. There are very practical issues that faculty members think too little about.

Conflict of interest is another area that needs to be explored. Should one obligate oneself to one's students? This is a temptation particularly in graduate education. I had a graduate student at the University of Southern California, way back in the 1960s, who happened to be the clergyman for a Hollywood star who was quite prominent at that time and who would always give his clothes and his cars and other things he no longer needed to this fellow who was our Ph.D. student. This fellow was continually trying to give us tickets to the Lakers professional basketball game or other events -- tickets given to him by the movie star. We had a small faculty in the graduate school and we all refused to accept any of these gifts.

152

He would pin them to our doors with thumb tacks and we would return them to him. We declined to obligate ourselves to a student. Another way of stating it is in terms of professional distance between the faculty and the student. It is a very important matter, I think, because as it turned out this fellow never made his Ph.D. -- we had to fail him along the way. If we had obligated ourselves to him by accepting all sorts of gifts, I think we would have been in an intolerable situation. Luckily our faculty made the right choice in that particular case. So there are serious issues of that kind, of obligating oneself to students.

Dr. Russ touched on the exploitation of students in a number of ways. I am not sure if she mentioned specifically something that bothers us humanists more than it seems to affect the social scientist, namely the use of students' research and the issue of giving credit, and I suspect in some cases not giving credit, for the ideas that have come up as well, as the issue of using students to do the research. In the humanities this probably will become more common, but over the years it has been a relatively uncommon thing. We usually do our own work. More social science methods are being applied to the humanities, and since computers are being used and there is more machinery and more data, more students are needed. Humanists, I suspect, will face these issues much more directly in the future.

An area I think may not have been touched upon quite as much as it might is what I call the academic environment. For example, do we provide an environment that encourages cheating? We do not have an honor system here, though people are working on it. How "ethical" is an honor system? Does the way that we give exams, does the way that we give assignments, encourage cheating? We do not have the problems that some of the Big Ten Universities and others have with athletes not being educated, that is, facing actionable cases about not being educated because they were given favors, and so on. I wonder about the implications of relinquishing the in loco parentis status that colleges always used to have. What are the ethical implications of that? I never wanted to go into a student dormitory when I was an academic dean because I'd rather let somebody else worry about those problems. That is not a very good response, I admit. But what are the

153

implications of just relinquishing all responsibility of that kind as colleges did almost universally around the late 1960s and early 1970s?

Next, let me come to those things that I started with. Plagiarism is not a serious problem for faculty but it does crop up. A far more common problem -- looking at these negative things now -- is the theft of time. Faculty face this temptation all the time: stealing time from the university to do something that is really quite unrelated to their work, and theft of supplies and equipment. I have mentioned a couple of instances of that. The language in the University is that materials and equipment are "converted" to personal use. That is a constant problem in all of industry and in all of business. I suspect it exists in the university as well. Telephone misuse I have mentioned. Fraud in travel expenses is another: if you read The Chronicle of Higher Education there is a constant warning applicable to any chairman or administrator. In almost every case where high-level administrators are convicted of crimes it has to do with the misuse of travel funds or the misuse of funds in general. And that is a real temptation when people have control of money; it can sift down to the departmental level to some extent as well.

Finally, a very subtle and difficult problem among many, many others that could be mentioned is the use of the university name for one's own benefit. Perhaps a trivial example is the use of the letterhead. I suspect I often misuse the letterhead myself when writing letters because I do not have a personal letterhead. Thus, we tend to pick up the University stationary and use it and, even though we pay our own postage on that letter, we are still often using the university's name improperly when our correspondence is not in any way university-related. There are, of course, many more serious examples of using the name of the University for one's own benefit.

If nothing else, one thing that should be clear is that the range of ethical issues in this field is enormous. Though many faculty members take such matters seriously and have thought through their own positions, I suspect that faculty in general are not sufficiently aware either of the breadth or depth of ethical issues affecting their everyday work.

THE PROFESSOR

THE CONSUMER:
DANIEL J. LINKE
PRESIDENT OF THE WESTERN RESERVE COLLEGE
CLASS OF 1986, CWRU

I want to speak first about the student-professor relationship, since this is something we can relate to on a day-to-day basis. Personally after four years of being at Western Reserve College, and this being a relativly small liberal arts school, I have some very good friendships with professors. As long as it is an out-of-class friendship, I have no problem. But when I take a course with that professor I feel awkward. I don't want the friendship to interfere with my learning or with the professor's performance, or the classroom atmosphere. This is something that is always a concern to the student; where is the line between "brown-nosing" and the legitimate interaction between students and professors? I'm not really quite sure.

An example I can give comes from my work on the University student newspaper. Often the professors will know I am on the staff and will have ideas for me and give them to me. And then in my mind I have to question if this is a legitimate news tip or is the professor trying to get help or publicity for his or her pet organization or group. This comes more into the play of newspaper ethics, if there are any, but the student role is also involved.

Something Dr. Epp brought up made me think of something that just happened recently. I'm applying to nine different graduate schools for their programs in History. That required, on the average, three recommendations for each school. To spread the work out, I asked nine different professors to write recommendations for me. Just a few weeks ago, after the process of sending out applications and transcripts and GRE scores was done, I started receiving notices that all the materials were received. I wanted to thank those professors for putting the time in, so I prepared individual thank you notes. Then I thought that professors probably get this sort of thing all the time. So, to really express my appreciation for what they had done for me, I bought some roses and gave each

155

one a single rose. I currently have three of these professors for class. I didn't mean this to be interpreted in any particular way as far as my classroom performance goes, but it could be looked on by someone who is not involved in the situation as, "Oh, he is brown-nosing or going for the A." I certainly hope not. This was not my intention, but it could be conceived as an ethical problem by some.

Moving now to another point that Dr. Russ brought up about moral relativism, namely being able to express one viewpoint while also making sure all the other theories are covered. There is the flipside of that from the student's point of view, namely being able to do the work and use your moral system and your values and ethics and not be penalized by the professor, as long as you are doing legitimate work. This comes into play, especially in the field of English, where the humanistic approach may be in conflict with a person who is Christian, or Moslem, or whatever religion, and may make a different interpretation of the literature. As long as the person does valid work, using those guidelines, this student should receive credit, and the professor should not only give credit but also encourage that different point of view.

Along the same lines, Dr. Russ and Dr. Epp mentioned how the professor must make the student think but avoid indoctrination. This is really "a given". I don't think there are any professors that brainwash, though there is definitely a lot of persuasion at times. I have never had a class where the professor's personal views were so overwhelming that he or she stifled any class discussion. Polemic professors will not draw large classes. Students vote with their feet, it is said, and this is true. As long as the professors encourage a wide range of thinking, they will always have a fair size class. I think bad professors are reflected in poor class size. I'm not talking about high level courses, but of course in introductory and intermediate courses this is certainly true.

An important role that professors play is that of a role model, especially for underclassmen. This is something that neither Dr. Russ or Dr. Epp talked about, so maybe I can go into this a little bit more. When students come into a university, especially one

156

like Case Western Reserve, they are 17 or 18 years old and while intellectually skilled, they are emotionally undeveloped. Their parents, for the most part, are now out of their lives. They are now looking for another role model; another father-figure, another mother-figure, an adult-figure they can identify with. Although the professor may not always be aware that this is happening, he or she should certainly be careful about how he or she deals with students. Tact and diplomacy are needed, (not implying that tact and diplomacy aren't always used), but especially with the underclassmen. The point of this is that the role model has room for abuse; it can lead to sexual exploitation and other types of exploitation. The professor should be aware of this and strive to be more sensitive towards the reactions and needs of the freshmen or sophomores in their classes.

But of all the ethical burdens a professor has, I think the most important role he or she has is that of being an inspiration for his or her students. The most important learning occurs, for the most part, outside the classroom. It is there that the reading occurs, the problems are worked out and the thinking about what is being taught takes place. It can't all be done in the 50-minute period three times a week. What the professor must do is convey his enthusiasm for the subject so the student will do the learning outside of class. They have to show students why the subject is interesting, why it is important, and why it should be learned. This is really important today when the liberal arts are being questioned in terms of their relevancy. The professor has to show that, although the subject may not have a concrete and applicable use in a banking job or at a computer terminal, it does contribute to the development of a significant life. Dr. Russ mentioned that you can have a computer just sit there and spit out the facts. But the computer won't do it. The computer will present everything and it won't forget any notes; but it won't convey the enthusiasm. And that is the ultimate job the professor has. They have to encourage the thinking which will be important, once the class is done, once school is done, once you are out in the real world. The responsibility can't be taken lightly, though it is often easily ignored. There are lots of times professors consider their scholarship and their research over their teaching. Since we are talking about ethics, I think this can be called a sin.

Presently there is an example of the opposite of this on our campus. A chemistry professor teaches introduction to freshman chemistry. He has two sections of classes, usually 200-300 people in each section and he teaches part one and part two. He has been doing this for about five years, but he doesn't do research. He enjoys the teaching and gets the material across well. The students like him. Yet he is not on the tenure track because he doesn't do research. As far as the "burning out" in ten years which has been referred to, I don't know. Ten years ago I was 11 years old so I don't claim to have a great knowledge of academics and the workings of them. But this is a freshmen chemistry course. It is not Chemistry 475, the intricacies of the carbon atom. Freshman chemistry is something that could be taught by someone who doesn't research. I personally hope that this professor will be given some sort of contract so he can remain here, because freshmen chemistry taught properly is a course on which a lot of students base a career decision, or choose to stay in the science field. It is a critical point in their lives. If they are going to get a professor that will be doing research and doesn't really care about freshmen chemistry with 'those dumb 18-year-olds who don't understand the basic concepts', it's going to hurt those people taking that course as well as the institution.

The importance of inspiration can't be underestimated. The university should produce thinkers, and not calculaters. And when I say university, I mean that in the broadest sense. If the university is only going to put out human computers, we are going to lose the human half of ourselves. Anything that is worth living for will be gone.

Chapter 7

THE LAWYER

THE PRESENTER:
ROBERT P. LAWRY, J.D.

THE WILL TO POWER: NIETZSCHE AS LAWYER

In Nietzsche, the concept of the Will to Power begins as a psychological hypothesis.[1] Whether it should have remained as such, and not developed into a monist philosophical principle, I leave to other, better minds. For myself, I think there is much to be learned from studying the concept as a psychological matter. In this paper I plan to use this psychological hypothesis as a launching pad from which to project some notions about the moral problems the Will to Power presents to lawyers. I will also suggest guidelines to aid the lawyer in protecting both the moral self and morally autononomous others from the potential abuses which exist because of the Will to Power.

The concept of power is readily understood in our work-a-day world. Like "time" for Augustine and "law" for H.L.A. Hart,[2] the concept "power" becomes troublesome if you stop and think about it, if you try to capture it in an ordinary definition, it you attempt to understand all its meanings and all its permutations. I do not want to venture an all-purpose analysis. I am content to try a working definition. Power is the ability to do, act or affect strongly. It is vigor, force, strength. It includes the ability to control or influence others,[3] even against their will. Succinctly, "power is the ability to cause or prevent change."[4]

We can begin to understand the concept of power if we start where Nietzsche did. He observed the common phenomenon that people do not want to be dependent and impotent. They want control over their lives. We take great joy as parents in watching our children overcome their limitations and achieve simple motor skills: walking, talking, the manipulation of simple toys and machines. To keep a child from developing his or her self-mastery is a cruelty. Power is seen here as the basic life urge to grow and develop. Parents who

159

continue to "do things" for children after they have passed the ordinary developmental stage for that specific activity are roundly and rightly criticized. At the political level, we observe an extension of this same truth. "Self-determination" is a key idea in international relations.[5] Nietzsche saw at the psychological level what Marx saw at the social level: the awfulness of domination. Marx projected an historical law which required the oppressed to throw off their oppressors. Nietzsche saw that the powerless tend to use whatever means possible to move from dependence to independence, from impotence to self-actualization, at least to break the chains that bind.

Nietzsche saw more. He saw not only the desire of people to achieve independence in the world, he saw also the Will to Power as the dominant psychological motive of human beings. He explained even ordinary moral concepts in terms of the Will to Power. In his book, Human All Too Human, Nietzsche wrote of the virtue of gratitude:

> "The reason why a powerful person is grateful is this: his benefactor has... intruded into... [his] sphere.... It is a milder form of revenge. Without the satisfaction of gratitude, the powerful man would have shown himself powerless and hence be considered so. Therefore every society of the good, i.e., originally of the powerful, posits gratitude as one of the first duties...."[6]

Lest the point missed, Walter Kaufman explains:

> "There is an implication that I was powerless and needed his help. I am degraded in his eyes and in my own. Then I thank him and the implication is reversed: he has done something for me, as if I were the powerful one and he my servant. In that sense, gratitude may be considered a mild form of revenge. More important: Nietzsche has explained a moral valuation as prompted by the will to power."[7]

Nietzsche took a large step from a fundamentally sound

psychological insight to the reductive notion that one important aspect of our psychological make-up explains the entire moral and biological life of human beings. The step is at least as large as Marx's from domination to revolution as historical determinism. In both cases, I think the step too long, too simplistic to explain the much more complex phenomenon that is humanity and history. However, I do not deny that our seeming-virtues may often mask a different motivation, often a venal one. This is one of the crucial power problems for lawyers. When a senior partner in a large law firm commandeers a half dozen associates and a like number of support personnel to work round-the-clock, leaving no stone unturned in the client's best interest -- I wonder how much of the partner's conscious mind is blocked from considering the avalanche of billable hours he has unleashed down the mountain...and behold, the snow or rock cascades into gold -- the partner's gold, of course. Still, we have not even mentioned the affect on other people.

Now, a last point concerning the Nietzschian concept of Will to Power before we look at its application to the art of lawyering. Nietzsche believed that the powerless would use any means to achieve power. Nietzsche was no liberal, so language like the "easy morals of the poor" may have appealed to him. At least he seemed to think of the thief and the murderer as a barbarian, at the lowest echelon of history and culture. At the top of the heap appears the powerful one. The weak and oppressed want to hurt and see others suffer. The powerful one has no desire to hurt others. He or she hurts incidentally, almost accidentally, "without thinking about it," (to quote Nietzsche), simply in the exercise of his powers, out of an overflow of fullness and creativity.[8] In Nietzsche's mature thought, the Will to Power becomes total self-realization or self-actualization[9] -- terms often used to describe Aristotelian ethics, though having an entirely different meaning for Aristotle. I shall not follow Nietzsche along the whole road, but shall later return to several of the places we have already been. I shall also have something to say about the Will to Power as self-realization.

II

For now let us switch gears to look directly at the two most general forms of moral criticism that have been levelled against lawyers. Each takes the form of a concern over the abuse of power. In Richard Wasserstrom's words: "The first centers around the lawyer's stance toward the world at large. The accusation is that the lawyer-client relationship renders the lawyer at best systematically amoral and at worst often immoral in his or her dealings with mankind."[10]

The problem is familiar enough. In acting for the client, in doing the client's will in the legal universe, the lawyer does not care who he or she hurts nor how they are hurt. "Whatever it takes" is not merely a theme to rally athletes to greater effort. It is the litigator's battle cry too. If the "little old lady" is telling the truth on the witness stand, but the truth damages my client, I may cross-examine her vigorously to confuse her or make her look stupid or ridiculous. In defending a rapist, I may elicit intimate details of the complaining witness' sex life to suggest perhaps "she asked for it." Representing a large, wealthy corporation against a lone, non-affluent adversary, I may innundate the opposing side with paper, demand answers to lengthy interogatories, playing the discovery game, in short, as if resources and time (and talent) were equal. I may do these things, and more, because my role as "advocate" within the "adversary system" demands this of me. I may not even not do them or their rough equivalents. My job is to zealously represent my client, to accomplish my client's aims, without breaking the law of course, but also without regard to the consequences of my efforts on others. Some have called this the Adam Smith Theory of Adjudication -- and for good reason. This stresses the "competitive" nature of the fray and asserts, as against its critics, that in the end the greatest happiness for the greatest number will occur magically by a wave of the wand in the magician's invisible hand.

I share the concerns of the critics. However, I also share the belief that the adversary system is not a bad method for resolving disputes. I will say more later about how I try to justify the lawyer's role in the system in the face of this serious moral criticism. For now I want only to assert that my prior description of what a lawyer may or must do as "advocate" in the "adversary system" is a wrong-headed caricature of the true professional role. However, before returning to the first general moral criticism, I need to say something about the second.

The second general form of moral criticism levelled against lawyers focuses (again in Wasserstrom's words):

".... upon the relationship between the lawyer and the client. Here the charge is that it is the lawyer-client relationship which is morally objectional because it is a relationship in which the lawyer dominates and in which the lawyer typically, and perhaps inevitably, treats the client in both an impersonal and a paternalistic fashion."[11]

Paternalism is a temptation for all professionals. The rise of the doctrine of informed consent in the field of medicine within the very recent past is the first sustained, public reaction opposing the long-standing practice of allowing doctors to do pretty much what they want to do, both to and for the patient, because "the doctor knows best." Indeed, is that not why we seek professional help, because the professional does know best? Traditionally, the professions dealt with matters of great personal concern to clients or patients. People were, and are, often in a particularly vulnerable physical, psychological, emotional, spiritual or economic state when seeking professional help from doctor, lawyer, teacher, or minister.[12] How comforting it is to have someone take your burden from you, assuring you they possess the magic to make it right or make it better. How comforting it is for the client-patient, at least initially, but how dangerous for the professional. The Will to Power lurks behind every decision, every professional move. "I am in control," says the professional to himself or herself. "I will exercise my powers to achieve the desirable end." But who determines what is the desirable end? Moreover, who determines what are means appropriate to that end? Often there is a multiplicity of both ends and means possible in a given situation. Some of those belong to the lawyer: more money, less effort, or less criticism or more power over someone or something else.

So clearly do we understand the dangers of paternalism in the American professional scene in the 1980's that the literature scarcely has a good word to say for paternalistic behavior. This is not to suggest that professionals do not continue to practice their acts paternalistically, even for very good reasons. We often try to do things for others "in their best interests." Sometimes we have good reason to believe they do not want us to do what we do. This is true paternalism. Often, however, we do it "without thinking about it." We do not know whether the client wants us to do it or not. We act this way, in part out of our own Will to Power, seen now as perfectly consistent with our training and with one of the central ideas in professionalism: that the professional is in <u>control</u> of his or her practice in ways that mere workers, time punchers and the like are not. One of the sweetest sounds I heard as a young lawyer was the managing partner in the firm I was with say to me my first day at the office: "you are a professional. You are responsible for your own time. If you want to get a haircut at lunchtime or take an afternoon off to play golf, that's your business."

"You are in control." How delectable those words are... even if they hide the brutal reality of responsibile professional practice: long hours, too much work, the real demands of a host of others (clients, senior partners, judges, even clerks and especially bureaucrats, who of course, are so dominated by system and bosses themselves, that their only avenue to express the Will to Power is to go painfully slowly, or to take a coffee break, or to insist -- even though you are a powerful, rich and unconscionably successful attorney -- that it is the blue form you file, and it is to filled out in this way and not that way and if you have to go back to your office to accomplish this and your office is in New York and this is Cleveland, well, then...ah, "isn't that too bad?")

The above bureaucratic flight of fancy may seem a tad extraneous. I don't think it is; but I am ready now to return to the next, perhaps more logical, point. If the problem is paternalism (the domination of the client by the lawyer), who is really hurt and how are they hurt? This question is apt because the lawyer is often genuinely acting in ways that are designed to advance the client's interests. Obviously, the first answer is the practical one. Unless there is real understanding and real communication, it is not always possible to know whether the end or the means is truly "in the client's best interest." So the client is the one hurt. "Yes, I want the divorce," says the wife; "and I want alimony of $2,400 per month, but I do not want it at the cost of alienating my children from me or their father. I don't want the kind of rancor you, Mr. Lawyer, seem to think is best calculated to obtain my divorce and the $2,000 per month." No-fault divorce came about in no small measure because true understanding of the total person and what was in the best interest of that client-person was a subject that was not being adequately explored. But, as so often is the case, the obvious and the practical simply mask the hidden and the more significant problem. The mask must be thrown off, even if the practical problem rightly understood brings about similar behavior. This is because behavior is not the whole of the problem. The problem is one of attitude. The literature talks consistently of the paternalism of the professional thwarting the exercise of the autonomy of the client.[13] The value here is the power of the professional to empower the client to exercise his or her own sense of self-mastery, to obtain some control over his or her own destiny as it becomes entangled in matters "legal." The American Bar Association's Code of Professional Responsibility recognizes this value at least partially when it asserts: "... the lawyer should always remember that the decision whether to forego legally available objectives or methods because of non-legal factors is ultimately for the client and not for himself."[14] On the other hand, the Code states that the lawyer may make some decisions "on his own," so long as they do not "substantially prejudice the rights of a client" nor adversely affect the merits of the cause."[15] The potential conflict in decision-making is addressed explicitly by the criminal defense bar in their American Bar Association Standards. Certain decisions are ultimately for the client to make, others ultimately for the lawyer, so reads Standard 4-5.2.[16] What plea to enter, whether to waive a jury trial and whether to testify on his or her own behalf are client decisions. All strategic and tactical decisions are the lawyer's. Each should consult with the other before the decision. If the client protests too much about the lawyer's decision, to protect himself from a malpractice suit or a charge of ineffective assistance of counsel (clients sometimes turn on their lawyers) the lawyer should make a record of the reason for the advice and the conclusion reached.[17] Presumably this means that the lawyer should bow to the client's wishes even if the lawyer's advice is contrary. The ideal is clear enough. The lawyer explains all the options, predicts consequences, and gives advice on what should be done. The client chooses, exercising his or her own moral autonomy, and the lawyer helps to effectuate the choice. Happily, advice and choice coincide. When they do not, the lawyer protects himself or herself, then does what the client wants.

If that model is reality (and it sometimes is, but often is not) then the second general form of moral criticism of lawyers is largely muted. This pushes to the forefront the first major moral criticism: that the lawyer's conduct vis-a-vis the world is amoral at best and immoral much too often. A lawyer who simply executes his or her client's own choices is allowing the self -- his or her own self -- to be used as a thing, as an instrument, quite contrary to Kant's dictum and surely in violation of not only the best moral thinking but the ordinary moral position espoused by the average person. "Even if I love you, my dear, I cannot, I will not, shoot the person you hate for you." Of course you may not do such a thing. However, that is not what lawyers say they do. Lawyers simply enable the client to obtain his or her due. This is a justice argument that dates back to the 5th century B.C., at the very least.[18] The client needs help to make his way through the system and is entitled to a lawyer's help. That is why we have professional lawyers: to assist the lay person in obtaining his or her legal rights.

At this point, let me summarize where we have been. In Nietzsche's Will to Power we find a psychological hypothesis that reminds us how naturally and strongly we wish to control our lives and environment; how power is exercised often without thinking, just for the joy of its exercise. Moral criticisms have been levelled against lawyers on two fronts, both on the basis of an abuse of power. The first criticism is the lawyer's stance vis-a-vis the world: in working for others, the lawyer may push other moral agents around. The second criticism is an attack on paternalism, because the professional is quite susceptible to the temptation to ignore his own client's aims in the exercise of his Will to Power through the professional skills he has acquired and wishes to hone and develop. To solve the second is to be victimized by the first.

We have looked at some psychological underpinnings and some general moral criticisms. Let us probe more deeply now the classic defenses of the lawyer's use of power.

III

The justifications for the lawyer's behaviors vis-a-vis the non-client world lie almost entirely with the nature of the work lawyers do and their understanding of that work. Ordinarily, we do not allow a person to say "I was just doing my job" if that is the excuse for immoral behavior. A hired assassin was truly "just doing his job" when he pulled the trigger. The difference between a hit man and a lawyer, however, is that we say the true hired gun (the assassin, not the lawyer) is engaged in an immoral occupation. The lawyer is engaged in a noble occupation, the practice of law, which brings justice and order to society and empowers citizens in the exercise of their rights. If the lawyer can excuse what otherwise seems to be immoral work by saying "I was just doing my job," he or she is engaged in what is called "strongly role-differentiated behavior." The claim is made that certain roles entitle those occupying them to behave in ways inconsistent with normal moral rules or principles because of the nature of the role. The relationship between parent and child is offered as the paradigm example of "strongly role-differentiated behavior." We expect extreme favoritism from parent to child not only because those who are closer can help better (an instrumental value only), but also (in Alan Goldman's words) "from the intrinsic value of the relations that define them." Goldman goes on:

> "From the point of view of a theory of value, human intimacy is a primary source of value and self-realization for almost all persons. And from the point of view of a theory of obligation or right, it is doubtful that individuals could develop moral capacities at all, capacities to act morally toward those in whom they show no special interest, if these capacities were not allowed to develop from affective interests in particular other individuals."[19]

Goldman argues further that professionals typically claim that their patients or clients are almost like children. Thus their roles are parental in nature.[20] We have already looked at the problem of paternalism. Whatever its value in the medical context (and there the real issue typically centers on the capacity of the patient to exercise automony rather than on true paternalism) the "paternalistic" lawyer has little defense. The entire rationale of the system really depends upon clients being able to do what they want to do, but being powerless vis-a-vis the system to effectuate their autonomous desires. It is just that problem, however, that puts us back to square one: the lawyer helping another to do immoral things.

The justification is the work we do and the way we understand the work we do. Well, what is that work?

Goldman sees lawyer's work as that of an advocate based on what he calls the Principle of Full Advocacy.[21] According to Goldman, lawyers are required to pursue the legal interests of their clients, regardless of their moral consequences or values. He cites the American Bar Association's Code of Professional Responsibility in myriad ways to support this thesis. I think he does not appreciate the ambiguities of the Code nor the complexities of law practice. No matter, he says no more than a good many lawyers say. What those lawyers say is simplistic and often quite wrong. If I asked the average doctor wherein lies his or her primary obligation I have little doubt the answer would be "to my patient." If I asked the average lawyer the same question, I am just as certain the answer would be "to my client." In one sense, these answers reveal the commonplace understanding of both professional and ordinary person. The follow-up question might be: "but does that primary obligation ever give way to a higher obligation?" The doctor may say that in cases of communicable diseases "it very well may." The patient may have to be quarantined, quite against his or her own wishes. People may have to be told, a spouse warned, for example, if the other spouse has contracted a disease which is likely to be transmitted through sexual contact.

If the same question were asked of a lawyer, there would also be some exceptions. The use of false evidence at a trial is one obvious limitation. No client's desires have any weight here. The lawyer simply "shall not...knowingly use perjured testimony or false evidence."[22]

These two examples are adduced to suggest that in common understanding the doctor and the lawyer have

168

similar professional roles. There are certain limitations on helping patients or clients but they are really just small exceptions to the general rule. Insofar as this commonplace understanding applies to doctors, I do not quarrel with it. As it applies to lawyers, however, I think it dead wrong, and damnably so. We can make sense out of the doctor-patient relationship as an ordinary moral matter. Respect for moral autonomy; an agreement to lend a hand and help someone who is ill; or even without an agreement, the ordinary moral principles of beneficence (do good) and non-maleficience (in the Hippocratic oath... "above all, do no harm") -- these moral matters can be understood and worked through without undue stress on context and setting. With the advent of DRGs and modern technological advances, questions of economic and social justice may soon throw over my current opinion on medicine but, historically, I think my position holds up. The doctor-patient relationship can be assessed by ordinary moral methods and principles, however difficult they might prove to be in application to a given set of facts.

It is otherwise with lawyers. It is, in fact, so far otherwise with lawyers that Lon Fuller claimed that:

> "The lawyer's highest loyalty is at the same time the most intangible. It is a loyalty that runs, not to persons, but to procedures and institutions. The lawyer's role imposes on him a trusteeship for the integrity of those fundamental processes of government and self-government upon which the successful functioning of our society depends." [23]

Such a statement denies the Principle of Full Advocacy. It gives the lie to Lord Brougham's famous words:

> "(A)n advocate, in the discharge of his duty, knows but one person in all the world, and that person is his client. To save that client by all means and expedients, and at all hazards and costs to other persons, and among them, to himself, is his first and only duty; and in performing this duty he must not regard the alarm, the torments, the

destruction which he may bring upon others. Separating the duty of patriot from that of advocate, he must go on reckless of cosequences, though it should be his unhappy fate to involve his country in confusion."[24]

To paraphrase Jeremy Bentham in another context: that is not just nonsense, it is nonsense on stilts.[25]

The lawyer-client relationship has meaning at all only within a true, deep, realistic understanding of the legal system. Our adversary system is based on a theory of adjudication which separates the function of judge and partisan advocate.[26] However, the adversary system is but a part of a network of interrelated institutions and processes, procedures and traditions which, in turn, form a central but still partial piece of a wider social and political whole.

Nietzsche's reduction of the whole of biological and moral life to the Will to Power has its analogue in the attempt to reduce the lawyer's obligation to "advocacy", and worse, to an even more limited Principle of Full Advocacy -- as if that is all we do and that is all we are about.

Let me try to suggest what else lawyers do; and how our work as advocates has a place within the full panoply of all that lawyers do.

IV

In the first place, a lawsuit is a rare thing even in litigious America.[27] The trial of a law suitfiled is even rarer. So whatever the lawyer's role is as advocate in an open forum, whether at trial or in some judicial or administrative analogue, or on appeal, it is a fraction of what lawyers do. Much more time, energy, and talent is spent doing a variety of other things: negotiating, drafting, putting together deals, organizing cooperative ventures. Perhaps the most significant role of the lawyer is as counselor. In this capacity, the lawyer has several different tasks. He or she is required to try to the utmost to keep the client compliant with the law.[28] This is often accomplished by explaining what the law requires or what is the danger of noncompliance or how disruptive or dangerous is a lawsuit. More often, the lawyer accomplishes law compliance simply by being a symbol of law itself. The lawyer has been called "an officer of the court;" but that formulation is based on the pervasive overemphasis on the lawyer as litigator. The lawyer is really an "officer of the law and of the legal system." In addition, the lawyer does empower the client to exercise moral autonomy. Notice the phrase is <u>moral</u> autonomy. In presenting his or her counsel to the client, the lawyer introduces non-legal factors into the decision-making process: economic, psychological, practical, and, of course, moral factors. Sharply distinguishing what might be legal from what is moral is not easy and often not particularly desirable. Even Holmes, who wanted to banish all moral words from the legal universe, admitted that:

"The law is the witness and external deposit of our moral life. Its history is the history of the moral development of the race."[29]

Of course some clients will resist even the sagest counsel, legal, moral or otherwise. One option is for the lawyer to resign. I do not advocate this option in many cases. Sometimes, of course, it is the best answer, perhaps even the only answer to a certain kind of moral quandary. However, the purpose of this paper, and of lawyering generally, is to explore how lawyers can help clients, not abandon them, and how this can be done morally without simply giving in to the urge of the Will to Power.

I want to present a case now, one in which the lawyers involved did resign. I think they acted well. They acted on principle. I applaud them. Yet I want to suggest how they could have stayed in the case and also acted well, consistent with principle. In exploring this case I want to highlight a strongly held conviction of mine, that there is sometimes no single right answer to a moral dilemma. There are often many wrong answers, but there are also sometimes more than one right answer. I must begin with a caveat.

Too often we conduct business in the law school world and in moral analysis generally on the basis of hypothetical cases, posing the <u>question for decision</u> as if it were the only relevant moral matter. It is reductionistic to suggest the moral life consists simply of making a morally correct decision, the <u>right</u>

171

one as opposed to the wrong one, as if, in Holmes' words, damning another truncated view of decision-making, "it meant simply that one side or the other were not doing their sums right."[30] Character is important too. Virtue is important. Indeed, Aristotle's Ethics treats character and virtue as the significant moral concerns, and decision-making subordinate to those concerns. With this important caveat in mind, let us examine the following case:

> "For many years, the outside General Counsel for The New York Times was an old and distinguished New York law firm. In 1971, the editors of The Times informed their General Counsel that they had obtained possession of secret documents involving America's involvement in Vietnam -- the Pentagon papers -- and the editors asked counsel for an opinion as to whether the materials could be published. Counsel reportedly advised The Times that if they published the documents before they were declassified there was a risk of criminal prosecution. The law firm reportedly advised the editors not to publish on the grounds, among others, that it would be contrary to the "public interest" to do so. The Times editors determined to publish notwithstanding this advice. When the Department of Justice notified The Times that it would seek a preliminary injunction to restrain further publication, the law firm informed The Times that the firm could not represent the newspaper. The Times was represented by other counsel in the litigation which followed."[31]

The question, "Did the lawyers do the right thing in resigning?" can only be answered after a complex analysis. Then the answer may be either yes or no, either of which may be correct. It depends on factors most often hidden in these matters.

We might begin by saying that it is hardly possible to argue that the decision not to represent was wrong. After all there is no obligation to represent any particular person or group in the United

States. Legally, of course, that is right. It should be remembered, though, that British barristers do not enjoy a similar right.[32] Nevertheless, what if the sole motivation of the law firm was to damage The New York Times because the lawyers were staunch political supporters of the Administration and they had many corporate clients who were reaping large profits from the Vietnam War? What if the lawyers wanted to exercise their Will to Power as much as they could, knowing that a new firm would have a much more difficult time gearing up to fight an injunction suit than they would, familiar as they were with the newspaper business and The Times' operation in particular? If these constituted their motives, then that particular exercise of the Will to Power would have been immoral and a blight on the legal profession.

However, let us assume what apparently was the case: that the firm of Lord, Day & Lord was motivated by moral outrage that classified government documents, pilfered for political motives, would be published by a newspaper whose motto was: "all the news that's fit to print." It was the firm's position that the newspaper's decision was wrong in every way. The Times would be profiting by a theft and the public interest would be severely damaged. The end was wrong and the means deplorable.

Louis Loeb, senior partner at Lord, Day & Lord, who had been the Times' general counsel for twenty-three years, said this was the advice given:

> "We told them...that they were running the risk of being criminally sued and it was our advice that the *Times* should not knowingly participate in a breach of the law. We advised them that they should not publish and that they should apply to have the material declassified."[33]

The evidence is reasonably clear that the law firm resigned as a matter of principle. The lawyers did not want to stand up for a client they believed was doing something legally and morally wrong, something as Loeb later was quoted as saying, "not in the public interest." Of course, there were other decent people who believed that the Pentagon Papers should have been published. The Times' in-house counsel thought there was a legal (constitutional) right to publish; and many believed that the revelation of massive governmental duplicity regarding the conduct of the Vietnam War and the attempt to cover-up that duplicity by hiding relevant information under the cloak of "a top secret classification" was immoral to boot. Nevertheless, even holding the position they held, could Lord, Day & Lord have continued the representation? If the matter had been thoroughly discussed; if the Times' editors and publishers believed they were legally and morally right; if they were convinced that the "theft" of these papers, though not a good thing in and of itself, was excusable in this case; and if the Times was willing not to hide the truth of the escapade and their involvement in it, then a decision to represent and represent vigorously seems to me to be justified. I do not list these "ifs" to suggest that these conditions constitute the only morally necessary set upon which a decision to represent could be justified. I list them only to suggest how the counselling function may be utilized in complicated circumstances. This particular case shows how good and evil, right and wrong are often inseparably linked in a lawsuit as they often are in life. It is a salutary lesson, one blurred by those who quickly jump to the final decision, presuming the whole moral experience may be captured there. The issues in the case were major constitutional ones. They needed to be litigated, and litigated well.

To probe this matter further: what if the Times had resisted all attempts at counselling by telling the law firm, "do what I say or you are fired." It is arguable that the firm would have acted immorally if it had continued the representation under those circumstances. There are two reasons for saying this. Both reasons are central to understanding the lawyer's work and the exercise of power entailed in that work. The first reason has to do with the lawyer's primary obligation to processes and institutions; the second has to do with the nature of the lawyer-client relationship itself.

Fuller's comments on the lawyer's primary obligation comes in a section of his article which is headed: <u>The Lawyer as a Guardian of Due Process</u>. Fuller goes on to say this:

> "All institutions, however sound in purpose, present temptations to interested exploitation, to abusive shortcuts, to corroding

misinterpretations.... Everywhere democratic and constitutional government is tragically dependent on voluntary and understanding cooperation in the maintenance of its fundamental processes and forms.

It is the lawyer's duty to preserve and advance this indispensable cooperation by keeping alive the willingness to engage in it and by imparting the understanding necessary to give it direction and effectiveness."[34]

If the Times had not believed it had a legal or moral right to publish, but had told its lawyers simply to use whatever devices they could to delay a ruling on a preliminary injunction "so circulation goes way up", then the firm must decline to do so even though the methods used may be "perfectly legal." Though "legal", they would be unethical means to an unethical end. Though our professional codes could be clearer on this, delay for the sake of delay or harassment is professionally irresponsible. The 1983 tightening of Rule 11 of the federal Rules of Civil Procedure points to a deep concern that lawyers are "abusing the system." In amending the rule, the problem of delay was cited as a major concern.[35] The point is quite clear: lawyers may be disciplined in the courts or before disciplinary boards for "improper motive," even though what they attempted to do was perfectly "legal." Just doing what is "legal" is not what lawyering is about. Witness the case of William Gahan.[36] In 1979 the Minnesota Supreme Court denied admission to the bar to Gahan, who was otherwise perfectly qualified for practice, on the sole ground that he declared bankruptcy for himself "perfectly legally" in order to discharge his student loan obligation. This young lawyer managed to maneuver the system so that he was able to keep his 1959 Jaguar by cleverly mortgaging it to a friend. Thus the only debts he actually discharged were his federally insured student loans. If this makes a person unfit for the practice of law, then similar work for "clients" ought also to make him or her professionally unfit.

This last example already slides us over to my second point. If the Times had said: "do what I say or you are fired" then the law firm has been told flat out it is to bend to the Will to Power, exercised by anyone paying anyone else "for services rendered." There is a name for this when the exchange is money for sex. Is it impolite of me to suggest the name might fit here too? Remember the larger thesis. The name fits not because a lawyer represents a client he or she believes to be in the wrong. It fits, as I have just suggested, if the system is abused. It fits also if the lawyer, as moral agent, is abused. One response to an arrogant client that Nietzsche might have argued, consistent with the Will to Power, would be for the lawyer to refuse to represent by saying: "I am more powerful than you. I fling the money back into your face. I cannot be bought." I wince at that response, while acknowledging its possibility. The moral response, however, must be otherwise. It requires the lawyer to treat the client as an equal moral agent. The lawyer-client relationship is not fundamentally contractual, nor is it fundamentally that of principle and agent. At its core it is a fiduciary relationship wherein each party respects and appreciates the moral worth of each -- or else it becomes the Will to Power.

I want to change the Pentagon Papers facts one more time. What if Lord, Day & Lord was one mind with the Times in this matter, acknowledging the moral value of publishing the material and convinced of the strong constitutional argument for being allowed to do so? What checks the Will to Power of lawyer cum client when both are sympatico? Processes again. Only that. The lawyer must still insist the client obey the letter and the spirit of the law. What if the Times wanted to hide the fact that it knew the documents were stolen because it would "make our motives look even better." If a client suggests perjury, then even the most passionate liberal lawyer who marched with worn shoes against Lyndon Johnson and Richard Nixon's conduct of the Vietnam War, must say: "No. I am an officer of the law. I cannot go that far."

V

Some recent sociological work on the legal profession yields some fascinating insights into the realities of the Will to Power as I have been exploring them in this paper. A British writer, Terance Johnson, suggests that occupations might be classified according to the allocation of power between the producer and the consumer (the lawyer and client for our purposes). Johnson classifies as "collegiate" those occupations in which "the Producer defines the needs of the consumer and the manner in which those needs are" to be met. He calls "patronage" those occupations in which "the consumer defines his own needs and the manner in which they are met." Applying this classification to the American legal profession, Edward Lauman and John Heinz found that part of the legal profession is "collegiate" (the lawyer is in charge) and part is "patronage" (the client is in charge). Lawyers who serve corporate clients are in a patronage occupation. Lawyers serving individuals are more "collegiate." Heinz explains the phenomenon this way:

> "The corporations that are the clients of corporate law specialists have vast wealth and social power; though their lawyers are also wealthy, as lawyers go, and enjoy high social status, the power of the corporate clients will outweigh that of their lawyers. The lawyers are often dependent upon receiving repeat business from a few, large corporate clients, and they will thus be reluctant to do anything that would offend those clients. In the personal client sector of law practice, the opposite tends to be the case. Though some of the persons who are the clients in noncorporate legal practice are wealthy (undoubtedly, a disproportionate number of them are, especially in fields of practice such as probate), the social power of clients in the fields of law that deal primarily with personal problems more nearly approximates that of the lawyers themselves. In some specialities within the personal client sector, fields such as criminal law, civil rights, consumer work, divorce, and personal injury plaintiffs' work, the clients include large numbers of persons of lower social status. In those areas of practice, the lawyers will usually have higher socioeconomic standing than their clients, and the clients will be much less sophisticated than are the corporate clients, much less able to monitor or evaluate the performance of their lawyers.

Moreover, the personal client lawyers will serve a much larger number of clients and will be much less dependent upon receiving repeat business from any one of them. They may, therefore, be more willing to act in ways that are contrary to a particular client's wishes. In short, in the personal client sector the lawyers will be in a much stronger position to define the clients' needs and to determine the manner in which those needs will be met (Johnson's definition of a collegiate occupation). They may well modify their clients' goals -- as, for example, in determining the amount to be accepted in settlement of a personal injury claim."[37]

What is odd about the Pentagon Papers case is that the law firm resigned "on principle." J.P. Morgan's lawyer protested a certain course of action with a "But you can't do that, Mr. Morgan." Whereupon J.P. replied: "Your job is to tell me how to do what I want to do."[38] Perhaps the corporate world is not so crude as the story implies, yet I dare say it is the corporate lawyer's often very proud position that he or she did find a way to do what the CEO wanted. An analogue is to be found in the famous Ford Pinto case. It is not that some engineers did not suggest the unusual safety problem in the placement of the gas tank. It is just that a cost-benefit analysis showed it was cheaper to pay damages for the approximately 180 people who would be killed and the 180 others who would be seriously burned than it was to spend $11 per car to fix the problem. It was just that nobody made a fuss because Lee Iacocca, whose baby the Ford Pinto was, had a motto: "Safety doesn't sell." It was just that, whatever the problem, lawyers for Ford were hard at work in Washington arguing against higher safety standards because that's what they were supposed to do, "without thinking about it."[39]

The little guy has a different problem. Here the lawyer often assumes stupidity or weakness or both, and therefore will not consult with the client. The Will to Power here is, in part, paternalism. It is also sometimes an awful arrogance and selfishness that allows the lawyer to push others around if he can, or allow his client to be pushed around if he must, all in the pursuit of some semblance of control over his or her own affairs, again, "without thinking about it."

My final salvo is brief. The bottom-line for lawyers, as for all of us engaged in the moral life, is that there is no bottom-line. There is the Will to Power and checks on the expression of Will to Power. As Charles Frankel pointed out in a review of the Code of Professional Responsibility: ..."when the specialized codes depart too frequently and radically from commonplace notions of acceptable behavior, demoralizing tensions are created within individuals and in society at large."[40] Our code is less our problem than our understanding of how to integrate our special tasks within an overall moral framework. What I have argued will not do that whole job -- but it is a start. Actually recognizing the dangers in the Will to Power is a big start, all by itself.

FOOTNOTES

[1]W. Kaufman, Nietzsche, 185 (1974).

[2]H.L.A. Hart, The Concept of Law, 93 (1961).

[3]Webster's Seventh New Collegiate Dictionary, 666 (7th ed. 1961).

[4]R. May, Power and Innocence, 99 (1972).

[5]Mentioned almost in passing as an acknowledged principle of International Law in Article 55 of the Charter of the United Nations, the right of self-determination is the first right granted in the important International Covenant on Civil and Political Rights. International Covenant on Civil and Political Rights, Part I, Article I, Para. I, as reprinted in The International Bill of Human Rights, 32 (1981).

[6]W. Kaufman, supra at 183.

[7]Id. at 183-84.

[8]Id. at 194-95.

[9]R. May, supra at 20.

[10]Wasserman, Lawyers as Professionals: Some Moral

Issues, 5 Human Rights, 1 (1975).

[11] Id. at 1.

[12] Named in the text are the four historically classic professions as denominated by Roscoe Pound. R. Pound, The Lawyer from Antiquity to Modern Times, 5 (1953).

[13] See generally, Miller, Autonomy & The Refusal of Lifesaving Treatment, The Hastings Center Report, Aug. 1981, at 22-28.

[14] American Bar Association Model Code of Professional Responsibility (hereinafter ABA Code), EC 7-8, (1987).

[15] Id. at EC 7-7.

[16] American Bar Association Standard Relating to the Administration of Criminal Justice, The Defense Function, Standard 4-5.2 (1987).

[17] Id. at Standard 4-5.2.

[18] The use of the phrase "to give the other fellow his due" is standard fare in the commentaries on Aristotle's theory of justice. Copleston, A History of Philosophy, 83-4 (vol. I, part II 1962).

[19] Goldman, The Moral Foundations of Professional Ethics, 4 (1980).

[20] Id. at 4-6.

[21] Id. at 92-112.

[22] ABA Code, supra at DR 7-102 (A) (4).

[23] Fuller and Randall, Professional Responsibility: Report of the Joint Conference, 44 A.B.A.J. 1159-1162. (1958).

[24] Kaufman, Problems in Professional Responsibility, 274 (2nd ed. 1984).

[25] Bentham said: "Natural rights is simple nonsense: natural and imprescriptible rights, rhetorical nonsense -- nonsense upon stilts." C.M. Atkinson, Jeremy Bentham His Life and Work, 109 (1969).

[26] Fuller, The Adversary System, in Talks on American Law, 34 (2nd ed. by H. Berman, 1971).

[27] P. Mishkin and C. Morris, On Law in Courts, 1 (1965).

[28] Fuller, supra note 23, at 1161.

[29] Holmes, Path of the Law, 10 Harv. L. Rev. 459 (1897).

[30] Id. at 465.

[31] Krash, Professional Responsibility to Clients and the Public Interest: Is There a Conflict? 55 Chi B. Rec. (Special Centennial Issue) 33 (1978).

[32] F. Phillips, The Evolving Legal Profession in the Commonwealth, 94 (1978).

[33] P. Hoffman, Lions in the Street, 100 (1973).

[34] Fuller, supra note 23, at 1162.

[35] Fed. R. Civ. P. 11. The amended rule reads in part that a lawyer must certify that the document presented "is not interposed for any improper purpose, such as to harass or to cause unnecessary delay or needless increase in the cost of litigation." See generally 1983 Amendments of the Federal Rules of Civil Procedure, 97 F.R.D. 165 (1983).

[36] Application of Gahan, 279 N.W. 2d 826, 832 (Minn. 1979).

[37] Heinz, The Power of Lawyers, 17 Ga. L. Rev. 899 (1983).

[38] Id. at 900. There is another side to the tradition. Elihu Root said: "About half the practice of a decent lawyer consists in telling would-be clients that they are damned fools and should stop." P.C. Jessup, Elihu Root 133 (vol. I 1964).

[39] Dowie, Pinto Madness, reprinted in Ethical Problems in Engineering, 167-174 (2nd ed. by R. Baum, 1980).

[40] Frankel, Review of the Code of Professional Responsibility -- American Bar Association, 43 U. Chi.

L. Rev. 883 (1976).

THE LAWYER

THE PRACTITIONER:
JAMES R. SKIRBUNT, J.D.

Let me state at the outset that I am a divorce lawyer. As a practicing attorney I am pleased to have the opportunity not to respond but to concur in part, and to dissent in part, with Professor Robert Lawry's remarks and to expand, or take the next step if you will, regarding some of his comments.

What I would like to do is share with you some of my thoughts concerning the institutions and procedures to which Professor Lawry refers and to which I believe Professor Lawry would suggest that we owe our first loyalty as attorneys. I would then like to share with you some of my impressions on the attorney-client relationship with a special focus on the client's expectations and how those expectations may impact on the creation of what is then perceived as the attorney's will to power. I would also like to share my impressions on how paternalism impacts on the attorney-client relationship. And, finally, I would like to share a few of my thoughts on what the actual role of the attorney happens to be.

I gather from Professor Lawry's presentation that the anchor which focuses us as attorneys is the larger system of which the legal system is a major part but which interreacts and interfaces with other institutions and systems as well. This anchor prevents us from drifting into a mode of "full advocacy" which is advocacy unbridled, advocacy without thought as to moral or ethical considerations, advocacy based upon the outcome or result for the client with no mitigating factors whatsoever.

The perspective that I have as a practitioner is that sometimes our anchor slips; sometimes the anchor is not secured at all. As the anchor begins to drift, what happens then to our loyalty? Let me give you a couple of specific examples of what I am talking about. Within this framework of institutions and systems one of the major roles would be played by substantive law. You would think that the substantive law that you are studying here at law school and focusing on in your endeavors would at least give you an amoral position with respect to the will to power. I suggest that this is not correct. My practice area, family law, is probably as good an example as any.

Ohio is an equitable distribution jurisdiction. We are moving continuously further into the arena of no-fault divorce. But prior to the statutory realignment in 1974 creating the Dissolution of Marriage procedure and the subsequent advent of Ground K, which is living one year separate and apart as an absolute entitlement to divorce in the state of Ohio, "who did what to whom" was a critical factor in determining what amount was going to be obtained by which spouse. As a result of this reality the substantive law was the very knife that was cutting loose the anchor to which we were supposed to be fastened. The substantive law said that, beyond how you will be viewed by your client, the system itself will base its results on the degree to which you exercise the Nietzschian will to power: the extent to which you abused the other party and were successful in breaking down the other party in showing that they had done something wrong; you were successful in obtaining favorable results for your client from the court.

I am pleased to say that with the introduction of no-fault divorce a lot of the notion of "who did what to whom" is now removed from consideration as far as financial results in Domestic Relations Court. But there is a lingering problem that exists in the practice, namely, that there is a generation of lawyers who continue to practice in a way that produced results under the prior substantive law and who do not shift gears overnight. At the same time, there is a new generation of divorce lawyers who want to put an end to this old fashioned style of practice.

What we really want to do is to say that family law right now is really about evaluation. Cherry vs. Cherry says that the starting point in Ohio is 50/50 division of the marital estate for an equitable distribution in a divorce. If I got the six leading practitioners of divorce law in Cleveland together, we would all say to you that we think that the starting point ought to be 50/50. The key is, "50% of what?" Is the pension plan part of the marital estate? Deferred compensation, closly held stocks, something

184

that the husband inherited, the wife inherited, or the something that someone received by gift -- are these part of the marital estate?

The new generation of attorneys may very well be more inclined than the prior generation to be familiar with experts: economists, actuaries to value pension plans, or accountants to value closly held businesses and compute tax consequences. But the fact is that that prior generation of lawyers did not disappear in 1974 when the legislature waved the magic wand over the Ohio Revised Code. They are still there. And they still practice based upon "who did what to whom" because that is the way they got results and became very successful in their own practice.

So as we look at the system that anchors us, I would say as my first point for your consideration that we must look at substantive law and say, "Isn't the substantive law itself at least partly responsible for what is perceived as 'full advocacy' or unbridled advocacy? Has it encouraged, or has it in some way made successful, certain practices and designed certain practices, or procedures, to be successful without regard for ethical or moral concerns? And once that substantive law has been in place, what then can we do with those attorneys who have become successful under it once the law is finally changed?"

The second part of the legal system that I would like to discuss, as far as the system being an ethical anchor for attorneys, is the judiciary at the state level. You are all aware that our judges in Ohio are elected. If they are elected that means that they are political. If they are political I think that we must conclude that, to at least some extent, they are politicians; and politicians are neither amoral or unethical. They are not part of ameritocracy. They are part of the political arena, and as such, are they sufficienty in place to be our anchor? I have a problem with that as a practicing attorney. In addition to the substantive law which sometimes rocks our anchor, the very political nature of the judicial system raises questions about whether we can look to legal institutions and systems to guide us in our ethical decision making.

Let us turn now to the attorney-client

relationship. I would certainly agree that full advocacy is at best amoral. I would certainly agree that it is frequently not in the client's best interest. And I would also concur that full advocacy can cause damage to others. What I am not convinced of is that such advocacy exists solely because of an attorney's will to power. I think that in great measure such advocacy stems from the expectation of clients that this type of advocacy is necessary, or at least important, in adequately presenting their case.

I had a fairly substantial case with one of the prior generation of divorce lawyers. When it became known who was going to be on the other side, I remember having a conversation with my client. He was very up-front with me. He said, "I now know who is going to be representing my wife and I suspect we are going to be in a dog fight. What I want to know is, do I have a big enough dog for the fight?" He was very serious and it was a legitimate question. It was something he needed to ask and he needed to know the answer. I suggested to him that he had to make his own decision about style, progress and results that would be obtained in the case as it went along.

I wasn't going to change my style for this client's case, nor could I, and we ended up establishing a good attorney-client relationship. But it was a very illustrative experience for me in realizing that the expectations of a client in these matters is very important in terms of how your role as attorney is perceived and what the client may feel is required to be done in a particular matter.

Recently I had another similar experience. I am representing the daughter of a client who might be considered to be part of the patronage system. He is part of the corporate community. The father made a point of talking to several other divorce lawyers in Cleveland, again to basically find out if I was mean enough, tough enough, dirty enough, to try his daughter's divorce case. I'm not sure what exactly the response was; but that woman is still my client, so I assume that the answers were somehow satisfactory. It again points out, though, that the client's expectations have a lot to do with what is going to be happening in the case and in terms of what kind of legal services are being demanded.

There is a perception by the consumer of legal services that this type of aggressive advocacy is what is going to produce the best results for them. This is what is very disturbing. You may agree and I may agree and Professor Lawry may agree that such unbridled advocacy is generally ineffective and sometimes destructive. But the consumer still believes that for you to be a litigator, you have to be able to "chew glass!" And unless you manifest that kind of attitude, you may not have the full confidence of your client.

As a footnote to this, I would like to go back to the court because I have had this conversation with several judges. And what I have said to them is simply this, "You know that you have to start operating your courtroom the way we operate our law firm. In order to get the kind of behavior you want, you have to reward certain kinds of behavior. If you don't want screamers in your courtroom, then don't reward them. If you want a new generation of divorce lawyers in your courtroom, make sure that they are welcomed and that they are rewarded." How does a court do that? There are a couple of ways. The most direct is called a motion for attorney fees. When it comes time for the court to set fees, and the known screamer is on the other side -- let's call him the "full advocate" -- the court is well aware from monitoring this case that this particular attorney has been an obstructionist in respect to discovery, that this attorney has filed unnecessary discovery, that he has done everything but Rule 11 types of behavior. When it comes time to look to fees for that particular attorney, the court has got to say "no." When it comes time for the attorney who has bent over backwards to get the matter resolved, the attorney who has not exercised the will to power, but the attorney who has tried to quietly and effectively resolve matters for his or her client, that attorney must be rewarded by the court. As long as there is the demand for this type of representation -- the "full advocacy" -- it will be provided. It is going to be provided, not only because certain attorneys grew up with a different substantive law in a particular area, but it is also economically beneficial for the attorney.

Professor Lawry referenced the partner in the law firm commandeering six associates and how the six associates' work turns into an avalanche of gold. This points to the ethical questions involved in how attorneys generate fees. There is no question but that war in litigation generates more dollars than quietly resolving the matter for your client. If you go to court a couple of times on various motions you very well may generate more fees than if you don't. If you work to stabilize the situation in order to commence effective negotiation it is less expensive for the client than automatically filing pretrial motions.

How then can I generate fees and still be moral and ethical? I think part of the answer is found in your fee agreement with your client. I think that there is no problem with saying to a client, "If I'm going to be representing you and we are able to resolve this without a trial, that is worth more to you than if we have to go through a week of embittered testimony in the courtroom on this particular divorce. My fee to you is going to be primarily an hourly rate. But if we are able to resolve this because of my profile in the community, my expertise, my reputation, and my knowledge of opposing counsel, that is going to have an impact on your fee, which is certainly allowed under the Code of Professional Responsibility to be a factor taken into account when we come to final billing." I think clients need to know that. I guess one of the most important things that we as attorneys can do for them is to tell them, to educate them, that they don't need, and don't want, the type of "full advocacy" that we all might conclude is, at the very best, amoral.

The next item I would like to address is the paternalism issue. I am collegiate in my practice and in dealing with individuals. Therefore paternalism is something that more naturally is a danger or a risk. Professor Lawry stated what should happen in the attorney-client relationship is that the lawyer explains all the options, predicts the consequences, and then gives advice on what should be done. After receiving the advice, the client chooses. My emphasis is on the part of the process where the lawyer gives advice on what should be done. I would suggest to you that, without paternalism, the wheels of justice would come to a grinding halt. Why? Because the recommendation of an attorney, the advice on what should be done, is, in most situations, what the client is paying for.

In litigation there is very little that goes to trial, but everything gets discussed. When you get to the pre-trial what happens? Clients are there in a courtroom. The attorneys for each side go into chambers; and in chambers the judge will attempt to resolve matters for the clients by bringing the two attorneys together. The judge does that by knocking heads together, by trying to get both sides to articulate what exactly their best position is going to be. At that point the attorneys are going to be asked by the judge, "What is it that you really want? What is it that you really need for your client?" And the attorney is going to have to say something to the judge which then has to be communicated back to the client. If, at that point, the attorney does not know the parameters of settlement, and if he or she is then unable to market those parameters to the client, that is what is known as the attorney who does not have control of his or her client. That is always construed as something very negative. The court requires and expects your use of paternalism in order to settle the case. It is not just the court that is going to be pressuring you. The statement, "the lawyer explains all options, predicts consequences, gives advice on what should be done, and then the client chooses equally," is not a fair appraisal of what actually takes place. The client hangs on every word the attorney says, every nuance. The client wants to know what you are feeling about it, not just what you are thinking about it. The client wants to have a great sense of comfort because, when all is said and done, what the client, in many situations, is going to want to be able to do is to say, "My lawyer did a great job for me. This is what we got. This is what happened." And the enthusiasm in which they can embrace that statement depends upon the degree of paternalism that you may or may not exercise in that case. I am not sure I feel wholly comfortable with this. I confess to you that it is something that is an uneasy balance. But it is a necessary part of the procedures of the judicial process that we now have and enjoy. It is certainly a critical part of the attorney-client relationship as the case matures and moves towards trial.

Finally, what role does the attorney play in all of this? I was delighted to hear Professor Lawry say that the lawsuit is a rare thing and a trial is rarer still. Just absolutely delighted! The reason is simply this. I'm going to go to confession now. I'm going to tell you that I have settled 98%, maybe more, of the cases that I have handled. But yet when you sit down with lawyers and you talk with them, they never tell you about that 98%. They only tell about the 2% that got tried. The more lawyers you know the more you will find this to be true; we tell war stories. And all the war stories deal with the 2% of the cases that got tried. I rarely exalt, "Boy! Did I settle a case today! It was really interesting." But I can tell you stories about custody cases -- things that have happened in the courtroom. That is the shared experience that we as lawyers tell one another. We don't tell each other, "I settle 98% of all my cases. How many did you settle?"

When you are in private practice you get promotional materials for seminars on a daily basis. If you are in the divorce area you are inundated with seminar materials that are about how to cross examine an actuary, a psychiatrist, and all kinds of other experts. And practitioners say, "I have to go to that because I don't know anything about that and I may have a case like that someday so I better find out exactly what I'm going to have to do to that actuary." You never see seminars that are geared toward "How to effectivly handle your client, stabilize the arena, and negotiate the settlement." Yet that is what we deal with on a daily basis.

We are trained as advocates. We do not see ourselves as counselors or problem solvers. We are litigators and we are not comfortable talking about the quiet resolution of a case. You are being socialized as law students and people are viewing you as advocates. They want to know how your thought processes are developing and they do not want to hear, "I really don't like to solve all my cases because I want to abuse the will to power." They want to know if you are sharpening your teeth and if you are getting all the latest, greatest, and the newest motions and procedures to reduce your opponent to rubble. That is what they want to know about. And that is what you are happy to tell them, because that seems to be the thrust of our psyches as lawyers.

Unfortunatly from the practice standpoint, I must

inform you that Professor Lawry is correct. What you are going to be doing is working on quietly dissolving a marriage for your client. Let's examine that a little more closely to see why. I will stipulate that there are some divorce cases that must be tried. There are some cases that present novel issues with respect to valuation; marital and non-marital assets; custody cases where clearly the matter must be resolved by a trier of fact. Now would you agree with me that it takes a significant amount of pathology on the part of any human being in a marital relationship to want to have their case tried before a complete stranger for four or five days in order to have all the wealth they accumulated during the marriage divided; have levels of support established; and have the relationship with their children defined for all time by that stranger? That is what a divorce trial is and I will suggest to you that every client that comes into my office does not want it. No one comes to me and says, "I want to be in the courtroom for a week. I want my most private activities exposed. I want to have this person talk to my children to see where my children are going to be living for the rest of their minority." They don't want that! As a result, to be effective in representing clients, I find that there is an increased emphasis on my ability to quietly resolve the matter, to stabilize the arena, and negotiate an effective settlement.

You have to get on the same wavelength with your client. And if that wavelength is totally unreasonable, bring that wavelength down to a manageable level. What do I mean by that? Let me be specific and give an example from my practice: custody cases. Every practitioner knows that the first time a client enters your office, that client will be on his or her best behavior. They want to impress you as much as you want to impress them. And they want to impress you with the righteousness of their cause. When a client comes in and says, "Custody is going to be an issue here", I explain to them that I handle two very distinct types of cases: divorce cases and custody cases. They are very different, because in custody cases we are probably not going to be able to resolve it without trial. So if we are talking about custody cases I just want them to make one commitment to me, one commitment only. That commitment is that they are concerned about the best interests of the children and not just about winning. And I write that down in my notes. Of course, a client at the first interview is going to say, "Well that's what I want. I am not interested in winning, I just want what is best for my children. That is why I am here to see you because being with me is going to be in their best interest." That's terrific! I pull a different color pen out of my pocket and I put a check mark in front of my note. As the case wears on, and expert testimony starts to shape up, and we really don't have a case, and there are going to be two experts testifying against us in trial and none for us, I have the opportunity then to sit down with the client and remind the client as to what we talked about in the beginning: "You're not about winning, you are about what is in the best interest of your children. It is right here in my notes. I checked it in green pen. Do you remember that?" Now if the client says to you, "I still want to try the case", there ought to be a red flag. Things are starting to erupt all around you because this client is interested in winning and only in winning. And you know what? You can't win this case. And when the case is lost, you will have lost it from the client's viewpoint. As a result you are not going to get paid. So my suggestion would be to immediately say, "I think we ought to try this case, but in order to go forward and for me to set foot in the courtroom, it is important for you to understand that I am going to have to have "x" number of dollars right now as an additional retainer." Now my "x" is sufficiently high so that no one has ever said, "O.K. let's do it!" And this is one way I think that we can work with our clients to maintain something that is reasonable for them and ethical and moral for us.

Responsiveness of an attorney to the needs of the client requires the attorney-client relationship to be based on being on the same wave length as our clients so that we can determine what appropriate exercise of power actually is on behalf of our client's best interest. And what that exercise of power is -- to make something happen or prevent it from happening -- is the practice of law.

Chapter 8

THE DENTIST

THE PRESENTER:
GLENN KEIPER, D.D.S.

Dr. Keiper presented this paper on the occasion of the annual Professionals Day at the School of Dentistry at Case Western Reserve University.

Professionals Day is a very auspicious occasion for the presentation of this program dealing with the power of the professional person. I understand that this day has been devoted entirely to the scientific aspects of the profession of dentistry. I also understand that there is some anxiety among promoters of this day's events as to the interest this program in humanities will hold for dentists who are in the habit of finding a purely scientific program on Professionals Day. However, a quick review of the definition of our profession will show we are practitioners in the art and science of dentistry. The demand for equal time, if we are going to draw sides then, for the art of dentistry, allows for this glitch in a purely scientific Professionals Day.

So as not to disappoint the purely scientific I, as ethicist presenter, will attempt to display the power of the professional person as dentist in an analytic, therefore scientific, manner.

My purpose, according to the format set by the Center for Professional Ethics at CWRU, is to define and describe ethical issues arising from the practice of dentistry vis-a-vis the power of the dentist as professional. I suppose some of you, the students in particular, being subjected not only to the demands of the dental school curriculum and faculty but the personal financial burden as a part of your becoming a professional, wonder what possible power might accrue to you. Today I want to have you realize that there is considerable power already available to you, and more coming. Those powers provide a means for you to overcome your financial burden. Those same powers will place upon you an awesome responsibility. It is the responsibility accruing to you through professional obligation that I want to analyze today. In so doing, I hope to elucidate the nature of the relationship between dentist and patient, making it a major component of the nature of the work of dentistry. This relationship is the ground for the power of the professional. It gives rise to authority, efficiency, economic superiority, and monopoly through organization and self government. I would, finally, attempt to show the effects of the changes brought about in the health professions as a result of government intervention into the tradition of professionalism, and what our attitude must be if we are to retain the idea of a profession of dentistry.

It is immediately obvious to me that at least a small book is in order, but an attempt must be made in thirty minutes of talk.

Therefore, let "power" be defined as "the ability to do."

Let "dentistry" be defined as "the science and art of preventing, diagnosing, and treating diseases and malformations of the teeth, jaws and mouth."

In defining "profession" we have the DNA of the power of the professional. Given the support of a nurturing environment, the double helix of DNA gives a phenotype in biology and power, when applied to the person as dentist.

What is profession? Chester Burns, writing in the Bulletin of the History of Dentistry, (December 1974), says of the evolution of profession, "No person is value-free; we are all bundles of values; we are all our own top value stamps.... It has not been possible for most American dentists to create patterns of professional ethics without relating them to their values about individuals and groups." Early ideas of profession were grounded in the tenets of Christianity culminating in a statement of the Golden Rule -- "Do unto others...." Additionally, a professional was to be a gentleman. This entitlement was to have the effect of self-acceptance of a code of behavior. This gentlemanly behavior was extended to groups, as dentists called for patriotism on the part of the growing profession. G.S. Dean in 1894 said, "Without a lengthy analysis I will divide the duties of dentists into three groups: First his duties to his country and to the general cause of humanity...." Thus early dentists chose values of personal and social obligation. Leaping into the early twentieth century ideas of profession, the medical reformer Abraham Flexner established six cardinal tenets of profession. According to David Nash, writing in the JADA, (October 1984), Flexner's six virtues can be condensed. He writes, "These traits can be summarized, as is done in the preface of the ADA "Principles", into three: service to humanity; education beyond the usual level; and self improvement/self-regulation." He cites William F. May as further resolving these characteristics of profession into the moral, intellectual and organizational components of profession.

The moral component espouses an ideal of service above personal gain. It is addressed in the latest version of the ADA "Principles and Code" in Section I of the "Principles":

"Service to the Public and Quality of Care. The dentists' primary obligation of service to public shall include the delivery of quality care, competently and timely, within the bounds of clinical circumstances presented by the patient. Quality of care shall be a primary consideration of the dental practitioner."

Let us look for a moment at the opening word: "service." Defined by the New Universal Unabridged Webster's Dictionary, service is, among other meanings: "the occupation or condition of a servant; work done for a master or superior; respect, attention, devotion, as of a lover to his lady; helpful, beneficial or friendly action or conduct; an act giving assistance or advantage to another; the result of service: benefit, advantage."

Service is derived from the Latin SERVITIUM, from SERVUS meaning SLAVE.

Continuing to define the nature of the work of dentists, through the doctor-patient relationship, let's explore briefly the concept of a "contract" relationship, as described by Robert Veatch in his book A Theory of Medical Ethics, and then of "covenanted" relationships, as described by William May.

Veatch says people acting from a moral point of view can be expected to formulate a basic set of ethical principles. These govern moral actions in their daily lives. Regardless of their source, they represent what is thought to be right in a given community. They may be called a social contract.

Assuming this basic contract to be in order, Veatch goes on to describe a second set of principles, or contract, to govern acts between these people when acting in the doctor-patient relationship. He says this second contract would be a reasonable assumption. It would "bind lay people and professionals in trust and understanding, in equality of human dignity and respect." However, it is highly idealistic, as Veatch recognizes when he says a contract "containing these principles and rules necessarily requires full participation by all who can approximate the role of reasonable people." Furthermore, allowances must be made for particular situations lying outside the scope of the contract.

Regarding a covenantal relationship, Nash writes:

The metaphor of covenant has been used by May in conceptualizing the relationship entered into by professional and patient, and as significantly between the profession and society. In its ancient and most influential form, a covenant between individuals or groups included an exchange of gifts or services, a pledge or promise based on this exchange, and finally but significantly, a change of "being" of the convenantal. May argues that the according to a group by society of the status of professional is the establishment of a covenant. In the exchange of gifts, society gives the gifts of education and the privilege of

196

self-government in return for the profession's inherent talents and abilities... The profession promises to serve society fairly and faithfully. In this convenantal relationship the nature of being is changed. Professionals become dentists and individuals of society patients. The health professional is transformed from "ordinary citizen" to "healer." When individual professionals are initiated, they agree to the existing covenant with society, and become healers. The shapes of their entire lives and relationship with others are changed.

Without further comment here, I assert that the nature of the relationship between the dentist and patient is best described by the word <u>fiduciary</u>. "Fiduciary" is defined, again in the <u>Universal Unabridged Webster's Dictionary</u> as "from the Latin FIDERE, to trust; designating or of a person who holds something in trust for another...."

What the dentist, as professional, holds in trust for the patient is established by, and through, the intellectual component of professionalism as previously described. The attainment of an education beyond the usual, a highly specialized knowledge of the science of dentistry, once attained by the dentist, is held in trust for his or her patient.

The patient trusts that you as doctor will use your knowledge and skills for the benefit, for the good, of the patient. The fiduciary responsibility of dentist to patient comes with the attainment of skills of practice. The trust obligates the dentist to keep current on advancing technical knowledge. The dentist will always be superior in the technical skills of the profession of dentistry to his patients. This is the essence of the fiduciary relationship.

Problems of judgment arise when, in this fiduciary role, the dentist prescribes and gives care. The term "paternalism" comes into play here. Paternalism is best described by the trusting relationship between a loving parent and his child. The father, or pater, will always do what is best for his child.

In the doctor-patient relationship, paternalism is an unavoidable facet of proper care. The doctor uses his or her special knowledge to educate the patient to a level where an autonomous choice can be made for or against proposed care. A competent, fully-informed patient must be understood as an autonomous being whose rational choice is the determining factor in treatment rendered. Autonomy means self- government. It comes with being a competent, therefore rational, being.

Of course, we recognize situations where autonomous choice is not possible -- in the case of a young minor or mentally retarded person. Paternalism may be properly used in exercising the fiduciary relationship for those persons. The doctor does good for the patient, using his knowledge and skill. However, it cannot be morally correct to override an autonomous choice with paternalism.

Therefore, establishing the ground for autonomous choice is primary to your fiduciary role.

The nature of the work of the professional in dentistry is, then, the application of the technology of dentistry, within the boundaries described by the definition of dentistry, to a person as patient, in a fiduciary relationship.

"Duty" has been defined as a job you try to avoid, do a lousy job of, and then brag about forever. It is not that sense of duty to which we adhere when we say that the ethics of dentistry encompasses the duty of the professional to act in accord with the professional virtue of servitude and beneficence toward a person as patient. This duty is discharged while holding in trust a superiority in knowledge and skill that comes with the attainment of a special education.

Having defined the nature of the work of dentistry and the source of power of the dentist as professional, we now must concern ourselves with specific powers and how their improper use injures the ethics of profession and hence humane treatment of patients.

The special knowledge, as a source of power, becomes manifest in the professional through the authority that comes with his or her education. The dentist has power through authority. Authority means power or prestige coming from special knowledge, the proper use of power.

Authority is given by the learning institutions of dentistry in the pre-practice of the professional. The title "Doctor" is used in the schools by students prior to the earning of the degree. Its early use is a not-so-subtle psychological conditioner for the student dentist and the patient. It confers authority by connotation. Throughout the life of the dentist person there is an identification with that authority. It is intensified by growing technology and continuing education.

However, unauthorized power is there as potential. Its use can result in less humane care for patients. These patients are the very society that grants authority through professional education. Accepted as paternalism, "doctor knows best", the inhumane and unethical use of authority can override competent autonomous choice and distort informed consent. Insightful help from assistants and paraprofessional hygienists and advanced assistants can be stifled by authority while, in misconception, the doctor delivers what could be more humane care to patients.

Technology and skill are the servants of the professional's authority. The combination allows for a highly efficient operation. The practice of dentistry, in all its technological glory, has become a highly efficient enterprise. Given enough fully equipped operatories and personnel to surround the dentist, a maximum number of patients can be given good technological care in a segment of office time.

What can happen to the art of a highly efficient practice? A consideration of human aspects of care is well described by David Hilfiker in his book Healing the Wounds. Hilfiker is a young Minnesota family-practice physician working in a four-man clinic. His description of efficiency may have an analogous ring for many of us.

He writes,

>   The morning was hectic and I've just returned from a semi-monthly hospital medical staff meeting,

scheduled over lunch hour so as not waste any time. Now it looks like I'll need to hurry through the afternoon, too.

My first patient is Bill Martin, who needs an insurance physical. As I enter the examining room, he's sitting on the exam table, undressed except for his shorts. He hands me his papers. I glance at them and notice he hasn't filled out his medical history. "Didn't Marge have you fill out these forms?" I asked impatiently.

"No, I, uh, just got here, I guess. I thought you were supposed to do that."

Over the next ten minutes Bill tells me that, no he hasn't had recent surgery, rheumatic fever, malaria, or gonorrhea; that his parents died at seventy-two and sixty-seven of heart disease; that he's not sure when his last tetanus shot was. I feel somewhat foolish interviewing Bill without his clothes on, but I certainly don't want to waste any more time in the examining room while he dresses and undresses.

The afternoon crunch has begun as Hilfiker finds himself fifteen minutes behind, with a broken wrist, lacerated hand, abdominal pain and other problems awaiting him in various areas. He says, "The purpose of all this confusion is to use my day efficiently."

Translated into an efficient dental practice, the details may change, but the concept is familiar.

Hilfiker goes on to say, "On a different level, the perceived need to be efficient and productive gave us, as physicians, a large measure of control over others. The rest of the office staff clearly had to structure itself to maintain the doctor's highest efficiency. Routine tasks could always be passed along to one of the office staff on the grounds of making the doctor's time more efficient. Patients, too, could be manipulated by my need to be efficient. Practically any interchange could be cut short on the basis of busyness. All I had to do was stand up, and patients knew they had only a little time left."

What causes all this perceived need for efficiency and the feeling of power that Hilfiker describes? Our practice-management journals are full of articles on how to get the most efficiency out of your office. Our fee for service system, which we realize is being changed, but which, nevertheless, is still the dominant method of exchange in dentistry, dictates that the more service that can be crammed into a time slot the higher the income. We, at the same time, disallow that quality of care suffers in the processing of patients. If quality is thought of as the technical means to a satisfactory end product, this may be true.

Anthony J. DiAngelis, in the Journal of Dental Education, (June 1984), describes the structure, process, and outcome phases of a model for assessing quality of health care. He says,

> Considerable controversy exists over whether quality of care is better judged by focusing on what is actually done (the process of care) or the resulting health status (the outcome).

In other words, is the smooth-margined, anatomically-correct, glistening inlay more important than the manner through which the inlay was delivered?

He goes on to say,

> Two cautions are in order here. First, in striving for specificity and completeness in criteria, we must not allow the definition of quality to become so restricted, that the elements of interpersonal or "art of care" concerns are ignored.

"Efficiency" has great potential for disallowing time for the proper exercise of this caution.

Hilfiker ends his critique of efficiency with these thoughts....

"The attempt to respond to the pressures of medicine by becoming more efficient inevitably damages both the physician-patient relationship and the physician's own concept of self. Yet the issue is a subtle one. It is simply not possible to refuse to consider the demands to be productive and efficient, for they are important issues in our task of caring for patients -- yet these values have such a profound effect on the practice of medicine that the physician needs to remain constantly aware of the tradeoff between efficiency and deeper personal relationship, between productivity and medicine as an art. When the physician finds that he is not taking the time needed for reflective meditation upon the meaning of his job...at these points the physician needs to ask himself whether the values of efficiency and productivity have not in fact gained the upperhand, submerging other important medical and human values."

Efficiency is the handmaiden of economic power. The more procedures that can be performed in a segment of office time, the greater the income. Moreover, since we charge for the procedure being performed, and the time to perform it being a factor peripheral to the cost of the procedure, there is a tendency to do those procedures that can be done quickest. It is understandable that quality of care may suffer when doing procedures that produce a high fee and that can be accomplished in the least amount of time. It has been charged that the fee for service arrangement both guarantees the monopoly of profession over those fees and supports the perceived need for a high income for health professionals.

What should we do? We must bear in mind the obligation to an ideal of service over personal gain, addressed repeatedly in our professional literature from varied sources. The following examples are illustrative.

"Dedication to service rather than to

gain or profit from service", is stated by C.E. Rutledge, D.D.S., and Bernard J. Conway, Ll.B., to be one of the professional characteristics to be "constantly reflected upon." They wrote for the JADA in March 1961 in an article entitled, "The Ethics of our Profession."

Addressing The American Society of Oral Surgeons Educational Foundation (now American Society of Oral and Maxillofacial Surgeons) in 1974, Authur J. Goldberg, former U.S. Supreme Court Justice, said, "...your organization will indeed fulfill what should be the first Canon of your Code of Ethics: The quality and indispensable health care which members of this Society are responsible for providing shall not be rationed or denied to any person."

Maynard K. Hine, D.D.S., addressed the American College of Dentists on October 11, 1969 with these words:

"It is generally agreed that modern professional behavior may be defined in terms of four essential attributes which must be predominant." Among them he lists "A primary orientation to the interest of others rather than [our own] individual interest." He adds finally, "However, I am convinced that the time is long past due to add a fifth attribute; assumption of responsibility for developing methods of making the required services needed, available to those who need them, regardless of nationality, race, color, creed, location, or economic status."

In this light we need ask ourselves the following questions: Are the incomes of American dentists arbitrarily and irrationally high? In the 1985 Statistical Abstract of the U.S., incorporated dentists made $72,000.00, net of professional expenses. How do we justify an income close to three times the average income of a U.S. family of four? Does the length of time involved in reaching the professional degree and the costs of that professional education create a barrier that makes the ideal of service over personal gain impossible -- or travesty? Does the drive for efficiency and the resulting better income foment the problem of processing patients vs. caring for them?

Is the fee for service intrinsic to what we do, or is it a result of the monopoly of profession in restricting non-professional competition, controlling numbers of practitioners and, until recently, keeping government from interfering with our structure?

Is high income a distancing factor in patient care, vis-a-vis covert resentment on behalf of patients, leading to an expectation of perfection and guaranteed results that are impossible to deliver?

Once in practice, how many of us do any real charity work?

Insulated by comfortable surroundings, including excess cash, the best of health insurance, and perhaps substantial savings, can we remain sensitive to the impossibility of some patients to buy a necessary service?

Are we willing to reduce the personal stress caused by the intensity of efficiency by cutting patient load, or do we endure stress to support our financial condition?

Now the answers will likely be that there is no excess of patients for many; that third party involvement has intruded into the fee for service arrangement; that HMOs, PPOs, PPAs, IPAs have made inroads into the profession and are dictating what fees will be paid for certain service. Then there is a corresponding demand for quality of care. Capitation, as a way of forcing the profession to be prevention oriented, has altered incomes.

We may argue that these alternative methods of payment thrust upon the health care professions, along with the 1979 FTC ruling against restriction of advertising, has the effect of cutting income. Furthermore, it makes health care just another form of business in a free market economy. In response we arm ourselves with business acumen. If the government says we must compete in the open market, devoid of the monopoly of profession, then business we will be.

However, the fiduciary relationship which is a part of the nature of dentistry cannot be disavowed. It is an intrinsic part of applying special skills to suffering people. The ideal of service over personal gain must be constantly striven for. It is intrinsic to the trust which we cannot disown when we open our special knowledge to needing people.

Dentistry can be proud of its move into an area of health care that is largely preventive. The application of fluoride in several forms has, in a single generation, largely eradicated dental caries. Dentistry, through its research and clinical application of the results of that research, has benefited society greatly. The costs of this great service were minimal.

Ironically, a disease entity that supported and gave reason for being to much of the profession of dentistry has been largely eliminated. We are limited to the care of a small part of the human organism. The resulting tensions have, on the one hand, implications for intense care in the area of prevention through new technical and scientific insights and, on the other, opening of new areas of care. Orthognathic surgery, adult orthodontia and intense periodontal care are some of the fruits of these efforts.

We are in a state of extreme change in the traditional notion of fee for service. Reliance on skills and satisfied patients to build practice will fall to alternative methods of payment involving large businesses and corporations. They will have the ability to choose who they will pay and for what they will pay.

However, as I hope to have made understood, as a health service professional, there is no escaping an ideal of service over personal gain. It is a fitting support to a fiduciary relationship between professional and needing patient, which is itself intrinsic to the choice of giving special care to that needing patient -- the choice of the profession of dentistry.

THE DENTIST

THE PRACTITIONER:
DANIEL VERNE, D.D.S.

I greet all of you in the audience as professionals, powerful and ethical. I am honored to be here.

It is difficult to criticize Dr. Keiper's paper. It is a scholarly paper and he has done an excellent job in its preparation. If we all followed that which he suggests in his paper then we would have no need for this kind of a conference. Unfortunately, we do not adhere to the suggestions made in Dr. Keiper's paper. We would not have to worry about ethical behavior if we did.

It is my duty to comment on Dr. Keiper's paper as a practitioner of dentistry. I appear before you with some reservation because I cannot think of the good things I ever did. I can only think of all the unethical things I have done.

My first criticism is that I see an audience of dentists and one attorney and some other people related to the profession of dentistry. One does not see any Democrats at the Republican Convention and no Republicans at the Democratic Convention. I think conceivably this convention should have been made up of all of the professions that we are talking about so that we understand one another. I think we all realize that this is a human behavioral problem. This is not a problem entirely of dentistry. It is not a problem of the profession of law, it is not a problem of the nursing profession. It is a human behavorial problem which we will have to control one day or we will all suffer from its adverse actions.

I am going to give you an example of why we act the way we do under different circumstances. No matter what location we are in or how much money we make, we act good or we act bad. We act correctly or we act in an awful manner. I did graduate from here some years ago in the school over the railroad tracks. We could listen to the professors when the trains were not going by or when smoke wasn't coming in the windows.

Allow me to paint a picture for you to show you that ethical actions are a human behavorial problem. We knew our entire class, there were only 48 people in the class. We knew who the cheaters were; we knew who the good guys were; we knew who the bad guys were; we knew who wrote on their cuffs; and we knew who palmed cards; and we knew who the honest students were.

I don't know if some of you can remember Blue books. Blue books demanded essay type questions in a blue covered book. The professor had to grade it. Now the professor becomes a little bit lazy and want true and false quick answers so he can knock it off on a computer. Some students had material written on these Blue books before the Blue books were handed out. It was an amazing situation.

When we graduated we entered the Navy after marching in Severance Hall for a couple of years in the Army. It was a brilliant move! Interesting enough, most of us went to the same station in San Francisco during World War II. We practiced under a Captain in a rather large clinic. The Captain graded us on the number of restorations we put in a tooth. In other words, we didn't do one three-surface restoration if we wanted to get into the good favor of the Captain. One put in three separate restorations. It would make your record look much better. Now mind you, we were making $175 a month. We never had so much money in our lives: the drinks were 25¢ at the Officer's Club, and we had a wonderful time in San Francisco. Do you get the picture? The same dentists who were putting in three fillings in the Navy had cheated on the Blue books.

We all came back to Cleveland, started our practices and eventually became more affluent. We know all our own classmates who live in Cleveland. We are not now writing in Blue books; we are not in the Navy; we are now all in practice.

The same people are cheating; the same people are putting in three fillings when they should be putting in one; the same dentists are making more money than perhaps they should be. This is a human behavioral problem. And, it doesn't make a difference how we live or how much money we make, we are all performing the way we feel is an ethical way to work.

Ethics is something that we should be taught earlier in our lives, not at the time we graduate. Let me give you some examples of ethical problems that we encounter. When a patient walks into the dentist's office and the patient says to the dentist, "Do you know that I wouldn't have this infection from my first dentist if I would have had antibiotics." What do you say? What do we say? What do I say? Should we say, "Yes, you are right. You should have had antibiotics or you wouldn't have had that infection." Or do we calm this thing down and act diplomatically and ethically and not condemn the first dentist?

Do we wait for the litigation that occurs from a case so that we can have the insurance pay for our bridge work or dentistry that we are doing? Are you going to condemn the second dentist so that we can get paid for our own work? Do we act in a revengeful fashion when patients walk into our office and we are told that something happened to the first dentist or the dentist before that? How do we handle that patient? Do we make correct comments? Are we diplomatic in our relationships with that patient? Do we all realize when we criticize that first dentist we are attacking the profession? We really are insulting the patient when we criticize the dentist. The patient picked out that dentist; the patient picked out that physician; the patient picked out that attorney; the patient picked out that nurse. We didn't pick them out and yet we are attacking that individual. We wonder why the patient eventually leaves us too. The patient is insulted. The patient is the one who chose the dentist.

I am alarmed by the number of malpractice cases that I see now. Please excuse me, Professor Robert Lawry (professor of Law at CWRU), if I discuss the law profession and its relation to the following example.

The patient comes to the dentist's office and he finds out that he needs periodontal therapy. The dentist says, "You should have received periodontal therapy from the first dentist." This announcement can be done with more diplomacy. It can be done ethically. When it goes to litigation who do you think told the patient that he needed periodontal therapy and that the first dentist was wrong? Was is the garbage collector? No! It was another dentist who acted in an undiplomatic manner, in an unethical manner, and condemned the profession by his method of conversation. I don't think we realize that it costs all of us money when we act in an unethical manner. It makes us look bad and it makes dentistry look bad.

It is very easy for me to make a statement about how to correct all this. I just have to stand up here and make some suggestions. But it seems to me that with this fine beginning of an inspection into our professional life and the power that we have as professional people, we have ways of accomplishing better ethical standards. As dentists, we should begin to instill and promote participation in organized dentistry to a greater extent and participate in promoting scientific courses.

It is not the lawyers who are going to make us better dentists. I heard a statement that the consent form was going to improve the manner in which we treated patients. That is not true. We will be better dentists if we become more intelligent dentists. If we take more courses we become better dentists. We don't need another profession to tell us to become better dentists or become more ethical. All this does is make us more unhappy, not make us better dentists.

I think that perhaps we should start rewarding students and practitioners. We should start rewarding students not for making a better denture or a better bridge, or the quickness with which they remove a tooth, or the better manner in which they can write a paper. We should reward them for their ethical conduct throughout dental school.

Why not reward somebody in the Cleveland Dental Society for his ethical standards rather than his ability to give a speech or to do some research in the construction of a periodontal flap? We have a number of people in the city of Cleveland that must be worthy of a reward for being ethical practitioners. It would show the rest of us that perhaps we might win an award too.

We should move in the direction of insisting that if our licenses are to be renewed one must take a certain number of courses. Of course, it doesn't make educated ethical individuals out of everybody, but it will certainly help. In the undergraduate schools, as well as the graduate schools, there should be courses in ethics and courses in the power of the professional from the beginning day of enrollment. Minds are fresh and able to understand power and ethics. The courses are difficult to assimilate after graduation. It seems to me that every year a course should be administered the same length as courses in prosthetics or oral surgery. There should be courses every year from the undergraduate area through the dental school in how to be a powerful, ethical practitioner. We should all meet with other professions -- with the attorneys, with the nurses, with the medical profession. These meetings should be regular and involve everyone in the professions.

I can only refer to the poetry of John Donne, "No man is an island entire of itself. Every man is a piece of the continent, a part of the Maine. Therefore, do not ask to know for Whom the Bell Tolls, it Tolls for Thee - **Everyone.**"

THE DENTIST

THE CONSUMER:
MARLA COMET-STARK, J.D.

I would like to consider some of the points raised by Dr. Keiper from a consumer's point of view. First of all, let me start by saying, as a consumer, I endorse wholeheartedly the position taken by Dr. Keiper as to what the art of dentistry should mean and what the moral goals of such a profession should be, namely, ideal of service over personal gain. If a dentist followed that creed in his practice certainly the consumer would benefit greatly. Specifically, though, I would like to review what it is the consumer expects to find, or at least hopes to find, when seeking dental care, and in what manner we would like to see the dentist exercise his power as a professional.

In a strict commercial sense, a consumer is always looking for VALUE; in other words, maximum gain for minimum investment. In the context of a professional/patient relationship, the patient does not usually shop comparatively for his or her dentist as he may for a comsumer product, although shopping for price is being done more and more these days. In any event, there is an expectation that in exchange for the patient's time, money, and selection in you, the dentist, certain needs will be met resulting in actual and psychological gain for the patient.

What is it we want?

First, and probably foremost, we expect competence and technical excellence. We want to be able to trust that our dentist's skill and knowledge will enable him to provide us with quality care -- that he will provide proper solutions for our dental problems and provide proper preventive care.

We want to think the dentist enjoys what he is doing and that he is doing dentistry as an affirmative choice. We want to think he is self-confident and competent as a practitioner. We want him to be progressive, involved in continuing education and constantly keeping up with new technology and methodology. As consumers, we want to know we are

213

getting the newest, the latest, the best. We shy away from those conveying a sense of static, status-quo dentistry.

In the context of competence, when considering the ethical use of the dentist's power, one of the things that concerns the consumer is the growing specialization of dentistry. We need to feel assured that our dentist would never attempt a treatment that was outside his area of experience or competence just in order to keep the business. We count on proper referrals to specialists or, when appropriate, we expect our dentist to encourage us to seek a second opinion.

On the other hand, overuse of referrals to specialists can make consumers paranoid of collusion. Many of us yearn for the good old days when our dentist took care of all of our dental needs; the parallel exists in medicine where you can see the growing trend toward family practitioners. What's crucial is that you, the dentist, take the time to develop a rapport with your patient and supply him or her with the necessary information so that he or she understands the basis for the referral.

Another issue is the proper use of auxiliaries. The patient selected you because of your competence. If the patient perceives that you overuse your auxiliaries, resulting in your spending too little time with him, then he will grow to resent it.

Another issue arises when the dentist is part of a group practice. Your patient may be put in a position of seeing another dentist in your practice. There is nothing worse for a patient than to receive conflicting advice or inconsistent approaches from members of a group practice. It may result in undermining the patient's confidence in you and/or your office. So, when you select among individuals with whom you wish to practice, make sure they share your ideas about administering care, not only the scientific and technical aspects but also the humane aspects of your professional/patient relationship. If your patient questions the competence of a co-worker, or has problems with his personality, it may adversely affect your individual practice.

Unfortunately, I have a case in point. Recently my 18-month-old son was seen by a pediatrician who is not the doctor we usually use in that group practice. In fact we had never dealt with him before. During the examination, the doctor asked me to have Jacob walk toward him so that he can observe his walk. I told him, "Sorry Doctor, he doesn't walk by himself yet." He gave me a look and then tried to get Jacob to stand. I said, "He won't do that for you either." The doctor looked at me and said, "Your son is 18 months old. He should be walking. He should be walking." I was so taken off-guard that I said: "Doctor, why isn't he walking?"

He completed the exam, told me to dress my son and come in his office for a conference. Now, please be aware, there was a third-year medical student who was observing this doctor all week and who was present in the office at this time.

I went into the office. The doctor took Jacob's records, jotted down a few notes, looked at me and said, "Your son is behind -- he should be walking. All children should be walking by 14 months of age." At that point a nurse walked in (the door was open), the doctor left the office for a few minutes, and took two phone calls.

Mind you, I, at this point was shaking -- he laid a bomb on me -- a very anxiety-producing statement -- then left me hanging, absolutely unaware of how his message was being received. I turned to the medical student sitting in the room and said (so that the doctor could hear), "When you get into practice -- don't do this!"

When I finally got my doctor's attention I said, "Doctor what are you saying? Do you have a diagnosis? Is something wrong with Jacob?" "No nothing is physically wrong." said the doctor. "So what is wrong!" I said. And then it dawned on me -- I was the problem. He was about to scold me. Sure enough he said, "You are babying him!"

I said, "With all due respect, how can you say that? You don't know me or my family. I don't carry him around at home. He has every opportunity to walk; he just doesn't choose to. If you think he should be lying face down in the snow as he wiggles to the car, I'm sorry. I am going to carry him to the car!"

Looking back at this, if his remarks had been presented in a proper manner and after proper inquiry, they would have been considered constructive and insightful. But because of the way they were presented they were seen as paternalistic and condescending insults. If I was a first-time mother I would have been reduced to tears. In addition to all this, our Pediatrician is very "laid back" and not at all concerned. He has assured me not to be concerned. This is an example of conflicting approaches which made me upset with the entire office.

Secondly, in addition to expecting competence, we as consumers hope to be treated as total persons; we don't want to be seen just as a set of teeth. You, the dentist, need to show us that you are concerned for us personally. This concern can be conveyed in a number of ways.

The personality or manner of the dentist and his or her staff is very important. A patient is usually grateful for some "small talk" regarding the patient in matters outside of dentistry. The office atmosphere, team work, and mutual respect filter down.

In determining a treatment plan, you, the dentist, should take into account any unique problems or circumstances of the patient's total health or personal condition in planning for his treatment. I'm sure you are already well aware of how necessary it is to review the medical history of the patient. But additionally, you must tune into each individual's needs, desires, or concerns, as expressed by him, and take them into account. Examples are special fears regarding anesthesia or losing teeth.

Another very significant way that the dentist conveys her concern for the patient as a person, is the manner in which she does her scheduling. As Dr. Keiper pointed out, balancing office efficiency and the quality of your dentist/patient relationships is a very difficult task. When a patient has to sit in the office and wait for an unreasonable period of time he may well interpret that to mean his dentist values her office efficiency, in other words, the volume of her

216

business and the amount of money brought in that day, more than she does the patient's needs, time or concerns. And remember, as a consumer, if I don't feel someone values my worth, and, as a result, makes me feel unimportant, I'm not going to remain in the relationship. How long I have to wait to get an appointment in the first place is another issue. The availability of the dentist in an emergency is another concern.

Considering what hours the office is open is crucial in looking at whether the dentist is meeting the consumer's needs in a humane way and making ethical use of his power. Do families where both parents work, or where there is a single head of the household, have easy access to dental care? Conveniences for your patients' visits is another way to show you care. The location of your office, ample parking, and access for handicapped are some examples.

We as consumers really are your customers. Treat us as your guests. Make sure your staff does not act as though they've been interrupted from something more important when a patient calls on the phone or taps at the window. Let us know you're glad to see or hear from us.

Providing extra comforts shows a lot of consideration as well. Comfortable seating in the waiting rooms and office is important.

Placing pictures on the ceiling above the patient's chair shows literally and figuratively that you, the dentist, have the ability to see things from our point of view. At my last visit to the dentist, I was offered a radio with headphones to wear while my work was being done. It really made the experience much more pleasant and I appreciated my dentist going that extra distance to show concern for my comfort. Remember, allaying anxiety or discomfort through discussion or other means is a major part of humane treatment.

Another extremely important way in which a dentist can convey his concern for the patient as a unique individual is in allowing for flexibility in making financial arrangements so that inability to adhere to a strict financial schedule does not preclude anyone from receiving proper care.

Thirdly, when we seek dental care, we hope to gain knowledge from our dentist regarding our dental condition. This knowledge is important for two reasons: 1) in order to make decisions regarding specific treatment alternatives presented; 2) to have that understanding serve as a basis for motivation to maintain proper long-term preventive care.

This is a touchy subject. As Dr. Keiper suggested, it is difficult for a dentist to balance the use of paternalism and the need to lay the groundwork for the patient's autonomous choice. It is especially difficult because patients respond to the information very subjectively and the responses vary greatly. Some people are offended and find it condescending when a dentist explains everything in detail whereas some take offense when just told what to do without a basis for choice. Some people want to know more than others. For example, my dentist sets up separate appointments for consultations before commencing any treatment plan. In preparation for today's discussion, I've asked around among my social circle and discovered that people differed as to whether they appreciated such opportunities to review x-rays and share in the diagnosis or whether they just wanted to get the work done and have not wanted to waste the time with separate appointments and get a "junior degree in dentistry."

I bring this up because what's crucial here is not to make any assumptions. Get to know your patient. Ask if they would be interested in finding out about whatever the topic is; keep checking to see if they want to know more. If you stay tuned in to a patient you can reduce the risk of abusing your power as a professional and you pursue an ethical process leading to the patient's informed and automous decision.

Lastly, but of great importance is for us to be able to <u>trust</u> our dentist. You do have a fiduciary duty to us, as Dr. Keiper stated, and we do rely on it. You should be honest. We want to know that only necessary work is being done. Frankly, there is a growing suspicion among us consumers that, since there are so few cavities and that the nature of day to day dentistry has changed so drastically, dentists are getting too imaginative and creative in dreaming up things to do to our teeth.

Oppositely, we wonder if dentists are doing less than they should, for example, using cheaper or faster techniques or materials due to tight scheduling or money considerations. Sometimes we wonder if the work done in our mouths is similar to that done on our cars -- on the "self-destruct" theory; are our fillings intended to last only "x" number of years?

We want to be able to trust that our best interest is our dentist's first priority even when there is conflict with his own, or in some cases, another dentist's interests. For example, if I go to a dentist who sees sub-par work in my mouth, done by another dentist, I would expect her to tell me. In fact, it is my understanding that the new code of ethics for dentists obligates the dentist to make such a disclosure.

Certainly we also hope that your profession maintains its integrity and does not resort to misleading advertising tricks for the purposes of drumming up business. Too many consumers are vulnerable to advertising gimmicks and, as a result, would choose dentists for the wrong reasons. And, of course, we want to trust the fact that dental fees are not arbitrarily set high by the profession but are, in fact, kept as low as possible.

Up to now I've addressed the concerns of consumers as individuals; but it should be kept in mind that, as a society, we expect everyone who needs care to be able to get it regardless of money, age, education, race, handicap, location, etc.

So you've heard some of what we want -- keep it in mind as you develop into practitioners so that some of the attitudes and values we've talked about are so imbedded in you by the time you have full power as a dentist that you'll be the kind of dentist the profession and society in general can be proud of. And remember, if you adhere to the principles Dr. Keiper and I have discussed, it won't only make you an ethical and humane professional but it will most assuredly make you successful. Because if you treat me accordingly, I, as your patient, will accept your proposed treatment plans, follow your instructions, pay my bills on time, refer my friends and relatives to you, and -- God forbid -- if an error is made, I probably won't sue because I'll like you too much.

Appendix I

Biographical Data

In order to provide some background on the individuals who participated in the Center's 1985-86 Program, a brief biographical sketch of each participant has been added to this volume as Appendix I.

John D. Aram, Ph.D.

John D. Aram earned the Bachelor of Arts Degree in Economics with a specialization in Public Policy in 1964 from Yale University. In 1968 he received the Ph.D. Degree in Management from the Massachusetts Institute Of Technology specializing in Organizational Studies.

Currently, Dr. Aram is Professor of Management and Associate Dean for the Master's of Business Administration program of the Weatherhead School of Management at Case Western Reserve University. He joined CWRU in 1968 as an Assistant Professor of Organization and Administration in the School of Management. In addition to his administrative and scholarly duties, Dr. Aram is a business consultant and lecturer in the United States and abroad. Dr. Aram is the author of a number of articles and books.

In 1984 he served as Co-Chairman of the Doctoral Dissertation Consortium for the Social Issues in Management Division for the Academy of Management. He is also a member of The Academy of Management, The American Association for Advancement of Science, and the Society for the Psychological Study of Social Issues. Dr. Aram's civic responsibilities include Past Co-President of the Coventry Elementary School PTA, member of the Advisory Committee to the Cleveland Area Development Corporation for the Greater Cleveland Growth Association, and member of the Industrial Enterprise and Technology Board for the State of Ohio.

Gail E. Bromley, B.S.N., M.S.

Gail E. Bromley earned the Bachelor of Arts Degree in Psychology from Boston University in 1971. She received the Bachelor of Science Degree in Nursing and the Master of Science Degree in Psychiatric Nursing from Case Western Reserve University. During her educational years Ms. Bromley received the Sigma Theta Tau Nursing Honorary Society Award.

For the last ten years, Ms. Bromley has practiced nursing and has been a Clinical Nurse Specialist in the greater Cleveland area. Currently she is the Vice President of Nursing Services, Rehabilitation Services, and Social Services for Lakewood (Ohio) Hospital.

Ms. Bromley's professional affiliations include the American Nursing Service Administrators Association, the Cleveland Nursing Roundtable, and the Frances Payne Bolton School of Nursing Alumni Association. She has also published a number of articles.

Marla Comet-Stark, J.D.

Marla Comet-Stark is a native Clevelander. After receiving the B.S. degree in social work from the University of Cincinnati, she earned the Juris Doctorate from Case Western Reserve University School of Law. For five years she practiced criminal law with the Cuyahoga County Public Defenders Office, specializing in the area of juvenile deliquency.

For the past year, Ms. Comet-Stark and her husband, Robert, have been developing the Loehmann's Plaza Shopping Center in Willoughby Hills, Ohio, as well as raising their two sons.

Ms. Comet-Stark is a member of the Board of Directors of the Cleveland Bet Sefer Mizrachi School.

Susan Coverdale

At the time of her presentation, Susan Coverdale was the Director of Computer Services and Computer Education at Hawken School in Gates Mills, Ohio. Prior

222

to working at Hawken School Ms. Coverdale worked for the Olivet Corporation, an international company which sells computer equipment and accounting software. While raising her family she continues as a consultant for a number of business firms in the Cleveland area.

Ms. Coverdale earned the Bachelor of Science Degree in Mathematics and the Bachelor of Arts in Computer Science Degree from the Ohio University in 1976.

Lynn J. Ebert, M.S., Ph.D.

Lynn J. Ebert earned the B.S., M.S., and Ph.D. Degrees in Metallurgical Engineering from Case Institute of Technology, now Case Western Reserve University. While at Case he received the Tau Beta Pi National Honorary Engineering Society Award while still an undergraduate and the Sigma Xi National Honorary Research Society Award in 1941.

Since 1941, Dr. Ebert was employed by Case Institute of Technology as a research associate and professor. As of July 1985, Dr. Ebert enjoyed the status of Professor Emeritus. At the time of his presentation, Dr. Ebert was retained as a consultant for Erico Products, Inc., and the Weatherhead Company, a division of Dana Corporation. He had also worked as a consultant for Republic Steel, General Motors, Aluminum Company of America and many other major corporations. Dr. Ebert was also a distinguished lecturer. In the fall of 1977 he spoke at the Soviet-American Symposium in Kiev, Ukraine, USSR. His professional publications include eight books, 50 technical papers, and numerous magazine and periodical articles on Metallurgy.

In 1980 Dr. Ebert received the Carl F. Wittke Distinguished Teacher's Award and has been recognized in American Men of Science, Who's Who in Engineering, Who's Who in Education and Who's Who in America.

The University will miss Dr. Ebert who died at the age of 66, on July 27, 1986.

Eldon Jay Epp, S.T.M., Ph.D.

Eldon Jay Epp graduated from Harvard Divinity School in 1956 with the S.T.M. Degree and earned the Ph.D. Degree from Harvard University in 1961. Following graduation he taught briefly at Princeton Theological Seminary and in 1962 became Assitant, and then Associate, Professor of both religion and classics at the University of Southern California.

In 1968, Dr. Epp came to Case Western Reserve University, and in 1971 he was appointed Harkness Professor of Biblical Literature. He served also as Dean of Humanities and Social Sciences from 1977 to 1985 and is currently the Chairman of the Department of Religion.

Dr. Epp is widely published. He is the author or editor of three books and has contributed two dozen technical articles to scholarly books and journals. He has served as Associate Editor of the Journal of Biblical Literature since 1971 and is an editorial board member of Hermenia: A Critical and Historical Commentary on the Bible.

Thomas P. Holland, M.S.W., Ph.D.

At the time of his presentation, Dr. Thomas P. Holland was the Vice Dean and Professor at the School of Applied Social Science at Case Western Reserve University. Dr. Holland taught graduate level courses in Social Policy and Planning, and Social Welfare. In 1980 he received the John S. Diekhoff Award for Distinguished Graduate Teaching from CWRU, and the Award for Service on Behalf of Children from the Institute for Child Advocacy.

Dr. Holland graduated with honors in 1964 from Wheaton College with the B.A. Degree in Sociology. In 1966 he earned a M.S.W. Degree from the School of Social Work at Florida State University and in 1972 he received the Ph.D. Degree from the Florence Heller Graduate School for Advanced Studies in Social Welfare at Brandeis University.

Dr. Holland has published widely. He serves as a member on the Academy of Certified Social Workers, the

Center for Professional Ethics at CWRU, and the National Association of Social Workers; he is also a Licensed Independent Social Worker in the State of Ohio. His civic responsibilities include Consultant for the United Way of Cleveland, N.E.H. Fellow for the Institute on Moral Issues in Human Services, and a Research Consultant for the City of Shaker Heights Office of Aging.

Glenn L. Keiper, D.D.S.

Glenn L. Keiper earned the Bachelor of Science Degree from the University of Pittsburgh and the Doctor of Dental Surgery Degree from Case Western Reserve University. He completed his Internship at Cleveland Metropolitan General Hospital and his Residency at Saint Vincent Charity Hospital. Following his residency, Dr. Keiper trained as an Oral Surgeon at Boston University School of Graduate Dentistry.

Presently, Dr. Keiper is in the private practice of Oral and Maxillofacial Surgery in Akron, Ohio. He is also an Assistant Clinical Professor in the Department of Community Dentistry of the School of Dentistry at Case Western Reserve University. As a philosophy student at Cleveland State University, Dr. Keiper is doing graduate study in Medical Ethics.

Dr. Keiper is a Diplomate of American Board of Oral and Maxillofacial Surgery and serves as a member of the American Association of Oral and Maxillofacial Surgeons, the American Dental Association, and the Ohio Dental Association.

Robert J. Lally, B.P.D., L.L.B.

Robert J. Lally earned the Bachelor of Philosophy Degree in Marketing in 1952 and the L.L.B. Degree in 1953 from the University of Notre Dame. He played football on Notre Dame's National Championship teams of the late 40's. Mr. Lally practiced law in Cleveland for four years and then joined The Norton Brothers Company as Legal Counsel.

In 1966 he became President of The Norton Brothers Company, a roofing and sheet metal contracting firm founded in 1888 and the oldest of its kind in the Northern Ohio area. He is a member of The National Roofing Contractors Association and the Greater Cleveland Roofing Contractors Association and has been the Labor Contract Negotiator for the Greater Cleveland Roofing Contractors Association for the past twenty years.

Mr. Lally's civic responsibilities include Past President of The Notre Dame Club of Cleveland, Past President of The Cleveland Touchdown Club, Knights of Columbus and the Rotary Club.

He and his wife, Nancy, are members of St. Ann's Church in Cleveland Heights.

Robert P. Lawry, J.D.

Robert P. Lawry graduated with honors from Fordham University in 1963, where he earned the B.A. Degree. In 1966 he earned the J.D. Degree from the University of Pennsylvania where he also graduated with honors. He received his Diploma in Law in 1967 from Oxford University. Mr. Lawry practiced law in Pittsburgh for eight years.

In 1975 he joined the Faculty of Law at Case Western Reserve University, where he became a Professor in 1979. Mr. Lawry has published many books and articles and has lectured extensively on law and ethics both in the United States and Canada.

Mr. Lawry is extremely active in University and Law School committee work. A most distinguished accomplishment is his co-founding of the Center For Professional Ethics at CWRU. The Center grew out of a perceived need for dialogue on moral and ethical issues both within and across professional disciplines within the University and with professionals in the field.

Hugh J. Leslie, Jr., M.D.

Hugh J. Leslie, Jr. is Clinical Professor of Pediatrics at the School of Medicine of Case Western Reserve University, having been a member of the faculty since 1954. Also, since that date he has been practicing General Pediatrics in Cleveland, Ohio. In addition to being on the active staff of University Hospitals of Cleveland, he is on the staffs of Hillcrest Hospital, St. Luke's Hospital, and Mt. Sinai Hospital.

Dr. Leslie attended Oberlin College from 1943 to 1945 and graduated from the School of Medicine of Case Western Reserve University in 1949. His post-graduate training included a rotating internship at Cleveland City Hospital (now Metropolitan General Hospital) completed in 1950, and pediatric residency at the University Hospitals of Cleveland, completed in 1954. He obtained certification by the American Board of Pediatrics in 1955.

Currently Dr. Leslie is a member of the Northern Ohio Pediatric Society of which he was past-president, the American Academy of Pediatrics, the American Medical Association, the Ohio State Medical Association, the Cleveland Academy of Medicine, and the Pasteur Club.

Daniel J. Linke

Daniel J. Linke graduated from Case Western Reserve University in May of 1986 with the B.A. Degree in English and History. In Dan's Junior year he was Editor of the University student newspaper, "The Observer". In his Senior year he was President of the Senior Class. During his college years he also served on the Western Reserve College Curriculum Committee. Dan is a native of Lindenwold, New Jersey, and attended Overbrook Regional High School from which he graduated as salutatorian.

Mary Briody Mahowald, M.A., Ph.D.

Mary Briody Mahowald earned her doctorate in philosophy from Marquette University in 1969. Since then she has taught philosophy at Villanova University and Indiana University, and published articles and books concerning American philosophy, feminism, marxism, and ethics. Dr. Mahowald's post graduate work, along with her teaching and research in biomedical ethics led to an appointment in 1982 as

Associate Professor of Medical Ethics at Case Western Reserve University School of Medicine. This in turn led in 1985 to the establishment of the Center for Biomedical Ethics, of which she is the Co-director. At CWRU, Dr. Mahowald also holds an appointment as Associate Professor of Philosophy for Western Reserve College, and has served on the Steering Committee of the Center for Professional Ethics for the last four years.

Dr. Mahowald is very active in both the clinical and academic areas of medical ethics. Her work involves teaching medical students, residents and other health care professionals at CWRU and its affiliated hospitals, organizing and chairing several hospital ethics committees, consulting with hospital personnel on specific cases, and sponsoring and participating in conferences on medical ethics for the community.

Violet M. Malinski, M.A., Ph.D.

At the time of her presentation, Dr. Violet M. Malinski was the coordinator of the Nursing Doctorate Program and an Assistant Professor in Psychiatric-Mental Health Nursing at Case Western Reserve University. Dr. Malinski has taught courses in family and group therapies, ethics, health policy and planning, research, and conceptional models.

Prior to joining Case Western Reserve University, Dr. Malinski was a faculty member at the University of Delaware College of Nursing. She has served as a consultant for the American Indian/Alaska Native Nurses Association. She was also a family therapist and a public health nurse.

Dr. Malinski earned her B.S.N. Degree from Rutgers University College of Nursing. In 1971, she received her M.A. Degree with a major in Child Psychiatric Nursing from New York University. Her Ph.D. Degree was also awarded from New York University.

Professional organizations that Dr. Malinski belongs to include the American Nurses Association, Sigma Theta Tau National Honor Society in Nursing, the National Council on Family Relations, and the Hastings Center.

Deborah M. Miller, M.S.W., Ph.D. Candidate

Deborah M. Miller graduated from John Carroll University in 1975 with a B.A. in Philosophy. In 1980 she earned a M.S.S.A. degree with specialization in health from the School of Applied Social Sciences at Case Western Reserve University, and is currently is a Ph.D. candidate in Advanced Studies Program at Case Western Reserve University.

Ms. Miller is a social worker with a multidisciplinary evaluation, treatment and education team at the Cleveland Clinic Foundation's Mellen Center, an outpatient facility for Multiple Sclerosis research and treatment. She joined the Mellen Center in July 1985, previously working with outpatient dialysis populations. Ethical issues with which she has dealt include initiation and continuation of life sustaining treatments as well as family decision making for long term care of the chronically ill.

Barry A. Rogers, M.S.C.E., P.E.

Barry A. Rogers is a structural engineer and research associate in the Technical Services Division with The Austin Company in Cleveland, Ohio. He joined the company in 1978. Mr. Rogers graduated from Worcester Polytechnic Institute in 1978 with a Bachelor of Science Degree and in 1983 he earned the Masters of Science degree from Cleveland State University. In that same year Mr. Rogers became a Registered Professional Engineer licensed by the State of Ohio. In 1984 he received the American Society of Civil Engineers Daniel Mead Prize for Young Engineers.

Carol J. Rottman, Ph.D.

Carol J. Rottman earned her B.A. Degree in Elementary Education from the University of Michigan in 1960, the M.A. Degree in Special Education from Michigan State University in 1970 and the Ph.D. degree in Social Welfare from the School of Applied Social Sciences at Case Western Reserve University in 1985. Her dissertation topic is "Ethics in Neonatology: A Parents' Perspective."

Currently, Dr. Rottman is working at the CWRU School of Medicine as the Research Director of the Prevention of Low Birthweight Project. Ms. Rottman has had a long involvement in the education of handicapped infants, primarily blind, and is the parent of a disabled son. She has served on the Steering Committee of the Center for Professional Ethics for the past three years.

Sandra Walker Russ, Ph.D.

Sandra Walker Russ graduated with honors in 1966 from the University of Pittsburgh with the B.S. Degree in Psychology. She earned the Ph.D. Degree in Clinical Psychology from that same institution. Upon graduation Dr. Russ worked as a Staff Psychologist with the Arapahoe Mental Health Center and the Washington University Medical School Child Guidance Center.

In 1975 Dr. Russ began her teaching at Case Western Reserve University. Since joining CWRU, she has become a tenured Associate Professor in the Department of Psychology and is currently the Director of Clinical Psychology Training. Dr. Russ' work involves teaching both graduate and undergraduate courses and seminars, supervising graduate student's practicum placements in the community, and serving as major advisor for Master's theses and dissertations. Dr. Russ's University activities include past Co-Chairman on the Committee on Student Life, past member of the Advisory Committee on the Education and Status of Women, and Chairman of the Faculty Senate.

Since 1968 Dr. Russ has published 19 articles and manuscripts and currently is on the editorial board of two academic journals.

James R. Skirbunt, J.D.

James R. Skirbunt is currently a Licensed Practicing Attorney with the law firm of McDonald, Hopkins & Hardy Co. and is a shareholder of the firm. His practice is limited exclusively to family law. He has been a frequent lecturer at domestic relations seminars throughout the state of Ohio for various Bar Associations, the Ohio Legal Institute, and The Ohio

Academy of Trial Lawyers. Mr. Skirbunt also serves as Chairman of the Cuyahoga County Bar Association Family Law Section and is a fellow in the American Academy of Matrimonial Lawyers.

Mr. Skirbunt earned the Bachelor of Science in Foreign Service Degree from Georgetown University in 1971. He then received his legal training at the Boston College School of Law and graduated with the J.D. Degree in 1974.

Edward A. Steigerwald, M.S., Ph.D.

At the time of his presentation, Edward A. Steigerwald was vice president of productivity for TRW Inc. Prior to joining TRW in 1959, Mr. Steigerwald was an assistant manager of the Research Department of the Cleveland Twist Drill Company. He served two years in the U.S. Army, primarily at the Army Chemical Center in Maryland.

Dr. Steigerwald received B.S., M.S. and Ph.D. degrees in metallurgy at Case Institute of Technology, now Case Western Reserve University. At Case he was an International Nickle and Union Carbide Fellow. He is a member of the American Institute of Mining and Metallurgical Engineers, the American Foundry Society, and the American Society of Metals.

Daniel Verne, D.D.S.

Daniel Verne is the Chief of the Division of Dentistry, Oral and Maxillofacial Surgery at Mt. Sinai Medical Center in Cleveland, Ohio. He graduated in 1942 from Adelbert College, now Case Western Reserve University, with the Bachelor of Science Degree. In 1945 Dr. Verne earned his D.D.S. Degree from the School of Dentistry at CWRU.

Dr. Verne was called to the United States Navy where he practiced dentistry until he was dicharged in 1946. In 1948 he completed his Residency at Mt. Sinai Hospital of Cleveland. Six years later Dr. Verne was recalled to the United States Navy where he served at the U.S. Naval Hospital in San Diego, California. He also was sent to the U.S. Naval Hospital in Yokosuka,

Japan for two years.

In 1973 Dr. Verne was appointed as an Adjunct Assistant Professor in the Department of Anatomy at the Case Western Reserve University Medical School. He is a lecturer in Oral and Maxillofacial Surgery throughout the United States, Mexico, Israel and Japan. He is a member of Omicron Kappa Upsilon Honorary Dental Fraternity and served on the Hope Ship in Tunisia and Brazil.

Appendix II

Programs of the Center for Professional Ethics

There follows as Appendix II, a list of programs the Center has sponsored from March, 1979 through November, 1987.

1979-1982 Academic Years

March 31, 1979. "Personal Integrity and Professional Life: The Socialization of the Student." Edward Mearns, Vice President, Graduate and Undergraduate Studies, CWRU.

September 29, 1979. "Lying." Dr. Ruth Owens, Director of Pediatric Endocrinology, University Hospitals, Cleveland, Ohio, and The Honorable Richard Celeste, Governor of Ohio.

February 7, 1980. "Towards Resolution of Interpersonal Problems Resulting from Professional Pursuits" or "You Can't Call Your Profession 'Darling'." Student-prepared skits with responders.

April 12, 1980. "The Present Crisis of Confidentiality." Dr. Mortimer Kadish, Professor, Department of Philosophy, CWRU.

October 19, 1980. "Personal Well-Being and Professional Survival." Dr. Janeen Carroll-Brown, Psychologist.

November 18, 1980. "Women and Men Shaping Professional Roles." The Rev. James Leehan, Associate Director, University Christian Movement in Cleveland, Ohio.

February 28, 1981. "Professional Responsibility for Public Service: Choice or Mandate." Dr. William May, Professor of Ethics, The Kennedy Institute.

April 9, 1981. "Combining Career and Marriage." A program presented by three married couples.

November 11, 1981. "The Responsibility of The University Community For The Ethical Preparation of Professional Students." Dr. Daniel Callahan, Director, The Hastings Institute.

March 27, 1982. "Power and The Professional Person." Dr. Mary Mahowald, Associate Professor of Medical Ethics, School of Medicine, CWRU.

1982-1984 Academic Years

November 2, 9, & 16, 1982. "Ethics and The University Experience." Three afternoon conferences each with a moderator and three panelists.

February 1983. "Systems of Ethical Thinking." A four-week course offered by the CPE and The Office of Student Affairs, CWRU. Conducted by University faculty members and students.

March 16, 1983. "Combining Career and Marriage." A program presented by three married couples.

October 1, 1983. "Personal Ethics and Professional Responsibility: Conflicts and Resolutions." Dr. Samuel Gorovitz, Professor of Philosophy, University of Maryland.

November 5, 1983. Workshop: "Basics of Ethical Thinking." Dr. Mary Mahowald, Associate Professor of Medical Ethics, School of Medicine, CWRU, and Robert Lawry, Professor of Law, School of Law, CWRU.

March 26, and April 2, 9, & 16, 1984. "Systems of Ethical Thinking." A course co-sponsored with the Office of Student Affairs, CWRU, dealing with ethics as applied to business, law and medical care. Leaders: Tommy McCuistion, Brenda Aume, Robert Lawry, Julie Hambleton, Wendy Miano, and Robert Clarke.

March 31, 1984. "Moral Grounds for Ethical Practice." The Rev. Timothy Beal, Associate Pastor, Fairmount Presbyterian Church and Dr. John Boatright, Professor of Philosophy, John Carroll University, Cleveland, Ohio.

Preconference Seminars relating to the
March 31st Conference listed above:

February 20, 1984. School of Nursing, Rozella M. Scholtfeldt, Speaker.
February 28, 1984. School of Applied Social Sciences, Tom Holland, Speaker.
March 22, 1984. School of Law, Michelle Creger, Speaker.
March 29, 1984. School of Management, John Aram, Speaker.

April 10, 1984. Co-sponsored meeting with the Case chapter of the American Society of Civil Engineers. Videotapes: "The Truesteel Case." Martin Krist and Robert Clarke, Director, Center for Professional Ehtics, CWRU.

Spring Semester, 1984-1987. "Ethics In the Professions," an interdisciplinary credit course taught each Spring Semester by a faculty member from the Schools of Law, Nursing, Medicine, and Applied Social Sciences.

1984-1985 Academic Year

September 22, 1984. Workshops: "The Language of Ethical Thinking." Dr. Mary Mahowald, Professor of Medical Ethics, School of Medicine, CWRU, and Robert Lawry, Professor, School of Law, CWRU.

October 27, 1984. "Ethical Issues in National Political Campaigning." Oliver C. Henkel, Jr., Speaker, (Mr. Henkel was Campaign Manager for Senator Gary Hart).

January 22, February 5, & March 19, 1985. "Ethical Issues in Business: Dilemmas and Decision Making." A series sponsored by The Center and Weatherhead School of Management, CWRU. Resourse leadership: Dean Scott Cowan, School of Management; Mr. James E. Bennett, Manager of McKinsey & Company, Cleveland Office; and Mr. Norton Rose, President, Norton W. Rose Company.

February 2, 1985. Workshop: "Systems of Ethical Thinking." Co-sponsored with the Office of

Student Affairs, CWRU. Leader: Robert W. Clarke.

February 17, 1985. A Theater Party at the Cleveland Play House to view and discuss the play, Billy Budd, by Herman Melville. Leaders: Robert Lawry, Chairperson, Center for Professional Ethics, William Rhys and Don Westbrook, actors in the play.

April 19, 1985. Spring Conference: Ethical Issues Raised by the Bishops Pastoral Letter on "Catholic Social Teaching and the U.S. Economy." Leadership: Bishop James P. Lyke, Fr. Gerald F. Cavanaugh, Dr. J.B. Silvers, and Dr. Merl Hokenstad.

1985-1986 Academic Year
Conferences on "The Power of the Professional Person"

October 22, 1985. The Social Worker; Dr. Thomas Holland, Vice Dean and Professor, School of Applied Social Science, CWRU (1986). Dr. Deborah M. Miller, Social Worker, The Cleveland Clinic Foundation Mellon Center.

October 30, 1985. The Engineer; Dr. Lynn Ebert, Professor Emeritus of Metallurgy and Materials Science, CWRU (1986). Dr. Edward Steigerwald, Vice President for Productivity, TRW Inc. Mr. Barry A. Rogers, Research Associate, The Austin Co.

November 8, 1985. The Nurse; Dr. Violet Malinski, Assistant Professor of Psychiatric & Mental Health Nursing & Coordinator of the Nurse Doctorate Program, CWRU (1986). Ms. Gail E. Bromely, Vice President for Nursing Services, Rehabilitation Services & Social Services, Lakewood Hospital. Dr. Carol Rottman, Incorporator-Consultant for the International Institute for the Visually Impaired (1986).

December 6, 1985. The Manager; Dr. John Aram, Associate Dean & Professor of Management, Weatherhead School of Management, CWRU. Mr. Robert Lally, President, Norton Brothers Co. Ms. Susan Coverdale, Director of Computer Services & Director of Computer Education, Hawken School.

January 22, 1986. The Physician; Dr. Mary Briody Mahowald, Associate Professor of Medical Ethics, School of Medicine, CWRU. Dr. Hugh Leslie, Associate Clinical Professor & General Pediatrician. Ms. Karen Metzler, Visiting Scholar, The Hastings Center (1985).

February 19, 1986. The Professor; Dr. Sandra Walker Russ, Associate Professor of Psychology & Director of the Division of Clinical Training, CWRU. Dr. Eldon Jay Epp, Harkness Professor of Biblical Studies & Chairman of the Department of Religion, CWRU. Mr. Daniel J. Linke, President of the Western Reserve College, Class of 1986, CWRU.

March 3, 1986. The Lawyer; Mr. Robert Lawry, Professor of Law, School of Law, CWRU & Co-Director, Center for Professional Ethics, CWRU. Mr. James R. Skirbunt, Shareholder, McDonald, Hopkins & Hardy, Cleveland.

March 19, 1986. The Dentist; Dr. Glenn Keiper, Assistant Clinical Professor, Department of Community Dentistry, School of Dentistry, CWRU. Dr. Daniel Verne, Chief, Division of Dentistry & Oral Maxillofacial Surgery, Mt. Sinai Medical Center. Ms. Marla Comet-Stark, Developer for Loehmann's Shopping Plaza, Willoughby Hills, Ohio.

1986-1987 Academic Year

September 15, 1986. Forum: "Justice and the Rationing of Human Services." Dr. Marvin Rosenberg, Professor, School of Applied Social Sciences, CWRU.

October 20, 1986. Forum: "Is The Technological Imperative Ethically Compelling?" Ms. Janicemarie Vinicky, Department of Bioethics, The Cleveland Clinic Foundation, Cleveland, Ohio.

November 14, 1986. Conference on "Professional Power and Self-Regulation." Dr. Michael Bayles, Professor of Philosophy, University of Florida, and Dr. Alan Goldman, Professor of Philosophy, University of Miami (Florida), speakers. Responders: Mr. Ralph Brody, Dr. Fay Miller,

Dr. Margaret Grevatt, Mr. Norman Rice, and Dr. Joseph M. Foley.

November 17, 1986. Forum: "The Ethics of Plant Closings and Relocation." Dr. Eugene Beem, Professor of Corporate and Management Ethics, Baldwin-Wallace College, Berea, Ohio.

November 22, 1986. Seminar: "Systems of Making Ethical Decisions." Robert W. Clarke, Co-Director, Center for Professional Ethics, CWRU, leader.

January 26, 1987. Forum: "Contragate: The Moral Obligation to Obey the Law." Robert P. Lawry, Professor of Law, CWRU, Co-Director, The Center for Professional Ethics, CWRU.

January 28, 1987. "Systems of Making Ethical Decisions." Presented to Student Chapter of American Institute of Chemical Engineers. Robert W. Clarke, leader.

February 5, 1987. "Systems of Making Ethical Decisions." Presented to Beta Alpha Psi, National Honorary Accounting Fraternity. Robert W. Clarke, leader.

February 23, 1987. Forum: "Balancing Relationships, Paychecks, and Fulfillment." Dr. James Leehan, Director, University Christian Movement in Cleveland, moderating a panel of dual-career couples and single parents.

March 2, 1987. Forum: "Whose Babies? The Ethical Dilemmas of Surrogate Motherhood." Dr. Mary B. Mahowald, Associate Professor of Medical Ethics, CWRU; Co-Director, Center for Biomedical Ethics, CWRU.

March 23, 1987. Forum: "Health Care: Is it a Right or a Privilege?" Dr. David G. Miller, Director of the Hough-Norwood (Health) Center. Responders: Dr. Mary Adams, Professor of Nursing, CWRU, and Dr. J.B. Silvers, School of Management, CWRU.

March 26, 1987. "Systems of Making Ethical Decisions." Presented to the Student Chapter of the American Society of Mechanical Engineering. Robert W. Clarke, leader.

April 6, 1987. Forum: "Ethical Issues in Racism." Dr. Marvin Rosenberg, Professor, School of Applied Social Sciences, CWRU. Responders: Gwendolyn Johnson, Assistant Dean, Student Affairs, CWRU; Margaret E. Boulding, Director, MEIOP, CWRU; and Charles Bromley, Director, National Neighbors & Coordinator, Metro Strategy Group.

1987-1988 Academic Year

September 14, 1987. Forum: "The Japanese Ethical Experience: Principle and Practice." Dr. Lee Makela, Associate Professor of History, Cleveland State University, Cleveland, Ohio.

September 28, 1987. Forum: "Insider Trading: An Ethics Trap?" A debate between Mark Moran, Associate Professor of Management, CWRU, and John Boatright, Professor of Philosophy, John Carroll University, Cleveland, Ohio.

October 12, 1987. Forum: "Ethics and Aids." Dr. Eleanor Davidson, Medical Director, University Health Service, CWRU, and Dr. Thomas Murray, Director, Center for Bioethics, School of Medicine, CWRU.

October 22, 29, and November 5 & 12, 1987. "Four-Week Study Group on Ethics," an informal discussion group designed to enable those participating to learn the skills of ethical decision-making. Robert W. Clarke, Co-Director, Center for Professional Ethics, leader.

October 26, 1987. Forum: "Can a Good Person be a Criminal Lawyer?" Kevin McMunigal, Assistant Professor of Law, CWRU.

October 31, 1987. Conference on "The Media and Politics in Ethical Conflict." Sponsored by The Center for Professional Ethics, CWRU, and the Society of Professional Journalists, Sigma Delta Chi. Dr. Judith Lichtenberg, Research Associate, The Center for Philosophy and Public Policy, University of Maryland, speaker. David B. Offer, Managing Editor, La Crosse (Wis.) Tribune, panel moderator. The Panel: Oliver Henkel, Tim Smith David L. Marburger, Thom Greer, Brian Usher,

Robert Hughes, Ellen Miller, Timothy Hagan, Jim
Underwood, Mary Briody Mahowald, and Fred
McGunagle.

November 9, 1987. Forum: "The Ethics of
Individualism: A Constitutional Perspective."
Edward (Ted) Mearns, Professor of Law, School of
Law, CWRU.

November 23, 1987. Forum: "Ethical Issues in the
Current Economic Crisis." Dr. Bo Carlsson,
Professor of Economics, Weatherhead School of
Management, CWRU.

BJ 1725 .P67 1988

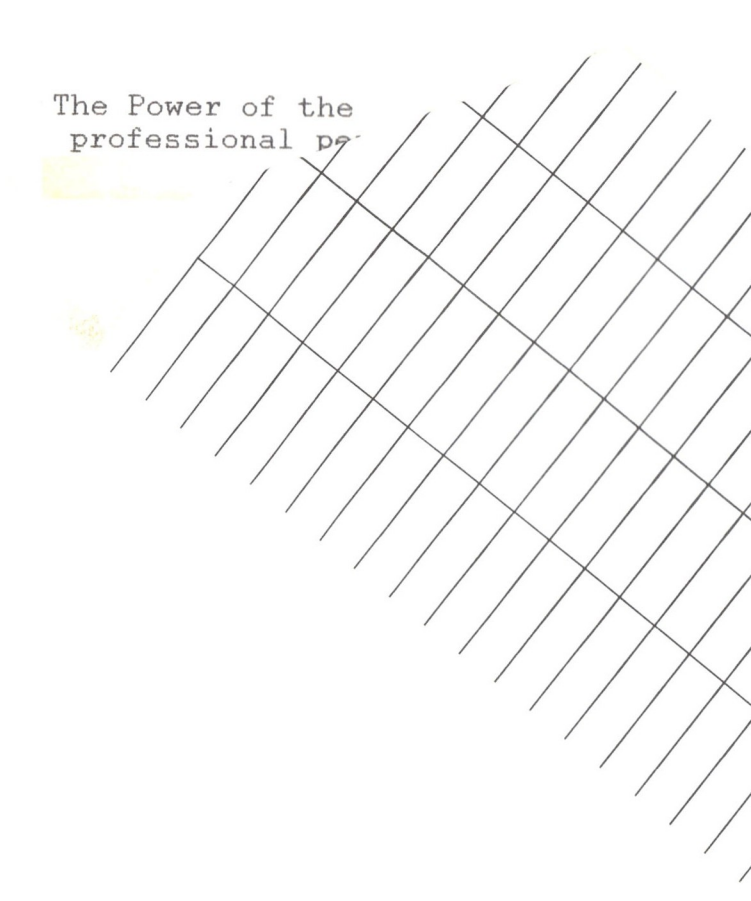

The Power of the
professional p...

CANISIUS COLLEGE LIBRARY